To my Loving Mother

Claudia 1981

My Stomach Goes Traveling

Also by Walter Slezak:

WHAT TIME'S THE NEXT SWAN?

WALTER SLEZAK

My Stomach Goes Traveling

Drawings by Franziska Bilek

DOUBLEDAY & COMPANY, INC.
GARDEN CITY, NEW YORK
1979

The chapter beginning on page 69 from WHAT TIME'S THE
NEXT SWAN?, copyright © 1962 by Walter Slezak. Reprinted
by permission of Doubleday & Company, Inc.

The drawings by Franziska Bilek are from Mein Magen geht
Fremd © R. Piper & Co. Verlag, München 1977

Library of Congress Cataloging in Publication Data
Slezak, Walter, 1902–
My stomach goes traveling.
Includes index.
1. Cookery, International. I. Title.
TX725.A1S552   641.5′9
ISBN: 0-385-11302-1
Library of Congress Catalog Card Number 76–42397

For Kaasi

CONTENTS

EXPRESSION OF GRATITUDE

My sincere thanks go to the manufacturers of Mongol No. 2 pencils. Without their valuable product this book could not have been written. My thanks also go to the Faber-Castell Corporation, makers of pencils and pencil sharpeners; the producers of Atlas typewriting paper with its smooth, silken finish; the Smith-Corona typewriter company with its wonderful red and black ribbon, and to the KO-REC-TYPE company, whose splendid product was used on every line I typed.

They all graciously permitted me to buy their products. My heartfelt thanks also go to the Swiss postal service, who kindly let me buy stamps so I could mail the manuscript to my publishers in New York, and to the postal service of the United States for returning the rejected pages to me.

But my SPECIAL thanks go to Chase Manhattan Bank of New York City for issuing the author's advance check, which enabled my wife and me to eat a warm meal twice a week.

FOREWORD

by Jean Kerr

I warn you. This is a dangerous book. I don't know what the Surgeon General would have to say, but I declare that *My Stomach Goes Traveling* will be a hazard to your diet. And not just because the recipes are so tasty and delicious. One could summon the strength to deal with that, stoically resisting the temptation to leap to the stove and—starting with *Snert,* a Dutch pea soup with sausage—prepare and devour all of these noble dishes in a single afternoon. After all, consider the number of excellent cookbooks that already lodge safely on your shelf without ever having caused an orgy. I myself have twenty-seven (I just *counted* them, is how I know), including the *Waring Blender Cook Book,* which I probably bought for a chapter entitled "Baby Will Eat Better Than Ever."

But back to Slezak. The problem here is that the *prose* is so tasty and delicious, the stories so charming and outrageous that you keep on reading and reading.

If, as used to be said, character is the ability to eat *one* salted peanut, then something even more rigorous than character would be required to stop after one chapter of Slezak. What we are here confronted with (nutritionally speaking) is the ultimate secret weapon—a cookbook that you can't put down. I would call it a wrong idea whose time has come. Fie on Doubleday (I never said "fie" before and I rather like the sound of it), fie on Doubleday, and a pox on Walter Slezak.

And why do I call it a wrong idea?

It was the astute Mayor Jimmy Walker who once said, "No girl was ever ruined by a book." But he was definitely talking about a different kind of ruination, or maybe a different kind of girl. Let me tell you how I was ruined by this book.

In all fairness I should admit that I had already eaten dinner before I started to read *My Stomach Goes Traveling*. For the record, I could say that the chops were rather overdone and the macaroni had seen better days—like on the weekend, when it was cooked in the first place. But that is not the point. The point is that I was adequately nourished, if not stuffed. Then I began to get involved in Slezak's sassy adventures: with a large fish (he literally gave the shirt off his back to an eighteen-pound trout); with young ladies (his account of how the *coq au vin* became accidentally *brulé* would alarm Escoffier and delight Maupassant); with airborne animals (I cannot bring myself even to hint at the dreadful end of two dear little chinchillas).

Through all of this our hero, our villain, is talking about food with the irrational passion I used to feel for Rhett Butler. Naturally, I got hungry. And since I could not, would not, put the book down long enough to pare and slice some raw carrots and celery, I just grabbed four chocolate chip cookies. An hour later, having concluded that I should have lost some weight (at least off my shoulders, from laughing) and being once more famished, I consumed (in its entirety) a forty-nine-cent bag of potato chips. And then still later—no, no, no, it's just too degrading even to reminisce about. All I can say is that the difference between a quick riffle through an ordinary cookbook to find still another way to disguise chicken and an evening spent with Slezak is about seven thousand calories. However, there is a happy ending. After three days of subsisting on nothing but hard-boiled eggs and grapefruit I was restored to what is, for me, normal. Not desirable, just normal.

And now, before I go, I want to give you a specific example of the Slezak menace at work.

First of all, here are the instructions for cooking blue trout taken from a standard and perfectly satisfactory cookbook:

"Combine all the ingredients, except the fish, and bring to a boil. Add trout and simmer for about seven minutes until fish flakes easily. Serve."

That's all. That's really all.

Now hear Slezak, who describes himself as "a trout fisherman and a trout eaterman." He begins with love's old sweet song. "The best, the tenderest, the gentlest fish is *truite au bleu* . . . that delectable aquatic friend." He doesn't just cook two or three, he cossets them, and then: "You have my permission to sing '*An einem Bächlein helle,*' from '*Die Forelle,*' the famous trout song of Franz Schubert, but it is not absolutely necessary." Nor does his vigilance wane once the first trout is cooked. "Being right-handed, I lay the fish with its head to my left on a prewarmed plate. I then address it with reverence as you would a golf ball at a championship match . . . I work toward me, being very careful not to disturb the fine bone structure that lies beneath the meat."

You see how the suspense begins to get to you. And if you don't necessarily want a blue trout, you want *something*.

What you've got here, all rolled into three, is Craig Claiborne, multiplied by a Fielding travel guide, divided by Robert Benchley.

Bon appétit.

My Stomach Goes Traveling

My Stomach Goes Traveling

This book is a memory of many meals!

With conscientious diligence I have researched the book market and, with the help of a small hand-held computer, have calculated that in the United States alone over 370,000 cookbooks have been produced during the last fifty years. Add to these the household magazines, the newspapers, and special home-orientated periodicals, and then consider that every other country in the world, in Europe, Russia and her satellites, the Middle East and Far East, Australia, and some countries of which no one had ever heard until they were admitted to full and equal membership in the United Nations, have been printing culinary tomes at a staggering rate.

Every manner, every procedure known to the human race, to prepare edibles, every combination of meats, fishes, game, crustaceas, mollusks, and birds: cheeses, vegetables, roots, fruit, animal products, spices, liquids: everything that nourishes us, that thrills us, the addition of every haunting flavor and fragrance that transforms an ordinary meal into a feast: from the most exquisite *haute cuisine* of France to the *equally* exquisite *haute cuisine* of the Far East, down to the intricate stewing and barbecue methods of the cannibals: ALL has been explained, catalogued, specified in print, with illustrations, with exact measures and time of preparation.

And yet—surprisingly—there is always room for another cookbook! Consider that a chessboard has only sixty-four squares and thirty-two chessmen, and that after the first four moves have been made you already have over two million different possibilities to push the chessmen around.

And then consider that we have, in our wonderful world, MILLIONS of different edibles and equally many ways to prepare them. You will be awed by the size of the territory that has *not* been explored.

The Masai, one of the great African warrior tribes, a tall beautiful species of human beings, enjoy as their favorite intake of nourishment a mixture of milk, blood, and cow urine, freshly milked, freshly drawn, and spontaneously rendered. Just think how we could enrich their lives if we taught them to add to that curdled delicacy a pinch of nutmeg, a dash of ground pepper, and maybe a squirt of Lea & Perrins Worcestershire sauce. Never having been overly fond of milk, I have not sampled that gruel-like mush, but I feel very strongly that if you *happen* to like milk, blood, and cow urine (freshly milked, freshly drawn, and spontaneously rendered), these few added ingredients might enhance your enjoyment and give it a healthy kick. (Letters from enraged Masai warriors should be addressed to my publisher and not to me.)

One of the glories of being a film actor and a compensation for being overpaid and underworked is the fact that we often have to travel! Films are being shot on location, and so—with all expenses paid—we have a chance to see a great deal of the world. I have always had a curious stomach, my palate is inquisitive, I am constantly trying to "find out," so I ask questions, and when I fail to get any answers, I analyze, experiment, and *sometimes* even manage to improve a dish.

Very few restaurants will tell you how they prepare a meal you enjoy: that's understandable; they want you to come back and pay again, and no imploring and cute promises that you will not open your own restaurant will induce them to part with their secrets.

For over forty years I have been an enthusiastic patron of Trader Vic's in Beverly Hills, Munich, and New York. And I have never been able to find out what it is that they do to their barbecued spareribs that makes them taste so much better than any other barbecued sparerib that has ever passed through my lips and been caressed by my tongue.

Unfortunately, that cult of secrecy reaches deep into today's social life. Nearly every hostess in our circle of friends and acquaintances clings to the belief that only she knows how to produce that masterpiece that evokes such an abundance of praise when served at her house for dinner. She is, of course, conveniently forgetting that *somebody* once gave *her* the formula. Maybe it was her mother, or—in times when help was still to be found—her cook, or MAYBE . . . that, under the dryer, she read it in *Good Housekeeping!* Nevertheless, now it's *her* patent, she really believes that she has invented it, and has therefore the right and duty to protect it as though it were the latest classified missile.

Some hostesses will tell you that they cook by FEEL. They do not exactly know how they concoct, they just throw a few ingredients together, it never comes out the same, and how surprised they are when people like it. My wife, who is a ceramist, has the same trouble when she is trying to duplicate a glaze she admires. No one will ever tell her the correct chemical composition, until she finds it in a book. She has given up on other ceramists and now concentrates on books. They are for sale and much less trouble.

I am acquainted with a certain mistress of the manor who, being gracious by nature, simply cannot say no to a dear friend; reluctantly she will give her creation to me, but *only* to me, extracting a holy promise that I shall never pass it on to anyone else. Then, dripping with goodwill, she will write out her prescription, omitting a few vital details and giving wrong measurements.

I—eternal optimist that I am—rush home and try it. It tastes like mud. So I slyly beg her to invite us again and to serve that heavenly dish I liked so much, because—inferior cook that I am—I could not do it as well as she had made it. Usually her pride overcomes her suspicion, as few people can fathom the abyss of deceit that creeps into my heart when I am on the trail of a good recipe.

Once more at home and with the help of my wife, whose taste-buds are superb and whose detective powers are tremendous, I try it again, usually discover what was missing and where my friend lied about the measurements. We experiment and, after we have it down pat, I turn into a real heel and s.o.b. I invite the gracious lady to our next dinner party, where—as a big surprise—I serve *her* dish. And while she pales, I put on a great show of exuberant and insincere gratitude for her generosity and kindness.

But being a culinary Sherlock Holmes is, most of the time, a trying business, fraught with many defeats and few triumphs.

If You Want to Lose Weight,
Write a Cookbook

One of the few sorrows of my otherwise happy existence has been the highly visible fact that I was FAT.

A tailor who took my measurements for a new suit once remarked, "You have an interesting shape!" Then, rubbing salt into that permanently open wound, he added that it was difficult "to drape a global form." "With a thin man," he said, "the suit just falls naturally from the shoulders down; that gives elegance."

For the last forty years of my life I have been waging an unsuccessful war against my expanding anatomy, a battle against my personal bulge.

I have been trying to shrink that all too solid flesh and to adorn my bone structure with the padding of a normal man, a man who conforms to those miserable charts which decree that if you are six feet tall and over seventy years of age you should weigh no more than 160 pounds. I am still a good stretch away from those 160 pounds, but finally—finally—I see light at the end of the tunnel. It isn't a very bright light, to be sure. No rays of sunshine break through the darkness of my fatty substance, but a faint twinkle, a touch of dawn, is becoming visible, and for me that is a big spark of hope, a spark that I owe mainly to the writing of this book. This collection embraces more than three hundred recipes. They have been tried and assembled through the years, gastronomical memories my traveling stomach has retained. They have been recorded by us in our own inimitable and mostly illegible shorthand, with key words and instructions in six different languages.

Then came Doubleday & Company—bless their corporate souls— to ask me to write this book. I was thrilled, I was elated. I saw a

chance to join the company of those immortal epicureans, the un-
surpassable Greats: the Savarins, the Escoffiers, the Charpentiers,
and Dione Lucases. I was floating on clouds, but the fantastic
dream turned into cold reality when the "lady cookbook-editor" of
that much blessed corporation entered the scene. Her enchanting
loveliness, her blond melting femininity was, so I was soon to learn,
nothing but camouflage for an iron will, an overpowering stub-
bornness, a fearsome perseverance. That lovely apparition informed
me in mellow tones that, if I really wanted the book to appear in
print, I would first have to obey all the draconic laws she would im-

pose on me. I would have to follow her instructions to the letter,
viz.:

RULE 1. *The manuscript must be neatly typed on sturdy white
bond paper 8½″×11″.*
Sturdy white bond paper of that size is not available in Europe.
They have different sizes, so I had to import all the paper from the
U.S.A., *and* I had to *learn* to type *neatly*.

RULE 2. *No smaller sheets should be used!*
Sometimes, in error, I used small sheets and felt ashamed for a
whole week.

RULE 3. *Staples, paper clips, and Scotch Tape should not be used.*
All my correspondence, for more years than I care to count,
consisted mainly of loose sheets held together by staples, paper clips,
and Scotch Tape. I felt frustrated and after every typing mistake
started a whole new page.

RULE 4. *Two carbon copies are required, the copies to correspond
EXACTLY with the original.*
I considered that demand completely unnecessary and could only
interpret it as a nasty way of picking on the author.

RULE 5. *For each recipe it must be stated for how many persons
the dish is intended.*
I know roughly how much our friends eat and how much I eat,
but how can I judge the eating capacity and devouring habits of
the average person? WHO is the average person? Is it a child, an
adolescent (they eat for two), is it a lady of leisure whose most
strenuous exertion consists of putting on make-up in the morning,
driving to the hairdresser, and switching channels on her remote-
control TV set? Or is it a person who does heavy work, either for a
living or as a hobby? One of my friends goes in for bricklaying! Another works every weekend as if his life depended on it, swinging a
pickax, sawing lumber, and shoveling earth, trying to plow, clear,
till, and cultivate the two acres of wilderness he owns next to his
house in the country. Yet another of my buddies is wild about boat-
building. Not the *small* boats, mind you, but the big seagoing craft,
the ones that sleep six. And what about the elderly? We need less
food to stoke the old furnace than an active middle-aged person.

RULE 6. *It is an absolute MUST that all the ingredients of every dish be listed on the upper-left-hand side AND in the order of their appearance in the finished product. And, of course, with the exact oven temperatures, measurements, and amounts!*

Rule 6 was the killer! It meant that I had to start from scratch. I had to recook everything! Dishes I knew so well that I used to be able to prepare them by feel.

Now I stand in the kitchen, to my left the scales, to my right a notebook, a pencil between my teeth, and I measure every quarter of a teaspoon of salt, of pepper, paprika, every stalk of celery, every handful of mushrooms I might need for a sauce; I count how many shakes of Worcestershire sauce I use and how many drops of Tabasco, all the while trembling with fear that I might overspice or underspice the future reader of this book. I also have to take into account the altitude at which I am cooking. Our house in Switzerland is 667 meters above sea level (that's well over 2,000 feet) and a four-minute egg in New York takes five minutes in Breganzona.

Most of our recipes are in European weights and measures, so I must convert kilos and grams into pounds and ounces. One kilo is 35½ ounces and a pound=454 grams. I must convert liters into quarts, pints, and cups: one cup is 2.27 deciliters and when changing grams into ounces I multiply grams by 0.035, and by changing ounces into grams I multiply ounces by 28.35. When I translate Fahrenheit into Celsius I subtract 32, multiply by 5, and divide by 9. It's all so simple, so easy, and *such fun.*

Then comes the moment when a dish is ready, when it's all down on paper and cooked in the pot . . . and it doesn't come out right! It's not as my taste buds remember it. I see red, I explode, and use the entire vocabulary that the great Ernest Hemingway compressed into that one word: OBSCENITY.

I obscenity into the obscenity of writing that obscenity book. Unkind thoughts about my lady editor in New York waft across the sea. It was *she* who remembered—and kept reminding me—that sixteen years ago, when Doubleday published that unforgettable "first book" of mine, *What Time's the Next Swan?*, I had casually mentioned that someday (how vague can you get?), that someday I might try to write a book with recipes. Now the boomerang has re-

turned. I am seriously considering chucking the whole project, of
NOT becoming one of the immortals of the kitchen. But my
money-minded, frugal subconscious filters the stark realities into my
brain: "You'd have to *give back* the *advance money* . . . you'd
have to give back the *advance money!*"

I know I am licked. I wail in self-pity. At night I lie awake:
"Where did I go wrong? Where did I miss? How big is a pinch?
How much does a dash weigh?"

Comes the morning and I plod on again, but slowly the thought
of all the food that has to be *prepared* begins to revolt me. I find
only raw edibles appealing.

One day I discover that my always too tight pants have become a
little looser, that the middle button of my jacket does not burst
away when I sit down, and "as spring has come, unannounced, on

little feet . . ." I begin to realize that I am *melting*. I consult the scales, that uncorruptible nemesis of obesity. It has slipped below the hundred-kilo mark. The joy of looking down on myself and being able to see my feet without having to bend over is indescribable. The old tailor who has been letting out my clothes for years now has to take them in. He takes them in at the back and all my pockets are now at the rear, next to my spine!

Dear, dear public, PLEASE buy this book (and do not lend it to anyone), give it away as a present—often; this precious book for which I paid with seventy-nine pounds of my bulk—help make it a best-seller so that I will be able to buy new clothes, turn into a fashion plate, and now—in my old age—experience the glorious feeling that I have become what I have never been before—ELEGANT!

I Consider Myself a Present
from the Emperor Franz Josef I
to the World

Let me explain that statement: I was born in Vienna as a subject of Emperor Franz Josef the First, Apostolic King of Hungary, King of Bohemia, Dalmatia, Croatia, Slavonia, Galizien; Archduke of Toscana, Cracow, and Salzburg, Duke of Steiermark, Kärnten, Lothringen, Krain, and Bukowina, Silesia, Parma, Piacenza, Ragusa, Tirol, Trieste, etc., etc., etc.

With all this tremendous power and awesome responsibility Franz Josef led a frugal life, his tastes were simple, and great was his loneliness. His marriage to beautiful Empress Elizabeth was a cold and formal relationship; she disliked life at court and traveled a lot. To ease his loneliness, she persuaded an actress of the Kaiser und Königliche (K. und K.) Burgtheater to look after the Emperor and, whenever possible, to keep him company.

The Emperor's life was crowded with work, appointments, conferences, and representative duties, and the only time he could reserve for Frau Katharina Schratt was early in the morning. He rose at 5 A.M., left the palace, and walked over to her house. There, away from the stifling, strict Spanish etiquette that for generations had been imposed on the House of Habsburg, he felt at ease and comfortable. Every morning he breakfasted with Frau Schratt on coffee and a special kind of roll that was to be known as *"Kaisersemmel."*

And it must have been during one of these breakfast sessions that Frau Schratt, who kept him informed on the nonpolitical news of Vienna and the happenings in the theatres and opera, mentioned

that on May 3 Kammersänger Leo Slezak, the famous tenor of his
K. und K. Hof Opern Haus, had, with the active participation of
his wedded spouse, produced a male child (me).

The aged monarch was a wise old gentleman and he knew that
sons of opera singers rarely made good soldiers, so he probably said,
"Okay, world! There's another one I can do without. Take him!"
And the world was kind. It took me.

I began my nomadic existence as a Thespian and started my
climb up the theatrical and celluloid ladder in Vienna, after that in
Berlin. From there I was snatched and shipped to New York by one
J. J. Shubert, bless his soul in heaven.

On arrival the immigration officer shook my hand, welcomed me
to the melting pot, and said, "When you have made your first million dollars, send me a bottle of champagne." I am afraid I still
cannot send him that bottle.

Emotional ties to the country of my birth still cling like a loose
umbilical cord to my obese person, but I have never known the
fierce pride in all things Austrian that local patriotism demands of
the natives. Several years ago I was being interviewed on television
in Austria and mentioned casually that in my humble opinion there
was no such thing as typical Austrian cooking. The startled and
disbelieving look on the face of the gentleman who interviewed me
should have alerted me to danger. But blithely I plowed on, eager
to show off my knowledge of history, expanding on my statement
that over hundreds of years the shaky structure that was once called
the monarchy had annexed, incorporated (either by trade, marriage, or conquest), and later partially assimilated many different
races: here I began to rattle off the titles of Franz Josef, and
claimed that all these nationals had left traces of their cooking,
traces that had been melted, combined, and converted into a com-
posite known as *Austrian cooking.*

When the interview was over, a gentleman from the TV station
walked over to me and, with ice-cold politeness, said, "Mr. Slezak, I
do not think it was very wise of you to say that there is no such
thing as typical Austrian cooking." Then he walked away, and it
began to dawn on me that I had stepped on one of their great national toes. I might as well have said that Johann Strauss, Mozart,
and Schubert were Russian composers.

The following day there began to arrive at the hotel where I was staying a deluge of letters and telegrams. Abuses, invectives, and insults such as I had never heard before were expressed, threats were made, and one letter writer suggested that I should do things to myself which even a trained acrobat could not possibly accomplish. My vocabulary of the Viennese vernacular was greatly enriched: "Have you never heard of *Wiener Schnitzel?*" "*Se verkalktes Rindviech*" (an allusion to bovine descendancy with arteriosclerosis). "Where would you get *Backhendl* [fried chicken] except in Austria?"

I was crushed, filled with shame, unable to take nourishment for four hours until, into the abyss of my depression, a ray of light penetrated and an idea kissed my brain: I hired a secretary and together we answered each and every letter. I deplored the deep well of misinformation that had guided me to say such unforgivable things in public: I asked for forgiveness and I even dared to beg the dear correspondents for enlightenment: Would they please ("please" underlined) enlighten a man who had lived for so many years in America and thus never had the chance to find out for himself *what* the typical Austrian dishes were, "and PLEASE send me YOUR way of preparing those dishes because only someone who is a dedicated great cook would care so much about the foolishness I have uttered."

Surprisingly about 180 people answered. A few stayed offended and angry, but the majority were nice and sent me their "typicals," a third of which turned out to be goulash.

Goulash, of course, had its origin in Hungary. There are many versions of how that dish was invented, all of them open to challenge and none verified.

VERSION 1

The Hungarians were blessed with wide open spaces that they call "the Puszta." On that Puszta roamed thousands of horses and cattle and a good many herdsmen to look after them. It was the custom that one of the herdsman (usually a senior citizen afflicted with rheumatism or an overly tender rear end that made it painful to him to ride herd) would sit all day under a colored umbrella in front of a large kettle. The kettle was mounted on an iron tripod and it was his vocation to keep a fire going under that kettle while IN the kettle there simmered water.

Every morning each herdsman brought with him a pig's bladder that had been filled with his favorite titbits, chunks of meat, onions, red and green peppers, tomatoes, and lots of sharp paprika. Each man marked his bladder (the pig's, that is), closed it tightly, and hung it into the kettle, there to simmer. Upon returning in the evening each fished out his bladder, ate its contents, and sang *triste* songs. One day, one of the herdsman said, "Oh hell, let's call it goulash!" and a name was born.

VERSION 2, probably equally untrue:

A band of gypsies, who were also roaming the Puszta, made a bet on how many ingredients for a stew they would be able to steal within an hour. Then they cooked the stuff and the winner called it goulash. Versions 3, 4, and 5, are too silly to mention.

I have personally eaten more than twelve kinds of goulash: beef, pork, lamb, chicken, turkey, fish, all *with* sauerkraut and *without* sauerkraut, *with* sour cream and *without* sour cream, with bacon, with potatoes. And there is one goulash that I believe I have invented.

Late one afternoon, many many years ago in New York, when I was young and a bachelor, I received a phone call from a ravishing young lady who had once hinted that she would not be averse to letting herself be seduced by me. It was always one of my noble principles that you also have to feed the girls. Unfortunately I was "out of funds" at that time and could not afford to take her to a restaurant. The stores were already closed, so I had to dream up a dinner with the remains of the icebox. I found green peppers, onions, garlic, tomato paste and tomatoes, potatoes, caraway seeds, and a can of frankfurters. I baptized it "frankfurter goulash," an apt name if there ever was one.

The evening turned out to be highly successful and so did the dish, so much so that the great Craig Claiborne found it worthy of inclusion in his celebrated *New York Times Cook Book.*

Viennese Goulash
(Wiener Gulyas)

2 pounds good quality beef shank
Salt
4 large onions, chopped
½ cup cooking oil or Crisco
2 or 3 cloves garlic, minced
1 teaspoon caraway seeds
½ teaspoon marjoram

2 large or 3 small tomatoes,
    peeled and chopped
2 tablespoons paprika
¼ teaspoon powdered ginger
Cornstarch if needed
Salt and freshly ground pepper
    to taste

Cut meat into 1-inch cubes and sprinkle with salt. Sauté the onions in the oil till golden brown. Add the meat, garlic, caraway seeds, marjoram, tomatoes, paprika, and ginger; let the mixture cook slowly in its own juice in a covered iron pot. When the juice has simmered down enough to cover half the meat, add boiling water to cover, cook for about 2 hours. If the gravy is too thin, you may thicken it with a bit of cornstarch. Season to taste. *Serves 5.*

Kaasi Goulash
(Kaasi Gulyas)

2 teaspoons salt
1 teaspoon freshly ground pepper
3½–4 tablespoons paprika
6 pounds stewing veal cut into
    1½-inch cubes
6 medium-sized onions, chopped
    coarsely

1 bell pepper, chopped coarsely
4 tablespoons Crisco
1 tablespoon tomato paste
1 teaspoon Worcestershire sauce
2–3 tablespoons sour cream
    (optional)

Rub the salt, pepper, and 2½ tablespoons of the paprika into the meat. Sauté the onions and bell pepper in the Crisco till the onions are transparent. Add the remaining paprika and stir. Add the meat and brown it lightly on all sides, being very careful not to burn the paprika, for if you do, everything will taste bitter. Add the tomato paste, Worcestershire sauce, and water to cover. Simmer, covered, for 1½–2 hours or till the meat is fork-tender. You may have to add more water as the liquid evaporates. Take the meat out of the sauce and run the latter through a blender. Return the sauce to the meat, and when the goulash has cooled, refrigerate it overnight. This goulash, as with any other, is best when it is made the day before using it. Just before serving you may add 2 tablespoons of sour cream to the sauce. Serve with *Spaetzle* (see the Index) or buttered noodles. *Serves 6.*

Chicken Goulash and Chicken Paprika
(Huehnergulyas und Huehnerpaprika)

Chicken goulash and chicken paprika are made exactly the same as the above recipe, substituting chicken legs and breasts for the veal.

Beef Goulash
(Rindsgulyas)

4 tablespoons paprika	1 bell pepper, chopped coarsely
1 teaspoon McCormick goulash seasoning	5 tablespoons Crisco or cooking oil
2 teaspoons salt	1 tablespoon vinegar
6 pounds beef chuck cut into 1-inch cubes	2 cloves garlic, minced
8 medium-sized onions, chopped coarsely	½ teaspoon marjoram
	1 tablespoon caraway seeds
	2 tablespoons tomato paste

Rub the paprika, goulash seasoning, and salt well into the meat. Sauté the onions and bell pepper in the Crisco till the onions are golden brown. Add the meat and brown lightly on all sides. Add the vinegar, garlic, marjoram, caraway seeds, and tomato paste, mix well. Add enough water to cover and simmer till the meat is fork-tender, 1½–2 hours. You may have to add a little water from time to time as the liquid evaporates. Take the meat out of the sauce, run the latter through a blender. Let the goulash stand overnight in the refrigerator, reheat before serving. This fine dish is usually accompanied by boiled potatoes or noodles. *Serves 6.*

Szekeler Goulash
(Szekeler Gulyas)

Oil for frying
1 medium-sized onion, chopped
1 teaspoon salt
1 teaspoon caraway seeds
1 tablespoon paprika
1 tomato, peeled and quartered
1 bell pepper, seeded and
  chopped

1 pound lean pork, cubed
¼ cup water
1 pound sauerkraut
1 slice bacon, chopped
Flour or cornstarch
½ cup sour cream

Heat the oil, sauté the onion in it until golden, and remove from stove. Add the salt, caraway seeds, paprika, tomato, and bell pepper. Place again on the stove and add the cubed pork and the ¼ cup of water. Simmer, covered, for ½ hour, until the meat is done. Cook the sauerkraut with the bacon in a little water, drain, and mix with the goulash, thickened with a little flour or cornstarch (if canned sauerkraut is used, put it in a colander and rinse it once under water). Add the sour cream. Reheat and serve. *Serves 4.*

Frankfurter Goulash
(Würstelgulyas)

6 medium-sized onions, cut in
  large slices
4 tablespoons Crisco
10 bell peppers
1 tablespoon caraway seeds
1 cup canned tomatoes
Salt and freshly ground pepper
  to taste

2 tablespoons paprika
1 pound skinless frankfurters, cut
  into ½-inch slices
Worcestershire sauce to taste
Tabasco sauce to taste
6–8 medium-sized potatoes,
  boiled, peeled, cut in half

Sauté the onions in Crisco or any other fat. When the onions begin to get glazed, add the bell peppers, which have been seeded and sliced into 2-inch-long, ½-inch-wide strips, cover, and steam for 5 minutes. Add the caraway seeds, tomatoes, salt, pepper, and paprika. Cook until the bell peppers are softened. Add the frankfurters. Boil for 3 or 4 minutes and, if necessary, thicken with a little cornstarch. Add the Worcestershire and Tabasco sauces. Add the potatoes. This very good plain dish should be made at least 8 hours before it is served. *Serves 4.*

Goulash Soup
(Gulyas Suppe)

1 medium-sized onion, chopped
   fine
⅓ cup Crisco
3 tablespoons paprika
1 bell pepper, chopped fine
1 carrot, chopped fine
1 tomato, chopped fine
2 slices bacon, chopped fine

1 pound best quality stewing beef
   cut into small cubes
1 teaspoon salt
1½ teaspoons caraway seeds
1½ quarts water
2 medium-sized potatoes, peeled
   and cubed

Sauté the onion in the Crisco till golden brown, lower the flame, and add the paprika, bell pepper, carrot, tomato, and bacon, stir well. Add the beef, salt, and caraway seeds and let simmer for a few minutes. Add the 1½ quarts of water, bring it to a boil, and let simmer, with the lid tightly closed, for 1½ hours or till the meat is fork-tender. About ½ hour before the meat is done, add the potatoes. Taste for seasoning, as the soup may need more salt. *Serves 6.*

Mushroom Soup
(Schwammerl Suppe)

½ pound fresh mushrooms,
   washed and sliced
1 tablespoon butter
1 10-ounce can Campbell's cream
   of mushroom soup
A little less than ½ soup can of
   milk

A little less than ½ soup can of
   water
Lea & Perrins Worcestershire
   sauce to taste
2 tablespoons dry white wine or
   dry sherry
Chopped parsley

Sauté the mushrooms in the butter in a saucepan. Add the soup with the milk and water and cook for a few minutes. Just before serving, add the Worcestershire sauce and white wine. Sprinkle with chopped parsley. For a creamed mushroom soup, purée all ingredients except the parsley. *Serves 4.*

WIENER SCHNITZEL

The origin of *Wiener Schnitzel* goes back to the first century A.D., when the Romans built a garrison on the banks of the Danube and named it Vindobona. The fortifications around that stronghold were called the *anus* (Latin: ring) and are today known as the "Ringstrasse."

One of the Roman legionnaires, who came from a small village on the Lombard Plain called "Milano," was the cook for the officers' mess in the Vindobona garrison, and one day he had the fancy idea of coating the slices of veal with flour, then dipping them in beaten egg and finally in bread crumbs. He named his dish *"scaloppinus Milaneus."* After the garrison evacuated the fort and countryside, the dish remained, and is today claimed to be of Austrian origin.

Through the centuries Vindobona became Wien (Vienna) and the "dobona" is today better known as the beautiful blue Danube.

Viennese Veal Cutlets
(Wiener Schnitzel)

2 *pounds veal sliced into thin cutlets twice the size of scaloppine*	½ *teaspoon salt*
	1 *cup bread crumbs*
	1 *cup Crisco (or half Crisco and*
½ *cup flour*	*half oil)*
2 *eggs, lightly beaten with 1 tablespoon water*	1 *lemon, thinly sliced*

Dry the cutlets with a towel, dredge them in the flour, then dip them in the beaten egg with the salt added. Drag them through the bread crumbs on both sides, patting them lightly so the breading stays on firmly. In a skillet that holds as many cutlets as possible without crowding, sauté them over medium heat for 1½ minutes on each side. Drain them on paper towels and serve them immediately with slices of lemon. Delicious! *Serves 4.*

Cabbage Strudel with Ham
(Kraut Strudel)

4 cups chopped white cabbage
1 medium-sized onion, chopped
    fine
3 tablespoons butter
½ teaspoon each salt and freshly
    ground pepper

⅛ teaspoon caraway seeds
1 cup chopped boiled ham
1 egg, beaten
1 package of strudel dough (2
    sheets), available at good
    gourmet shops

Wash the chopped cabbage and drain. Sauté the onion in the butter in a large saucepan until light brown. Add the cabbage, salt, pepper, and caraway seeds. Mix well and simmer, covered, for 30 minutes. Mix in the boiled ham. Taste for seasoning. Add the beaten egg. Roll out 2 sheets of strudel dough, brush the first sheet with melted butter, put the second sheet on top of the first, paint with butter, and place the filling on the strudel, folding in the sides and rolling up the strudel tightly, paint top with butter. Place on a buttered or oiled baking sheet and bake in a preheated 350° oven for 30 minutes or until the top of the strudel is light brown. With a sharp knife cut the strudel into slices. Serve as a main course accompanied by a green salad for luncheon. *Serves 4.*

Serbian Meat with Rice
(Serbisches Reisfleisch)

5 slices bacon, chopped
4 tablespoons Crisco
2 medium-sized onions, chopped
1 teaspoon paprika
1 tablespoon tomato paste
3 pounds shoulder or shank of
    veal cut into 1-inch cubes

Salt to taste
1 cup uncooked rice
Water or chicken bouillon for
    cooking rice
¼ cup grated Parmesan cheese

Fry the bacon in the Crisco, add the onions, and fry till golden brown. Add the paprika, tomato paste, veal, and salt, and let the meat cook on a low fire in its own juice till half done. Add the rice, cover with water or bouillon till it is 1½ inches above the rice, and let it simmer till the rice is done and the liquid has almost been absorbed. Mix half the grated cheese with the meat and serve the other half separately. *Serves 6–8.*

Hungarian Reindel
(Ungarisches Reind'l)

1 cup finely sliced onions	*1 bell pepper, seeded, membrane*
¼ cup butter	*removed, sliced*
1 teaspoon paprika	*2 medium-sized tomatoes, peeled*
1 teaspoon salt	*and sliced*
2 pounds round steak in one	*2 medium-sized potatoes, peeled*
piece, pounded thin	*and quartered*

In a Dutch oven sauté the onions in the butter, sprinkle with paprika and salt. Add the steak and barely cover it with water. Add the bell pepper and tomatoes, cover the Dutch oven tightly, and place in a preheated 300° oven for 2 hours. One half hour before the meat is done, add the potatoes. If necessary, the sauce may be thickened with 1 tablespoon of flour and ¼ cup of sour cream. *Serves 4.*

Boiled Beef Kaasi
(Tafelspitz)

3 pounds top or bottom round in	*2 stalks celery, cut into 2-inch*
1 piece	*pieces*
2 tablespoons salt	*3 sprigs parsley*
8 peppercorns	*2 carrots, peeled and cut into*
1 bay leaf	*chunks*
2 large onions, halved, of which 2	*¼ teaspoon marjoram*
onion halves are stuck with 1	
clove each	

The meat should be prepared the day before the dish is to be served. It is very important that the meat should fit tightly in the pot. Place it in the pot and cover with cold water, add the salt, peppercorns, bay leaf, onions, celery, parsley, carrots, and marjoram. Cover tightly and bring to a boil. Cook slowly for 3 to 4 hours, adding water when necessary. The meat should be very tender. Probe with a fork. This should be all done the day before. Cool and let stand in the refrigerator overnight. The following day remove the fat from the soup, take out the meat, and slice it—against the grain—into ½-inch-thick slices. Warm the jellied soup until it turns liquid again and run it through a sieve. Return the strained soup with the meat slices to the pot. Be sure that the meat is completely immersed. Leave the meat in the soup until it is ready to be served. Before serving, heat but do not boil again. Serve with fried potatoes, Apple and Horseradish Sauce (see Index), or either of the following two sauces. *Serves 4.*

Chive Sauce
(Schnittlauch Sauce)

3 hard-cooked eggs	1 teaspoon prepared mustard
2 raw egg yolks	1–2 tablespoons vinegar
1 cup salad oil	¾–1 cup yogurt
Salt and freshly ground pepper to taste	1 bunch chives, chopped

Mash the yolks of the hard-cooked eggs and add the 2 raw egg yolks. Beat with a wire whisk and slowly add the oil, salt, pepper, mustard, and vinegar, beat until smooth. Add the yogurt, egg mixture, and chopped chives. If the sauce is too thick, thin it with a little milk or consommé, but the sauce should be thick. Serve it at room temperature. *Makes 1 cup of sauce.*

Dill Sauce
(Dillsauce)

2 tablespoons butter
1 small onion, minced
2 tablespoons flour
1 cup beef broth (use the soup of
    the boiled beef in Boiled
    Beef Kaasi, above)
1 teaspoon chopped parsley

1 tablespoon finely chopped
    fresh dill
A few drops lemon juice
Salt and freshly ground pepper
    to taste
1 tablespoon sour cream
    (optional)

Melt the butter, sauté onion in it until golden brown. Add the flour, brown it a bit. Add the broth, stirring constantly, let cook until thick. Add the parsley, dill, and lemon juice, season with salt and pepper. Add the sour cream. The sauce should be served *warm!* *Makes about 2 cups of sauce.*

Calf's Liver Viennese Style
(Wiener Kalbsleber)

2 pounds calf's liver
½ cup vegetable oil
½ cup finely chopped onions
1 teaspoon flour
A pinch of marjoram

Chicken bouillon or water
Salt and freshly ground pepper
    to taste
Chopped parsley

Trim the liver, cut it into strips 3 inches long and ¼ inch thick. Heat the oil in a skillet large enough so strips of liver will not be crowded, sauté the onions until brown, add the liver, and fry, stirring, for 5 minutes. Sprinkle with flour and marjoram, stir, and slowly add enough bouillon (or water) to half cover the liver and to make gravy. Only when serving add salt and pepper. Sprinkle with chopped parsley. *Serves 4.*

Breaded Pork Liver
(Panierte Schweinsleber)

2 pounds liver of YOUNG pork
Flour
2 eggs, beaten with a little water

Bread crumbs
Vegetable oil
Salt

Wash and skin the liver, cut into strips 1 inch long and ¼ inch wide, and roll them first in flour, then in egg, and then in bread crumbs. In the oil fry the liver strips until they are brown on the outside and pink on the inside (a very short time). DO NOT salt them until you are ready to eat—they might become tough. Serve with a green salad or green vegetable. *Serves 4–5.*

Serbian Pork—A Meat Loaf
(Serbisches Schweinefleisch)

2 teaspoons oil for frying
1 medium-sized onion, chopped
3 tablespoons flour
1 pound lean pork, ground
Salt and freshly ground pepper
*   to taste*

1 egg
¾ cup uncooked rice
4 bell peppers, chopped coarsely
1 small can tomato paste
½ cup sour cream

Heat the oil, sauté the chopped onion in it until golden brown. In a bowl mix the onion with the flour, meat, salt, pepper, and egg; with moistened hands form the mass into a loaf and lay in a well-greased roasting pan. Boil the rice in salted water until half done, and set aside. Lay the chopped peppers around the loaf. Lay the half-cooked rice on top of the bell peppers. Now mix the tomato paste with a bit of water and fold in the sour cream, pour over the meat loaf, and bake the loaf in a preheated 350° oven until all the liquid has evaporated and the rice is done. Slice the loaf and serve with the rice and bell peppers on the side. *Serves 4.*

Viennese Breaded Fried Chicken
(Wiener Backhendl)

Chicken not over 6 weeks old,
*   allow ½ chicken per person*
Flour
Egg, beaten with a little water
*   and ⅛ teaspoon salt per*
*   chicken*

Bread crumbs
Half oil and half Crisco for deep
*   frying*
Parsley, not chopped

Quarter the chicken and skin the pieces, roll them in flour, beaten egg, and bread crumbs. Deep-fry them in oil (it should not be too hot) for about 5 minutes. When done they should be golden brown outside. Take a bunch of parsley and sauté the sprigs very lightly for ½ minute in the oil. Put the parsley over the chicken pieces just before serving.

Macaroni with Ham
(Schinkenfleckerln)

1 pound very small elbow
*   macaroni or medium-sized*
*   noodles*
1 pound or more cooked ham,
*   chopped, or 1 can corned*
*   beef*
¼ pound butter or margarine

4 eggs, separated
1 cup sour cream
1 teaspoon salt
Freshly ground pepper to taste
½ cup grated Parmesan cheese
Bread crumbs

Boil the macaroni (or noodles) in a lot of salted water. Meanwhile, cut the ham (or corned beef) into small pieces. Cream the butter with the 4 egg yolks, add the ham, sour cream, salt, and pepper. Beat the 4 egg whites until stiff, blend with the macaroni and Parmesan cheese. Put into a deep Pyrex casserole, sprinkle with bread crumbs, and bake in a preheated 400° oven for 1 hour.

KNOEDEL!

Everyone I know has the best hairdresser and the best podiatrist. And every opera house in the world has the best "Mime" (*Siegfried*) and the best "Beckmesser" (*Die Meistersinger*). And everyone who has ever wielded a wooden spoon or has pressed down on a rolling pin has the best recipe for *Knoedel*. The English word for Knoedel is "dumpling," but I find the German word more heartwarming.

Knoedel consists mostly of flour, bread, eggs, and milk. These nourishing ingredients are combined and are formed into round balls that are then immersed in boiling water or soup. The size of these balls depends on one's taste and the particular use the *Knoedel* is to be put to. They range from tiny to small, to medium, to large (the size of a basketball), and then to the giant sizes. These last are shaped into the form of a loaf, wrapped in a large napkin, and then boiled. There are therefore called *Servietten Knoedel*. This may sound confusing to the uninitiated, but there is wisdom behind that method: the napkins hold the mixture together until it is firm enough to live its own life.

When word spread among our friends that I was about to write a book of stories with recipes, I was suddenly besieged: by those ladies who entered their kitchen only on the maid's day off—and those who did their own cooking. Hostesses who usually guarded their gastronomic secrets with fierce determination became openhearted and wanted to share. And NEVER had their recipes for making *Knoedel* originated in a cookbook—ALWAYS it was a family heirloom—something handed down from generation to generation, usually whispered to the favorite grandchild by Grandmother on her deathbed.

Legends have been woven about the number of *Knoedel* some glutton managed to down in one sitting; and there's the story of a five-year-old who watched his mother breast-feed his baby brother. Wide-eyed and scared, he asked, "Does little Tommy have to eat that WHOLE knoedel?"

Friends of ours have a collection of antique cookbooks. I leafed through one that was written in 1756. It was dedicated, with endless expressions of devotion, to His Eminence, the Archbishop of Salzburg—submitted by his most subservient, humble cook, Hans Spelger.

In that book every dish is named after a saint, and cooking times are given only in prayers; very exact directions on how many Hail Marys would produce a soft-boiled egg and how many Our Fathers an omelette. One of the recipes starts: "Buy flour for 3 kreuzer, and for 2 kreuzer Semmeln [hard rolls], for 4 kreuzer eggs," and so on. I do not know the purchase price for a kreuzer in 1756, but I am sure that inflation has wiped out its buying power.

This book had everything—including forty-three recipes for *Knoedel,* fish *Knoedel* dedicated to St. Peter—yes, even matzo balls, an astonishing dish for a diocese.

Fool that I was, I believed that *Knoedel* was a Tirolean invention, but every country in Europe claims it as its own.

Individual Dumplings
(Semmelknoedel)

1 small onion, chopped	*2 cups milk*
½ teaspoon chopped parsley	*2 eggs, beaten*
¼ pound butter or margarine	*Salt to taste*
8 day-old white rolls, cut into	*A dash of white pepper*
½-inch cubes	*¾–1 cup flour*

Sauté the onion and parsley slightly in the butter, then pour onto the cubed rolls in a large bowl. Mix the milk, eggs, salt, and white pepper and pour over the bread mixture, let rest for 15 minutes. Mix in the flour, kneading well. With wet hands, form dumplings about 2½ inches in diameter and cook in boiling salted water till they rise—10–15 minutes. Do NOT overcook. In Bavaria, the leftover dumplings are sliced, dipped in beaten egg, and fried like French toast for breakfast. *Serves 6.*

Tirolean Bacon Dumplings
(Tiroler Speck Knoedel)

Use the same ingredients as in Individual Dumplings (see the recipe above), but add ½ pound diced bacon or smoked pork and ½ pound diced salami to the mixture. Form the dumplings and cook in salted water until they rise—about 12 minutes. *Serves 6.*

Farina Dumplings
(Gries Nockerln)

½ cup fine farina	1 teaspoon chopped parsley
1 egg	(optional)
1 tablespoon melted butter	⅛ teaspoon onion salt (optional)
Salt and freshly ground pepper to taste	

Mix all ingredients thoroughly, let the mixture stand for 10 minutes. Drop the mixture by teaspoonfuls into boiling salted water, let them simmer for 10 minutes, then turn off the flame and let the dumplings stay in the water for another 10 minutes. Then add them to bouillon or soup. *Makes 8 large or 12 small dumplings.*

Napkin Dumpling
(Servietten Knoedel)

18 slices of white bread, 1 or 2
    days old
1 cup milk
¼ cup plus 1 tablespoon butter
    or margarine
6 egg yolks

2 tablespoons salt
¼ teaspoon white pepper
2 tablespoons chopped parsley
¼ teaspoon onion salt
6 egg whites

Cut the bread into half-inch cubes, pour the milk over them, mix lightly, and let stand for a half hour. Beat the butter with the egg yolks, add the salt, pepper, parsley, and onion salt, and mix with the bread cubes. Beat the egg whites till stiff and fold into the bread mixture. Form into a ball or thick roll. Thoroughly wet a large napkin or kitchen towel and wring it out. Butter it, lay the dumpling on it, gather up the corners and tie them together. Suspend the bag from a wooden spoon across the rim of a large kettle, submerging the tied napkin in boiling salted water to cover. Cook the dumpling gently for 1 hour, then remove it carefully from the napkin, let the steam evaporate, and slice the dumpling into 1-inch slices. Serve with any roast or stew that has lots of gravy. *Serves 6–8.*

Wine Sauerkraut
(Wein Kraut)

1 large can of sauerkraut
3 tablespoons butter
1 large onion, cut into large
    pieces
1 large apple, cut into large
    pieces

1 teaspoon sugar
½ cup white wine
1 cup seedless white grapes cut in
    half
1 teaspoon cornstarch

Place the sauerkraut in a colander and rinse once with cold water, drain well. Melt the butter in a large saucepan, sauté the onion till it is transparent, add the sauerkraut, apple, and sugar, and cook for a few minutes more. Add the wine and enough water to cover the

sauerkraut, let it simmer, covered, for about an hour. Sauté the halved grapes for a few minutes in some butter. Meanwhile mix the cornstarch with a little water and add to the sauerkraut to thicken it. Then fold in the grapes very carefully. This dish goes well with roast pheasant and other fowl. *Serves 6.*

Bologna Salad
(Wurst Salat)

6 tablespoons oil
3 tablespoons vinegar
½ teaspoon sugar
2 pounds bologna, diced
1½ cups finely sliced cold boiled
    potatoes

3 large pickles, sliced fine
1 large onion, diced
2 tablespoons chopped parsley
Watercress for garnish

Mix well the oil, vinegar, and sugar and combine with the rest of the ingredients except the watercress, which is the garnish. This salad is often served as a first course with small slices of dark bread. Delicious! *Serves 4.*

Liptauer Cheese Spread
(Liptauer Kaese)

½ cup butter	1 teaspoon caraway seeds
½ pound pot cheese (or, less preferable, cream cheese)	1 teaspoon chopped onions
	1 teaspoon chopped capers
2 anchovy fillets, finely chopped	1 teaspoon chopped chives
1 teaspoon dry mustard	Salt and freshly ground pepper
1 teaspoon paprika	to taste
1 teaspoon chopped parsley	Cold light beer

Mix everything to the consistency of a spread with the cold light beer. Serve with dark bread or crackers. *Makes 2 cups.*

Liver Pâté Kaasi
(Leber Pastete Kaasi)

1 pound chicken livers	½ teaspoon allspice
Enough milk to cover the livers	1 teaspoon salt
3 eggs	¾ teaspoon white pepper
2 slices white bread, soaked in water and pressed dry	¼ pound sweet butter, melted
	Aspic (recipe given below)

Soak the chicken livers overnight in the milk. Rinse them under cold water in a colander, remove the stringy tissue, and pat them dry. Place them in a blender with the eggs, bread, and the seasonings, blend for 1 minute. Add the butter and blend for a few seconds more. Place the mixture in a buttered loaf pan, cover loosely with aluminum foil, and place in a large pan (a roasting pan is fine) of slowly boiling water, which should come to only half the height of the pan. Boil for 30–35 minutes till the pâté feels springy to the touch. Remove the pan from the water, cool, and put in the refrigerator, leave till the pâté is very cold. Remove the loaf from the pan by first running a knife around the sides, turning it upside down on a wooden board, and hitting it to loosen the pâté. Rinse out the pan with water and dry it.

Aspic

> 1 package unflavored gelatin
> ¼ cup cold water
> 2 cups chicken bouillon

Soften the gelatin in the cold water, add to the bouillon in a saucepan, heat and stir gently over low heat till the gelatin is dissolved. Pour this aspic ¼ inch deep in the loaf pan, leave in the refrigerator till the aspic is hardened. Cut a ¼-inch slice from *each* of the 4 sides of the pâté, invert the loaf, then set it down onto the aspic. Pour the remaining liquid aspic around the sides of the pâté till it is almost covered. Return the pan to the refrigerator to harden the aspic. To remove the pâté from the pan, set it in an inch or so of very hot water for a few seconds after running a sharp knife around the sides of the pan. Place the loaf upside down on a serving platter. When the pâté is served as a first course, cut it into half-inch slices and serve with white toast points and Cumberland Sauce (recipe follows). When served as an hors d'oeuvre, surround the platter with rounds of white toast or dark bread. This is an excellent pâté. *Serves 6–8.*

Cumberland Sauce

> 2 tablespoons jellied cranberry sauce
> 2 tablespoons currant jelly
> ½ tablespoon orange juice
> ½ tablespoon lemon juice
> ½ tablespoon grated orange rind
>
> 1 teaspoon grated lemon rind
> A pinch of dry mustard
> 1 teaspoon bottled horseradish
> Lea & Perrins Worcestershire sauce to taste

Mix all ingredients. If the sauce is too thick, add 1 tablespoon of dry red wine. *Makes about 1 cup with wine added.*

The following two dressings—Apfel Kren and Essig Kren—are both prized for use with boiled beef, poached fish, and cold meats.

Apple and Horseradish Sauce
(Apfel Kren)

8 small apples	⅓ cup sugar
⅓–½ cup freshly grated	1 tablespoon vinegar or
horseradish to taste	juice of ½ lemon

Peel and core the apples, grate on the small-sized teeth of a grater. Add the horseradish, sugar, and the vinegar or lemon juice.

Horseradish Vinegar Dressing
(Essig Kren)

Fresh horseradishes	Sugar
Beef bouillon	Salt
Vinegar	

Grate the horseradishes, add enough bouillon to make a sauce consistency. Add vinegar, sugar, and salt to taste.

Individual Cheese Soufflé Muffins

6 tablespoons butter	1 teaspoon flour
5 eggs, separated	¼ teaspoon salt
½ cup grated Parmesan cheese	6 tablespoons chopped ham

Beat the butter and egg yolks well together, add the Parmesan cheese, flour, and salt, blend well. Beat the egg whites until stiff, add to the mixture. Fill buttered and floured large muffin cups a quarter full with the mixture, add 1 teaspoon of ham, add more of the mixture until each muffin cup is over half full. Bake for 20–25 minutes in a preheated 350° oven. If 4 individual soufflé dishes are used, fill each dish a quarter full with the mixture, add a quarter of the ham, add more of the soufflé mixture to each dish, and bake for 20–25 minutes in a preheated 350° oven. Serve immediately. *Makes about 1 dozen soufflé muffins; serves 4 made in individual soufflé dishes.*

Apricot Dumplings
(Marillen Knoedel)

1 pound farmer's cheese	8 small ripe apricots
2 eggs	8 small lumps of sugar
4 tablespoons farina	1–1½ cups bread crumbs
2 tablespoons flour	browned in butter
A pinch of salt	Powdered sugar

Place the first 5 ingredients in a bowl—preferably one for an electric mixer—and mix well till you have a soft dough. Let this rest for an hour in the refrigerator. Roll out the dough on a floured board and cut into 2-inch squares. Cut open the apricots, take out the pits, and replace with a small lump of sugar in each fruit. Place an apricot on each square of dough, gather the corners, and press dough into 8 balls. Put into a kettle with lots of lightly salted boiling water, let them cook for 8–10 minutes. They must float for at least 5 minutes before they are done. Lift them out of the water with a slotted spoon, roll them in the buttered bread crumbs, pour a little melted butter on top of each, and dust as heavily as you wish with powdered sugar. These are delightful. *Makes 8 dumplings.*

Chocolate Soufflé
(Schokoladen Soufflé)

¾ cup sugar	Juice of ½ lemon
¾ cup chocolate softened in the	5 egg whites, well beaten
top of a double boiler	

Mix the sugar and chocolate well, add the lemon juice, and fold in the beaten egg whites. Place in a buttered 2-quart soufflé dish and bake in a preheated 375° oven for 10 minutes. *Serves 4.*

Döry Cake à la Helene
(Döry Torte à la Helene)

5 eggs, separated
⅔ cup sugar
¼ pound semisweet chocolate,
    melted in the top of a
    double boiler

1 stick of butter, melted
A pinch of salt
Grated sweet chocolate

Beat 2 egg yolks with half the sugar until fluffy. Add the melted and somewhat cooled chocolate, stirring slightly. Add the remaining egg yolks, melted butter, stiffly beaten egg whites, remaining sugar, and a pinch of salt. Bake half that batter until done. Remove the torte from the oven, and when it is slightly cooled, pour the other half of the batter on top of it. Sprinkle with grated sweet chocolate and place in the refrigerator. *Serves 4–6.*

Lemon Cream
(Citronen Creme)

2 packages unflavored gelatine
2 tablespoons cold water
⅔ cup dry white wine
5 eggs, separated

½ cup sugar
Juice and grated rind of 2
    lemons

Soak the gelatine in the mixed cold water and wine. Beat the egg yolks with ¼ cup of sugar, add the lemon juice and grated rind, beat again. Beat the gelatine mixture and add to the egg yolks. Refrigerate until almost firm. Beat the egg whites and remaining ¼ cup of sugar until almost stiff, add the lemon mixture. Cool in the refrigerator. This cream can be served with a vanilla or fruit sauce. *Serves 6.*

Emperor's Omelette
(Kaiserschmarrn)

2 cups milk	*A pinch of salt*
7 tablespoons flour	*7 tablespoons melted butter*
8 eggs, separated	*¼ cup raisins*
1 tablespoon or more of sugar	*1 tablespoon rum*

Mix the milk and flour well, add the egg yolks, sugar, salt, melted butter, the stiffly beaten egg whites, raisins, and rum. In an omelette pan melt some additional butter, pour in batter ¼ inch deep, fry till the underside has a crust, turn the omelette over and fry the other side. Then tear the omelette in pieces. Sprinkle lavishly with sugar and serve with a Compote of Plums (*Zwetschgenroester*), the recipe following. *Serves 6–8.*

Compote of Plums
(Zwetschgenroester)

4 pounds ripe dark plums	*¼ teaspoon cinnamon*
2 pounds sugar	*1 clove*

Wash and pit the plums. Put them in a heavy enamel or stainless steel kettle. Cover them with sugar, add the cinnamon and clove, cover with a cloth, and let stand overnight. Cook the plums for approximately 2 hours, stirring occasionally to keep them from burning. Cook until the fruit reaches a translucent state and the syrup is heavy. Remove the clove. Should the syrup not be heavy enough, drain the plums and put them into sterilized jars, then simmer the syrup to the desired thickness and pour over the plums. Seal and store. *Makes about 5 pints.*

Linzertorte Maria

¾ cup sugar
¾ cup melted butter
¾ cup finely chopped or ground
     almonds
1⅓ cups flour
1 egg

1 egg yolk
2 squares unsweetened chocolate,
     grated
Raspberry jelly and raspberry
     jam to cover cake mixture

Mix the first 7 ingredients well, spread a little more than half of the
mixture on the bottom of a buttered cake pan, keeping a little less
than half the mixture for latticework. Cover with a mixture of half

jelly and half jam (with seeds). Now make a rim and latticework to place over the sweet filling. Press the latticework into place with a fork. Bake in a preheated very slow oven for 1 hour or at 400° for 30 minutes. Linzertorte is better after 1 or 2 days.

Apple Strudel
(Apfel Strudel)

I am a lazy cook, too lazy to go through the long, tedious, and time-consuming procedure of making and rolling out the dough. When I feel like having strudel, I use the equally good ready-made strudel dough sheets that are available at many gourmet stores.

¾ cup unseasoned bread crumbs	*½ cup granulated sugar*
3 tablespoons melted butter	*Juice of 1 lemon*
4 cups peeled and sliced apples	*1 package strudel dough sheets*
(5 medium-sized green)	*(using only 2 sheets)*
⅓ cup chopped almonds	*1 tablespoon butter*
⅓ cup seedless raisins	*¼ cup powdered sugar*
½ teaspoon cinnamon	

Brown the bread crumbs in the butter, set them aside. In a bowl mix the apples, almonds, raisins, cinnamon, sugar, and lemon juice, set them aside. Open the package of strudel dough carefully (it should be at room temperature). Place one dough sheet on a large cloth or napkin, dampened, and paint it carefully with some melted butter, using a pastry brush. Sprinkle with half of the crumbs. Place the second dough sheet directly over the first, paint it with butter, and sprinkle it with the remaining bread crumbs. Place the apple filling on the end of the dough sheet nearest you in one strip 2½ inches wide, fold the right and left sides of the dough toward the center of the sheet, and, starting at the end nearer you, roll like a jelly roll with the aid of the cloth or napkin. Place the strudel carefully on a buttered cookie sheet and paint it lightly with butter. Bake in a preheated 400° oven for 25–30 minutes. When it has cooled a little, sprinkle it with powdered sugar, then cut it carefully into individual portions with a very sharp knife. This is a truly delicious dessert. *Serves 6.*

IMPORTANT NOTE: The same recipe can be used for cherries, rhubarb, or plums.

Orange Cake
(Orangen Kuchen)

¾ cup sugar
6 eggs, separated
Juice of 1½ oranges
Grated rind of 2 oranges

1 cup finely chopped or grated almonds
1 teaspoon bread crumbs

Beat the sugar and egg yolks until light lemon-colored. Add the orange juice, grated orange rind, almonds, and bread crumbs. Fold in the stiffly beaten egg whites. Bake in a buttered and floured snap cake pan in a preheated 350° oven for about 1 hour, or until a knife inserted comes out clean. Let the cake cool before icing.

Icing:

Confectioner's sugar
Lemon juice

Grand Marnier
Orange marmalade

Mix confectioner's sugar with enough lemon juice and Grand Marnier to make a thick and smooth icing. Cover the cooled cake with orange marmalade and then spread the icing over it.

Equilibrium Cake
(Equilibrium Kuchen)

1 cup sugar
4 eggs, separated
Juice of 1 lemon
¾ cup butter

1 cup flour
1 teaspoon baking powder
Sliced fresh fruit—apples, apricots, peaches, or plums

Beat together the sugar and egg yolks, add the lemon juice and butter bit by bit. Then add flour, beaten egg whites, and baking powder, mix well. Spread the mixture thinly on a buttered 16- by 10-inch cookie sheet. Lay sliced fruit on top. Bake in a preheated 350° oven for 30 minutes. *Serves 6.*

Nut Layer Cake with Whipped Cream
(Creme Schnitten)

6 eggs, separated
½ cup sugar
½ cup ground nuts (hazelnuts or almonds)

1 teaspoon rum
2 cups heavy cream
1–2 tablespoons powdered coffee

Beat the egg yolks with the sugar until lemon-colored, add the ground nuts and rum. Fold in the stiffly beaten egg whites. Set aside. Butter a 16- by 10-inch cookie sheet and cover it with foil, butter the foil, and pour in the batter, spreading it evenly. Bake in a preheated 350° oven for 25 minutes, or until brown. Remove the cookie sheet from the oven and cover it with a moistened tea towel. Let the cake cool slightly, then invert it onto a wooden board and peel off the foil. Trim the edges and cut the cake into four 4- by 10-inch pieces. Now whip 1¼ cups of the heavy cream until stiff, fold in the powdered coffee. Divide the whipped cream into 3 equal parts; cover the first piece of cake with ⅓ of the whipped cream; lay the second piece of the cake on top, cover that with whipped cream; then lay the third piece on top of the cake, cover with the rest of the whipped cream. Place the fourth piece of cake on top. Cover the cake with plastic wrap and keep in the refrigerator for at least 8 hours. Before serving, beat the rest of the heavy cream very stiff and cover the top and sides of the cake. When serving, cut into 1¼-inch slices. *Serves 6.*

Coffee Cake Ring
(Gugelhupf)

1 stick butter
1 cup sugar
3 eggs, separated
A pinch of salt
Grated rind of 1 lemon
¼ cup chopped blanched almonds

¼ cup raisins
¾ cup milk
Scant 2 cups flour
1 heaping tablespoon baking powder
Powdered sugar

Beat the butter and sugar in a bowl until creamy, gradually add the egg yolks, a pinch of salt, the lemon rind, almonds, raisins, milk, and the flour with the baking powder. Last fold in the stiffly beaten egg whites. Butter heavily and flour a deep fluted 1½-quart ring mold and bake in a preheated 350° oven for 1 hour. Turn out on a board and sprinkle lavishly with powdered sugar. Let the cake cool. It tastes best the following day. *Serves 6.*

Sachertorte

6 1-ounce squares semisweet chocolate	*6 eggs, separated*
¾ cup butter	*Apricot jam*
¾ cup powdered sugar	*6 ounces chocolate chips*
¾ cup sifted flour	*½ cup butter*
1 teaspoon baking powder	*Heavy cream as accompaniment*

Melt the chocolate in the top of a double boiler over boiling water. In a bowl cream the butter until fluffy and add the warm chocolate, mix well until the mixture has cooled. Then slowly fold in the sugar, flour, baking powder, and beaten egg yolks. Beat the whites of the eggs until stiff and fold into the mixture. Butter a 9-inch springform pan, sprinkle it with flour, and fill with the batter. Bake for about 1 hour in a preheated 350° oven. Let it cool, take it out of the springform pan, and carefully cut the torte horizontally in half (best use a long, thin knife than one you use to slice smoked salmon). Spread a thin layer of apricot jam on top of the bottom half, place the top half over it, and spread the *whole* cake with apricot jam—not forgetting the sides. *Serves 8.*

To Make the Icing:
Melt the chocolate chips in the top of the double boiler, add the butter, and blend, stirring well. When the icing has cooled, spread it evenly over the top and sides of the torte. Put in refrigerator. Do not serve it until it has completely cooled. Serve with whipped heavy cream—that way it's more nourishing! *Serves 8.*

Dessert Pancakes
(Palatschinken)

1¾ cups milk	1 cup flour
2 eggs, beaten	¾ teaspoon salt
1 tablespoon sugar	2½ tablespoons butter

Beat the milk, eggs, sugar, flour, and salt until smooth, let stand for at least 8 hours. Brush the 8-inch bottom of a hot skillet with melted butter and pour in a very thin layer of batter, tilting the skillet to spread evenly. Fry over medium heat until light brown on both sides. Use the fillings given below. *Makes about 16 pancakes.*

Fillings:

Number 1:
Spread apricot jam on each pancake and roll it up, sprinkle it with powdered sugar.

Number 2:
1 cup creamed cottage cheese, mashed with a fork, a dash of salt, 2 tablespoons sugar, and ½ teaspoon grated lemon rind; combine and use as a filling.

Vanilla Crescents
(Vanille Kipferln Jaegerwinkel)

2 cups flour	⅓ cup blanched, very finely
⅘ cup butter	ground almonds
6 tablespoons powdered sugar	1½ teaspoons vanilla extract
2 egg yolks	Additional powdered sugar

Sift the flour, mix with the remaining ingredients into a smooth dough, put in the refrigerator for 2 hours. Roll out the dough in long rolls one finger thick. Cut off 1 inch pieces, roll them till they become longer, then form them into crescents. Put them on a buttered cookie sheet and bake them in a preheated 350° oven for about 15 minutes. Dip the crescents into powdered sugar while they are still warm. *Makes about 2 dozen.*

Holland

One of the countries dearest to my heart is Holland. Not only has that small kingdom exported to our United States great men like Peter Stuyvesant, Vanderbilt, Knickerbocker, Roosevelt, and many more, and sent out into the world the thoughts and works of Erasmus of Rotterdam, Frans Hals, Van Ostade, Vermeer, and Rembrandt, just to mention a few. But to my personal life it has given constant bliss and joy by sending me one of its loveliest products, one Johanna van Rijn, who, thirty-six years ago, consented to change her name to Johanna Slezak. There is in her family a lingering suspicion that the great Rembrandt van Rijn might have been one of her forefathers; but as that so enviable descent would probably have been illegitimate, my mother-in-law, a moral, correct, and dignified lady, disputes that rumor in a most determined manner and proves, beyond the shadow of a doubt, legitimate ancestry back to the year 1616.

My first visit to Holland was in 1923, when the wounds and privations of the First World War were still painfully evident in Austria and Germany. The troupe of a play in which I was then appearing on the Berlin stage was invited to tour Holland, a chance we all accepted with joy. I arrived in Amsterdam late in the afternoon, dropped my bags at a hotel, and went on the town. Holland had never been touched by the war of 1914–1918, and to me Amsterdam was then a city of unbelievable opulence, with bright street lights and all shops open far into the night. When the war broke out in 1914, I was only twelve years old. Here I saw for the first time delicacies I had only heard about but had never tasted . . . I stood for a long time gazing on the display counters of foodstores where I saw caviar, pâté de foie gras, fresh lobsters and crabs, oysters and clams, eels live and smoked; I saw whole tubs filled with butter, crates filled with eggs, every kind of meat and game . . . all to be had for the asking.

During the last years of the war, my sister and I had bicycled into the Bavarian countryside, she with a guitar and me holding hopefully an empty canvas bag; we knocked at the doors of farms, we sang, told jokes, and sometimes as a reward we were allowed to buy a few eggs, half a pound of butter, and maybe half a loaf of home-baked bread.

My drooling in front of store windows of Amsterdam soon grew into hunger, and I entered a small, inexpensive-looking restaurant off the Nieuwe Zijds Voorburgwal. We were not to be paid in Dutch guilders until after the first performance the following day; I had changed just a few German marks at the railway station and had to economize.

The *spijskaart* was, of course, printed in Dutch, a language that was then unfamiliar to me, so I just studied the prices. A *Kellnerin* came and I pointed to something that was called *"Snert,"* the cheapest item on the bill of fare.

At the next table some fellows were served a colorless liquid that they seemed to enjoy. I pointed and the girl brought me a small glass filled to the brim. It tasted like gin, and actually was a gin called *Genever.*

Snert turned out to be pea soup. Floating on that pea soup were slices of *Boerenworst,* a smoked peasant sausage, and swimming inside the soup, trying to rise to the surface, were bits of pork and bacon. When I realized what I was about to eat, I ordered *Amstelbier van het vat,* at the end of the meal I said, *"Sigaar,"* and when the girl brought me a cigar I felt that I now spoke Dutch.

I returned to the hotel a happy man!

The following morning I consulted the hotel porter about inexpensive lodgings, and he recommended a Mevrouw Antje Geertruide Jelgerhuis, who would, he assured me, be kind enough to rent me a furnished room, breakfast included, for the short duration of my stay in the city, six days to be exact, the length of our playing time in Amsterdam and Den Haag.

A taxi took me into a long, narrow street where all houses were identical: sixteen feet wide, three floors high, plus a gabled roof where a beam with a set of pulleys protruded into the street. All the houses were painted the same color, with identical flowering win-

dow boxes gracing the narrow windows. I rang the bell, the door
opened and revealed a voluminous lady of heroic proportions. She
was the biggest Isolde I had ever seen, her frame filling the opening of the door in a tight fit; she was in her late twenties with blond
curly hair, a nice round moonface with *one* dimple on her left
cheek. Immediately under her face, actually below her ears, her
figure began. From then on she bulged downward, sideways, and
out front; especially out front, where a promontory protruded like a
hammock filled with sandbags. They were her mammary glands, a
joyous vision to behold.

After much smiling and an exchange of pleasantries that neither of us understood, I entered. She pointed upward and I followed her. The stairs were two and one-half feet wide and rose at an angle of sixty-five degrees. She walked ahead of me, blocking out daylight on the narrow stairs. We reached the first floor, continued to the second, and then on to the third, and then finally to what she called the *"dak kamer."*

The space between the bed and the opposite wall was one and one-half feet. Over the bed hung a print of tulips in bloom and a painting of a family of Dutch fishermen in their traditional Sunday garb, complete with long clay pipes, wooden shoes (*klompen*), benign expressions on their satisfied faces.

I had to go to the theatre to rehearse, so I dropped my bags and climbed down the hen roost preceded by Antje, and I marveled at the light-footed elegance with which she was able to navigate her bulk around that doll's house. At 7 A.M. the next morning she knocked at the door of my *dak kamer*, woke me up, and handed me a cup of tea. I was very disappointed at the meagerness of that breakfast, but at nine o'clock she reappeared carrying a huge tray with *ontbijt*. This consisted of the strongest coffee I had ever tasted, a pitcher of hot milk, five different kinds of rolls and slices of bread including *ontbijtkoek*, a honey bread that made a lasting impression. Then there were biscuits (Holland rusk), cold cuts, eggs, *pap* (cooked cereal), four kinds of cheeses, butter, three kinds of marmalade and jams. The pièce de résistance on that tray was a ceramic monstrosity in the form of a large bee: when it was tilted backward honey slowly oozed out of the stinger.

With a jolly *"Goede morgen, Mijnheer,"* Isolde left me to stuff myself. It caused her deep concern that I was never able to finish the spread and that a healthy young man should have such a poor appetite. I spoke German to her and she answered in Dutch until one day we found out that we both spoke English, and we became fast friends. I heard the sad story of her marriage, her husband, a *"rotvent"* (heel), if ever there was one, who had left her for another probably thinner, *Mevrouw*. She gave me a list of inexpensive restaurants in Amsterdam and, before I left Holland, presented me with old family recipes in case someday I should settle down, have a home and a wife, so that we wouldn't starve. We corresponded for several months; this later petered out into exchanging Christmas cards, and now only the recipes remain.

Amsterdam, Rotterdam, and Den Haag are very cosmopolitan cities and serve a great variety of international food, and I will therefore mention only the so-called national dishes; let's start with *Snert*—Dutch pea soup.

Dutch Pea Soup
(Snert)

½ pound split peas, soaked overnight in water	*Celery leaves, cut fine*
1 medium-sized onion, chopped	*1 ham bone, or ¾ pound pig's feet or smoked Polish sausage*
2 leeks, sliced	
1 small celery root (or 4 stalks of celery and tops), cut fine	*Salt and freshly ground pepper to taste*

Boil the peas in 1½ quarts water for about 1 hour. Add the onion, leeks, celery root, celery leaves, and ham bone and cook for another hour, or until peas are tender. Remove ham bone. Season the soup with pepper and salt, strain it, press the vegetables through a sieve or run them through a blender (if Polish sausage is used, leave it whole while cooking; when it is sliced, cut it into bite-sized pieces). If a more substantial dish is required, add a package of frankfurters, cut into ¼-inch to ½-inch rounds. Serve with croutons (given below) and fried onion rings. *Serves 5–6.*

Croutons
Bake small cubes of white bread on a cookie sheet in the oven until they are brown.

Some people—ill-advised people, I would say—run the finished soup through a blender. I prefer it the way it comes out of the pot. Sometimes I add cream to taste.

Remember, the Dutch insist that a spoon stuck into the soup must remain *upright*. That's a tradition and you'd better stick to it or they'll take away your wooden shoes.

HUTSPOT

This is is an historic dish, equivalent to our American Thanksgiving turkey. Every patriotic and self-respecting home in Holland serves this dish on the third of October in memory of the day they were delivered from a five-month siege by the Spaniards in 1574.

A variation of the story of the little Dutch boy who put his finger in a dike is the story of another little Dutch boy who slipped out of the city of Leyden right after the Spaniards left. No wonder they left. The clever Dutch had opened the floodgates on their dikes and 85 per cent of the Spanish Army couldn't swim. The little boy found a pot, still warm, with some mush in it, and he brought it back to his hungry parents.

Today they serve that mush with more sophistication: they add boiled beef and . . . potatoes, at that time unknown in Europe until Sir Francis Drake brought some back from one of his plundering expeditions on the South American Continent in the year 1580. The Germans, being great potato eaters, have even erected a monument to Sir Francis in memory and gratitude for that lovely bulb. It stands in Offenburg, Baden, where it is admired by the tourists and ignored by the natives.

Hutspot
(Hodgepodge Number 1)

3 pounds carrots, diced	2 tablespoons butter
1½ pounds onions, diced	Salt and freshly ground pepper
4 pounds potatoes, sliced thick	to taste
Chicken bouillon to cover	½ teaspoon powdered mace
vegetables	

Boil the carrots, onions, and potatoes in the bouillon till the vegetables are tender, then mash them. Add 2 tablespoons of butter. Add

salt, pepper, and the mace. If you feel exuberant, walk past the pot
with an open bottle of Tabasco sauce; if a few drops should happen
to fall in the mash, it's fine with me. *Serves 6–8.*

Hutspot
(Hodgepodge Number 2)

1 pound brisket of beef	*1 bay leaf*
½ pound onions, chopped	*2 cloves*
1½ pounds carrots, diced	*2 tablespoons butter*
2 pounds potatoes, sliced	*Freshly ground pepper to taste*
1 teaspoon salt	*¼ teaspoon powdered mace*

Boil the brisket in 1 quart of water for 1½ hours. Add the onions,
carrots, potatoes, salt, bay leaf, and cloves, boil slowly for another
¾ hour. Take the meat out of the pot, mash the onions, carrots,
and potatoes together, add the 2 tablespoons of butter, season with
additional salt, some pepper, and the mace. Remove the bay leaf
and the cloves. Serve the vegetables on a platter with slices of the
meat on top. *Serves about 4.*

I have an old family recipe for preparing crayfish in beer with
caraway seeds (my father used to prepare it). It's a lovely child-
hood memory, because first I was delegated to go to a little creek
near our home and *catch* the crayfish—*by hand,* mind you—and
then bring them home alive. The recipe comes from Czechoslovakia,
and few people except the Slezaks like it.

The Dutch also like cooking with beer, or so Mevrouw Jelgerhuis
assured me, and here are two of *her* family secrets.

Veal Stewed in Beer
(Kalfsvleesch in Bier)

2 pounds veal for stewing	*Beer*
Oil for frying	*1 lemon, sliced*
3 medium-sized onions, chopped	*Flour*
coarsely	*Salt and freshly ground pepper*
1 bay leaf	*to taste*
A pinch of thyme	

Cut the veal into bite-size cubes, fry them lightly on all sides in oil in a skillet. Place them in a stewing pot, add the onions, herbs, and the beer until the meat is partly covered. Stew slowly for about an hour. When the meat is tender, run the gravy through a sieve or a blender, return to the stewing pot. Add a few slices of lemon, thicken the gravy with a little flour, warm the meat again in the gravy, add salt and pepper. *Serves 4.*

Cold Beer Soup
(Koude Bier Soep)

1 quart light beer	*2 heaping tablespoons cornstarch*
1 quart milk	*1 cup heavy cream*
1 stick of cinnamon	*2 egg yolks*
4 cloves	*Sugar to taste*
Grated rind of 1 lemon	

Boil the beer with the milk, cinnamon, cloves, and lemon rind. Thicken with cornstarch. Add the cream, egg yolks, and sugar to taste, simmer for a few minutes, stirring constantly. Remove the bay leaf and cloves. The soup should be really *cold* before serving. *Serves 8.*

There are several other beer stews: beef, chicken, turkey, and pigeon, but frankly I prefer my beer straight, i.e., from the bottle or the spigot into the glass and down the hatch.

Holland, a country practically surrounded by the sea, is a great place for fish eaters. *Nieuwe haring,* raw and sweet as sugar, best eaten in the street off a vendor's stand, are a wonderful delicacy; and so are smoked young eel, about a foot long and no thicker than a fat finger. The first time I ate them was at a smokehouse I visited in Volendam. They were still warm and the smokemaster, or whatever his title was, explained the technique of eating them without the fat and juices running up your arm, down your sleeve into your collar, and smelling up your whole anatomy. You pull off the skin as you would take the cover off an umbrella, then you grasp the dear little eel with one hand by the head and, with the other hand by the tail, bend forward, and eat it as you would kiss a flute.

Of course there is no law against eating them at home, nor against ordering them in a restaurant, but, like *Burenwurst* in Vienna, they taste best in the street.

Fried Eel
(Gebakken Paling)

2 pounds eel, skinned	2 eggs
Salt	Bread crumbs
Flour	Butter or oil

Clean the eels, cut in sections of about 3 inches, score the pieces of eel at several places, for it takes quite awhile for eel to get tender. Rub the eel with salt and let stand for ½ hour. Dredge the pieces with flour. Beat the eggs lightly with a little water and dip the floured pieces in the mixture, coat with bread crumbs. Heat butter (or oil) in a skillet and when the butter is hot but not brown sauté the pieces until they are brown on all sides. Then cover the skillet and let the eels cook slowly, turning frequently, for another 15 to 20 minutes. One can serve this dish hot or slightly cooled. Eels are very rich. Serve with tartar sauce, mayonnaise, or tomato sauce. The eels should be eaten with a salad. *Serves 4.*

Braised Eel
(Gestoofde Paling)

2 pounds eel, skinned	Juice and slices of 1 lemon
Salt	Bread crumbs
½ stick butter	

Cut the eels in pieces 3 inches long, rub with salt, and let stand for ½ hour. Place the eels in a casserole with a cover, add water to cover bottom of casserole, add the butter and lemon juice, sprinkle with bread crumbs, cover the casserole and put in a preheated medium oven (or on top of the stove), and let cook (or simmer) for

20 minutes. For the last 5 minutes take off cover to brown the eels. You can add a few slices of lemon in the casserole in the beginning and cook them with the eel. *Serves 4.*

Gourmet Fish Fillets
(Lekkerbekjes)

Fish fillets	*Milk*
Salt	*Oil*
Flour	

Sprinkle small pieces of fish fillets with salt and dip in a thin mixture of flour and milk. Fry in hot oil. In Holland these are eaten on the street, at a fish stand, but you have the permission of the author to eat them at home.

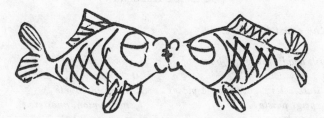

Sole Kaasi
(Schol of Tong Kaasi)

Take 2 whole soles, filleted, wash, dry, and rub with salt. Let them stand for 1 hour. Coat the fish with flour and fry them in half oil and half butter till light brown on both sides. Place them immediately on a serving platter and garnish with a choice of candied ginger, pineapple rings, canned asparagus tips sprinkled with finely cut boiled ham, sliced tomatoes, canned mandarin oranges, mustard, or curry sauce (3 tablespoons mayonnaise mixed with 1 teaspoon curry powder, a bit of whipped cream, and chopped parsley). *Serves 2–4.*

Fried Fillet of Sole
(Gebakken Schol)

6 fillets of sole	Oil or butter
Salt	Lemon juice
Flour	Chopped parsley
Milk	

Wash the fillets and rub with salt. Dredge them in flour or first dip
them in milk and then roll them in flour. Fry in hot oil or butter for
a total of about 5–6 minutes, sprinkle with lemon juice and parsley.
If the fish is fried in butter, pour the leftover pan butter on the
fillets before serving. Serve immediately. *Serves 4–6.*

Poached Cod
(Gestoofde Kabeljauw)

For the court bouillon:

Fish heads, tails, and bones of	1 quart water
any white fish	10 peppercorns, crushed
1 stalk celery, cut in large pieces	A pinch of thyme
3 sprigs parsley	1 small onion, quartered
½ bay leaf	1 teaspoon salt

Put all these together in a saucepan and boil for about 20 minutes,
then strain through cheesecloth. This will be more than enough for
the following recipe.

2 pounds fillets of cod	7 tablespoons butter
Salt	Court bouillon
Juice of ½ lemon	1 lemon, sliced

Rub the fillets with salt and let stand for ½ hour. Sprinkle with
lemon juice and put in an ovenproof dish. Add the butter and
enough court bouillon to half cover the fish. Bake in a preheated

350° oven for about ½ hour. Put the lemon slices on the fish and serve immediately. *Serves 4–6.*

Pork Fillet with Pineapple
(Varkensfilet met Sinaasappel)

Salt and freshly ground pepper
½ pound pork fillet
1 medium-sized onion, chopped
3½ tablespoons butter
Small glass of cognac
1 carrot, diced
Mace, basil, and rosemary to
    taste

¼ of a calf's foot
1 glass of white wine
½ cup chicken bouillon
Sauce (given below)
A can of pineapple chunks with
    juice
Parsley

Salt and pepper the meat. Sauté the meat and onion in a large skillet with a cover in butter till golden brown. Add the cognac and ignite; when the flame has died down, add the carrot, herbs, calf's foot, wine, and bouillon. Cover the skillet and simmer for at least 1 hour. When the meat is done, remove and keep warm.

Sauce: Remove the fat from the skillet and add pineapple juice to taste, heat. Pour the heated sauce over the meat, garnish with the pineapple chunks and parsley. *Serves 2.*

Peasant Dish
(Boeren Gerecht)

¼ pound bacon
2 tablespoons butter
1 medium-sized onion, chopped
6–8 medium-sized potatoes,
    peeled and cubed
1 bouillon cube
1 cup water

2 stalks celery, cut fine
Salt and freshly ground pepper
    to taste
Basil
Cornstarch
Parsley, chopped
1 cup grated Parmesan cheese

Cut the bacon into small pieces and fry in the butter with the onion in a large iron skillet. When the onion is golden brown, add the potatoes and the bouillon cube dissolved in the 1 cup of water. (Also add leftover gravy if you have any.) Add some water, but the potatoes and onion should not be completely covered. Add the celery, salt, pepper, and a pinch of basil. When the potatoes are tender, thicken the liquid with a little cornstarch. When the dish is served, sprinkle it with chopped parsley and the grated cheese. *Serves 2–4.*

Peasant Cabbage
(Boeren Kool)

6 medium-sized potatoes, peeled
   and diced
1½ pounds curly kale, washed
½ pound smoked sausage

⅓ cup butter
Salt and freshly ground pepper
   to taste

Put the potatoes in a large pot and half cover them with boiling water. Lay the kale on top of the potatoes and crown these with the smoked sausage. Bring the water to a boil again and cook for ½ hour or until the potatoes are tender. Remove the sausage. Mash the potatoes and kale with the butter. Season with salt and pepper. Add some milk if the mash is too dry. Cut the sausage into 2-inch chunks and serve separately. *Serves 2–4.*

Dutch Salad with Dressing
(Slasaus met Hard Gekookt Ei)

Dressing:

1 egg, hard-cooked
Dry mustard to taste
Salt and freshly ground pepper
   to taste

2 tablespoons salad oil
2 tablespoons vinegar
1 tablespoon sugar

Mash the hard-cooked egg with a fork, add some mustard, salt, and pepper, the salad oil, vinegar (I take half vinegar and half water), and the sugar. Mix thoroughly.

Salad:

> 1 large or 2 small heads Boston lettuce
> 1 small onion, minced
> Parsley, minced

Wash and drain the lettuce well. Add the onion and parsley or any other green herb. Just before serving add the dressing to the salad, toss, and mix well. *Serves 2.*

Brown Kidney Beans with Bacon
(Bruine Bonen met Spek)

> 1 pound kidney beans
> 10 slices bacon

Soak the beans overnight, then boil in water to cover for about 1 hour. Serve with freshly fried pieces of bacon and pour bacon fat over the beans. Serve with applesauce and salad, or pickles. *Serves 2–4.*

Cocktail Meat Balls
(Bitter Ballen)

> 1 medium-sized onion, chopped fine
> 1 tablespoon butter or margarine
> 1½ pounds ground pork
> 1 tablespoon parsley, chopped fine
> A large pinch of nutmeg
> Salt and freshly ground pepper to taste
> Bread crumbs
> 1 egg, beaten
> Corn oil

Sauté the onion in the butter or margarine until the onion becomes transparent. Add the ground pork, parsley, nutmeg, and a small amount of salt and pepper. Next, make little balls about 1 inch in diameter. Roll the balls in fine bread crumbs, dip them in egg beaten with a bit of water, then roll them again in bread crumbs and fry them in hot oil for about 10 minutes. A wonderful appetizer. *Makes about 24.*

A Bouncer—Open-faced Sandwich
(Uitsmijter)

Butter to spread on bread	*2 large slices tomato*
2 slices white bread	*2 eggs*
4 lettuce leaves, cut into strips	*4 sprigs parsley*
4 slices cold ham, roast beef,	*1 or 2 pickles, sliced*
roast pork, or roast veal	

Butter the bread, cover with the lettuce. Lay on the ham or other meat, add the slices of tomato. Fry the eggs sunny side up and place on top of the meat. Garnish with parsley and pickle.

Half a bouncer is just one slice of bread for one open-faced sandwich. *Serves 2.*

Hot Lightning
(Heete Bliksem)

2 pounds pears or sweet apples	*Salt to taste*
3 pounds potatoes, peeled and	*⅓ pound sliced bacon*
diced	*Milk*

Peel and quarter the pears or apples, core them, and cook for ½ hour in a small amount of water. Add the potatoes and salt and cook for another 30 minutes or until the potatoes and fruit are cooked and dry. Meanwhile fry the bacon slices. Mash the potatoes and fruit together, add a little milk, mix well, and serve with the bacon slices.

Hot Lightning was a favorite dish of the great dancer Anna Pavlova when she went to Holland. It is a peasant main dish. Without the bacon slices it is used as a main course by Catholics on Friday. *Serves 4–6.*

Puffed Pancakes
(Poffertjes)

For something really great the Guide Michelin shows three stars
and the legend "Worth a special journey." I consider well-made
poffertjes worth that journey. In Holland one goes out to eat them
as a treat, with a cup of tea or coffee.

If you want to make poffertjes at home, you will need a special
pan of cast iron with hollows about 2 inches wide and 1 inch deep.

3 cups milk	*Salt to taste*
1 pound flour, well sifted	*2 eggs*
3 tablespoons powdered yeast	*Powdered sugar*
Grated rind of 1 lemon	

Make a well-mixed dough of the milk, flour, yeast (started with a
little bit of warm water), the grated lemon rind, a pinch of salt,
and the eggs. Let the dough rise for about an hour. Grease the hollows of the pan *well* and put about 1 tablespoon of the dough into
each mold. Cook over a medium flame. Turn the pancakes once.
Serve very hot, dusted with lots of powdered sugar. *Serves about 6.*

French Toast
(Wentelteefjes)

8 slices two-day-old bread	*¼ cup sugar*
1 or 2 eggs, lightly beaten	*2 cups milk*
Grated lemon rind	*Butter for frying*
1 teaspoon cinnamon	*Additional sugar and cinnamon*

Cut the crusts from the bread. Mix together the egg(s), some
grated lemon rind, 1 teaspoon of cinnamon, ¼ cup of sugar, and
the milk. Soak the bread in this mixture, taking care that the slices
are completely soaked. Fry the slices of bread on both sides in hot
butter. Before serving, sprinkle generously with a mixture of cinnamon and sugar. *Serves 2–4.*

Salt Twists or Straws
(Zoute Krakelingen)

1 cup sifted flour	*4 tablespoons water*
⅛ teaspoon salt	*1 egg yolk, well beaten*
1 cup softened butter	

Blend the ingredients until smooth and chill for ½ hour. On a floured board roll the dough into a rectangle ¼ inch thick. Cut off strips ½ inch wide and 6 inches long, roll and stretch them. Twist the strips into knots or leave them as "straws." With a pastry brush, glaze them with beaten egg yolk. Bake in a preheated 350° oven until golden. *Makes about 36 twists or straws.*

Cream of Wheat Pudding with Raspberry Sauce
(Griesmeelpudding met Bessensap)

⅔ cup cream of wheat	*⅜ cup sugar*
1 quart milk	*2 eggs, separated*
½ teaspoon vanilla extract	*Raspberry Sauce (given below)*

Combine the cream of wheat, milk, vanilla, and sugar, bring to a boil, and cook till thick. Add the 2 eggs yolks. When the mixture has cooled a little, add the egg whites, stiffly beaten, blend well, and let cool. Pour into a 2-quart mold. *Serves 6–8.* Serve with Raspberry Sauce:

Raspberry Sauce:

1 cup raspberry syrup	*Sugar to taste if needed*
1 cup water	*Cornstarch to thicken sauce if*
½ teaspoon lemon juice	*needed*

Combine the raspberry syrup, 1 cup of water, lemon juice, sugar if needed and bring to a boil. Add a little cornstarch if needed. Stir well. Serve over the pudding. Cherry Sauce is equally good:

Cherry Sauce:

2 cups ripe, fresh cherries, pitted,
    or 2 cups canned cherries,
    drained
¼ cup water or cherry juice
1 tablespoon sugar

¼ cup orange juice
1 tablespoon cornstarch
1 tablespoon water
1 tablespoon butter

Bring the cherries, ¼ cup of water or cherry juice, sugar, and orange juice to a boil. Thicken with the cornstarch mixed with 1 tablespoon of water. Add 1 tablespoon of butter, mix well. Pour over the pudding.

Dutch Lemon Cream
(Hollandische Citroen Vla)

4 eggs, separated
1 cup confectioner's sugar
½ cup orange juice

⅓ cup lemon juice
1 pint strawberries

Beat the egg yolks and sugar in the top of a double boiler *off the heat* until thick and fluffy (5 minutes). Combine the fruit juices and add carefully to the egg mixture, stir until well mixed. Place the top of the double boiler *over* simmering water and cook, stirring constantly, until the mixture thickens, remove from heat. Fold in the stiffly beaten egg whites, replace over heat, and continue to simmer for several minutes, folding gently. Spoon into serving dishes. Garnish with the strawberries. Chill. Serve with Dutch Cookies (recipe follows).

Dutch Cookies
(Hollandische Koekjes)

½ pound butter
¾ cup sugar
1 cup flour

Mix the ingredients well until a smooth dough is formed. Roll out the dough on a floured board to ⅛-inch thickness, cut out the cookies with a cookie cutter, and place on a greased cookie sheet. Bake in a preheated 350° oven for 15–20 minutes. *Makes about 2 dozen.*

"Braggarts" in the Hague
(Haagsche Bluf)

3 egg whites	1½ cups raspberry juice
¼ cup sugar	½ pint heavy cream

Beat the egg whites with the sugar until they are stiff, carefully fold in the raspberry juice. Whip the heavy cream and spoon a dollop of it on top of the "Braggarts" in sherbet glasses. Wafers are just right for this.

Instead of raspberry juice, you can also use frozen raspberries puréed in a blender, with water added, if necessary, to make 1½ cups. *Serves 4.*

Max Schaute

When I first went to Berlin in 1923, I made friends with a German officer who was eight years my senior. In 1914, when World War I broke out, he had been given the rank of colonel and ordered to the front. He needed an orderly, and the Army issued him a private Max Schaute. The man was investigated, and it was discovered that he had a criminal record for petty thievery. But the colonel liked the open-faced young lad and called him into his presence.

"Private Schaute," he growled, "I know all about your past! Nevertheless I will accept you as my orderly. But I warn you: if so much as a cigarette is missing, I shall have you court-martialed. Is that clear?"

"Yes, Colonel," answered Max Schaute, standing stiffly at attention in his best military posture.

"That is all," said the colonel, and the subject was never mentioned again.

Two weeks later they moved to the front. In their first bivouac Private Schaute asked for permission to reconnoiter the terrain. After a while he returned with a donkey, which he had requisitioned as a draft animal. The following day they moved to another village. There Private Schaute traded the donkey for a side of bacon and a fat goose. And early the following morning, before they broke camp, he rerequisitioned the donkey as a draft animal. He kept up that jolly gambit as they moved through the countryside, never in need of chickens, eggs, hams, or fresh vegetables.

Nearly two years later the donkey was hit by an exploding mine and thus stopped being their provider. The colonel survived the war, and Max Schaute stayed on as his valet and cook. He gave me my first cooking lesson.

La Iettatura

I was hired to take part in a picture to be shot in Rome. It was a silent film, the year being 1925. The story was a very daring one, about an irresistible vamp who ruined every man who crossed her path, young and old alike. I played the young one.

In the cast was a struggling young actor. He didn't have to struggle very hard in his private life, as he was blessed with a very rich father whose motto was: "For Paolo, MY son, *nothing* is too good!" And to back up that conviction, he gave him a brand-new shining Lancia sports car for his twenty-fifth birthday. It was a sensational automobile. The hood alone was seven feet long; from its sides six silver tubes protruded, leading to a trumpet-shaped exhaust pipe. Two huge spare tires were mounted next to the running boards. The whole job was a dream in silver, chrome, and red upholstery. I turned olive green with envy.

Paolo assured me that when the top was down there wasn't a *bambola* (doll) in all of Rome who could resist being taken for a ride. Because he let me drive his car several times, he became my best friend.

After the picture was finished, he invited me to go along for a ride down the coast. "We'll stay for a couple of days," he said. "We won't take any dolls along; we'll pick some up on the way!" I was then twenty-three years old and most impressed.

The drive was beautiful. Paolo let me take the wheel because it left both his hands free for talking and indiscriminately waving at every female form we passed. The car drew many admiring glances. *"Che bella macchina!"* and *"Stupenda!"* were often called out, but the lack of attention the two of us received didn't dampen Paolo's adventurous spirit. His urge to conquer was great. *"Questa sera avremo un'orgia,"* he kept assuring me. At dusk we pulled up at an old hotel in a fishing village south of Salerno. The *bella macchina* was parked in the piazza and drew a big crowd. We scanned the assembly for available girls, but the outlook was grim.

Paolo decided we should go back to Salerno or to Naples, but I was tired and told him to go alone. After he had rounded up enough talent *"per un'orgia,"* he could bring them back and wake me up.

The only thing that woke me up the next morning was church bells. Paolo was nowhere in sight, so I had a nice quiet breakfast on the sidewalk terrace of our hotel and was served by Emilio, the *padrone*, a mustachioed and talkative man who was glad to chat with a foreigner. Across the piazza the Sunday Mass had just ended and the good folk were coming out of church. Many dropped in at Emilio's for an apéritif, and soon our little terrace was filled.

The last person to emerge from the church was a tiny and very, very old woman leaning on a cane, bent over and staring at the cobblestones as if she were counting them. When she passed our terrace, I noticed that quite a few of the guests turned their heads away from her and performed curious movements with their hands, the second finger and the little finger pointing downward in a stabbing movement. Before I had a chance to ask Emilio for an explanation, there was a big roar and in a cloud of dust and exhaust Paolo raced up the piazza and stopped with screeching brakes in front of our hotel.

He was full of tall stories about the wonderful wild time he had had in Naples, meeting a beautiful contessa and her two nieces, crowing about his prowess, and pitying me for not having shared his thrills and joys.

"But now," he said, "I want to return to Rome."

I called Emilio to pay my bill and asked him about the old woman. *"Ah, la vecchia,"* he said simply, *"è una iettatura."* I didn't know the meaning of the word, so he explained that it was "the evil eye" and told me that the movements of the hands were made so as to hold off the "spells." "But what has the woman done?" I asked. "Why is she a *iettatura?*"

"Everybody knows that—the whole village—for the last seventy years." Then his eyes lit up (he had found somebody who didn't know the story) and quickly he sat down. "Angela," he began, "that's the old woman, was only seventeen years old when it happened. She and her two older brothers lived with their parents in that old house up there on the mountain—you can see the roof from here. She is still living there alone; she just comes down for church every Sunday. Well, the family owned a fishing boat and every Friday morning they would bring in their catch and sell it here on the piazza (we still use it as a market place). Both her brothers worked the boat with the father, and in the evening Angela came down to the village to pick up the money and take it back to Mamma, who used to hide it so the father and brothers wouldn't spend it all. When it came to money, Mamma was a holy terror, her word was law, they were all afraid of her."

Here Emilio got up to fetch a glass of wine, returned, and began talking before he had even sat down again. "It was the seventeenth of October, 1851," he continued. "Everybody around here remembers that date. There was a big scare; bandits were around. They had come up from Sicily, robbing and stealing; the folks locked their doors. Well, on that day—the seventeenth—Angela came down to the village to fetch the money and take it back to Mamma. Her brothers had given her a pistol in case she should meet up with bandits. Before she walked home she stopped here to buy bread (our hotel was then a bakery). When she was paying, Nonno—my grandfather—saw that she had a pistol in her handbag. He examined the gun and smiled. 'That won't be of much help, *mia piccola;* it isn't loaded,' and he went to a drawer, took out five bullets, and shoved them into the chambers. 'I hope you get your mamma a rabbit,' he joked.

"It happened about half a mile before Angela reached her house. In a wooded area she was suddenly confronted by two masked bandits who said only one word: 'MONEY!' Petrified with fear, she reached into her handbag to hand it over when one of the men approached her. The gun was in her hand, she fired, he dropped to the ground. The other man raised his hand and ran toward her. She shot again at close range, saw the man stumble. She ran up to her house screaming hysterically, crying for Mamma.

"Mamma got the shotgun out, marched back to where the two bandits were lying. Resolutely she tore the masks off their faces, then moaned and fell to the ground in a dead faint."

After a long pause Emilio went on, "You see, Angela had shot her two brothers," and very matter-of-factly he continued, "The parents died shortly after that tragedy, but the old one, *la povera,* she lives on."

On the drive back I recounted the story to Paolo. "Ah, Madonna," exclaimed, "what a film that would make! I could play one of the brothers!"

Arlette!

Reprinted from *What Time's the Next Swan?* with kind permission of Doubleday & Company, Inc.

Her name was Arlette and she smelled of Houbigant's Quelques Fleurs.

She was terribly, terribly chic: limbs slim and endlessly long, eyes the color of deep chartreuse, hair of flaming amber, hands narrow and fragile, cheekbones high, complexion of pale porcelain. The voice low and melodious. I was in awe of her delicate beauty—but she ate like a horse. On our first dinner date she suggested that I take her to Hôtel Rond Point de Champs Elysées, whose restaurant was very famous. Arlette looked like a cover of *Vogue* and all eyes followed her when we were shown to our table. I felt proud.

I was handed what I thought was an exquisitely bound first edition. But it turned out to be the bill of fare. Rich, varied, elaborate, and elegant.

In fact, it was so elegant that the prices were not even mentioned.

The maître d'hôtel stepped up, his manner endearing and benevolent. He took the menu away from me, as if to say: *"We* won't need this, will we?" He winked at me. I didn't like him.

"Madame is open to suggestions?"

Madame lifted her finely chiseled chin and looked ahead . . . She was!

"Caviar Mollosol?" He sounded a little apprehensive.

She lowered her long eyelashes in agreement and inclined her head gently toward me, thus forcing me into silent acknowledgment.

"Potée bourguignonne?"

"Charmant." She smiled.

"*Langouste, grillée, à la crème?*"

She touched my hand. "You'll like that."

"*Faisan sous cloche, ris sauvage?*"

Down came the eyelids.

"*Petit filet en croustade, asperges à la sauce Molière?*"

She glanced him a small thank you as if he had just lit her cigarette.

He had gained confidence: "*Les crêpes flambées au Kirsch!*"

It sounded like a command.

"*Fromages variés!*"

"*Café diable!*"

"*Des petits riens . . .*" The last was said condescendingly.

"*Ahmm—les petits riens,*" she purred (they turned out to be candies).

The maître d' flashed his teeth at me and with a casual "*Merci, monsieur*" he was irretrievably gone. But in the place where he stood appeared the sommelier, smiling, jolly, holding—but not parting with—the wine list. Madame was not only open to suggestions, she was eager! Waiters are quick to recognize a pigeon when they see one; so before he was through ordering wine for us, practically everyone in the place was swarming around our table, setting dishes, silverware, and glasses. An atmosphere of general rejoicing could definitely be felt.

Way back, when *langouste grillée à la crème* had first been suggested, there had arisen in me a slight suspicion that I might not have enough money on me to pay for the feast. By the time the sommelier had descended into the cellar to search for the rare vintages he felt we should sample, that suspicion had ballooned into a horrible certainty. Now I KNEW that a swift current of adversity was swirling me further and further up the good creek—and no paddle in sight.

There is an old saying, "When rape is inevitable—you might as well relax and enjoy it." I found it small comfort.

Arlette was a lovely companion. Being nearsighted, she brought her face with those luminous eyes and that low voice quite close to mine. It was like having a conversation with an owl.

A large bubble of anxiety was growing larger and larger in my stomach. I couldn't eat much. But there was nothing wrong with *her* feeding habits. With the steady, resolute rhythm of a Channel

swimmer's strokes, her slender arms and fragile hands traveled from plate to mouth. She ate for both of us.

I lingered over my brandy and kept on lingering, until the solicitude of the headwaiter, inquiring again and again if there wouldn't be anything else we wanted, shamed me into asking for the bill.

It came to about five times the amount I had dreaded. With great nonchalance I got up and sauntered to the telephone in the hotel lobby.

I called the Pathé Film Company and talked to the night watchman.

I called my producer and talked to his cook.

I called my director and talked to his mother-in-law. It was a Saturday and everybody I knew was out. I even thought of calling Papa in Vienna, but somehow it didn't seem practical.

So I simply walked over to the room clerk and registered as a hotel guest. Only the presidential suite was vacant. I mumbled something about having my luggage sent over *"bientôt"* and tipped him all the cash I carried. I walked back to the restaurant, signed the check, and had it charged to Apartment 9.

Then I told it all to Arlette.

She laughed and found it *"très chic."*

I invited her up for a nightcap, but she was a woman of principle: "Not on our first date," she laughed, and hailed a cab.

But on Sunday afternoon she visited me—for a tea and *"amuse bouche."*

I found that *"très chic."*

Monday morning Pathé Film Company bailed me out.

That most pleasant encounter and memorable evening happened over fifty years ago, a time when I was still very young and nauseatingly beautiful—a condition that has since abated with frightening rapidity.

"Langouste grillée, à la crème" was simply broiled langouste with the completely unnecessary addition of *"crème."*

I have never tried *"faisan sous cloche"* because—I am deeply ashamed to admit—I have never owned a *"cloche."* But unless my *"mémoire de cuisine"* fails me, MY roast pheasant tastes every bit as delicious, and that also goes for my wild rice.

"*Petit filet en croustade,*" I remember faintly, was beef Wellington, a filet baked in bread, and "*asperges à la sauce Molière*" were tips of white asparagus with some sort of mayonnaise or *sauce hollandaise* that the chef blamed on the great Molière.

Finally "*les crêpes flambées au Kirsch*" were the same thing as *crêpes Suzette*—WITHOUT the Cointreau and the cognac!

Ginette and the Coq au Vin

In the spring of 1926 I went to Paris to act in my first French film, *La Girl aux mains fines,* script by the famous Maurice Decobra.

It was a small production and small was my salary, but I was so eager to see Paris, the REAL Paris, the Paris regular tourists never got to know.

Having heard the opera *La Bohème* too often, I had dreamt of living in the Quartier Latin, preferably next to L'Église du Sacré Coeur and close to the Café Momus, and there mingle with poets, painters, midinettes, and get to know a few bona fide "Apaches" and their "Apacheuses."

Arriving at the Gare St. Lazare, I took a taxi to the Quartier. Across the street from Le Rat Mort (at that time a famous cabaret), I spotted a small hotel and had the taxi stop there.

The room clerk was most astonished when he saw my three bags and wanted to know for how long I was planning to stay. When I said, "From three to four weeks," a smile lit up his face; he opened a curtain behind the *loge du concierge* and called, *"Alphonse, viens ici . . ."*

The curtain parted and Alphonse, the *patron,* appeared, a greasy little man in suspenders, chewing a cigar. *"Patron,"* the clerk announced, "this gentleman wants to stay with us for four weeks!" He could barely suppress his laughter.

"Give him numéro 14," *le patron* said, grinned, and disappeared behind the curtains. Numéro 14 had an oversized bed, no closet but a few hooks on the wall, and—as the room clerk pointed out—the bathroom, with W.C. and bidet, was just across the hall.

I dumped my belongings and rushed out to see the real Paree.

It was then about seven in the evening, I walked over to the Boulevard Rochechouart, where some kind of a fair was going on:

lampions illuminated open stalls, a carrousel with a huge calliope providing the grating music was filled with screaming children, a massive crowd of people slowly moved about, talking, laughing, jostling each other, and having a wonderful time.

I got hungry and walked over to a taxi stand because I had been told that taxi drivers the world over know all about their towns.

"Are you rich, *mon petit?*" a well-fed driver with a walrus mustache asked me, after I had inquired for good place to eat.

"No," I laughed, "I am poor, VERY *pauvre!*"

"*Alors,* you want to eat where we usually eat?" he asked, pointing to a group of chauffeurs. "*Oui,*" I said, sensing that the REAL Paree was getting closer. "Try Chez Rolland," he said, and pointed toward a side street. Chez Rolland was a small bistro; at the entrance hung a large sign: "*Ici tout est bon excepté le patron.*" The food was very *bon,* but the *bon*-est was the fact that *le diner prix fixe* with a carafe of wine cost only one franc eighty centimes.

Back at my small hotel I tried to go to sleep, but persistent noises drifted through the walls; grunts, moans, bangings, very loud arguments, and a steady flow of traffic to the W.C. and bathroom across the hall soon made me realize why the room clerk had been so amused when he learned that I wanted to be their guest for four weeks.

I stayed on at the sinful den of illicit amour for another few days, then moved to a decent pension where they served the blandest breakfast, stale rolls, thin coffee, rancid butter, and all this in a most depressing atmosphere. But it was inexpensive and, above all, it was quiet!

Filming had begun. My first day of shooting was at the Maison Poiret, at that time the reigning fashion house of France.

The producers didn't want to go to the expense of building an elaborate "showroom set" in the studio or to hire extras, rent expensive clothes, and teach the extras how to wear them; so they made an arrangement with Monsieur Poiret to let us have his whole establishment for three Sundays, including *his* clothes—pardon me, *créations*—and *his* models.

My role was that of a young student who was in love with one of the mannequins. The mannequin was played by the wife of the producer. She was the star, *on* screen ravishing, *off* screen a bitch who tried, successfully, to be difficult, obnoxious, and arrogant. Our assistant director called her *"une emmerdeuse."*

I was especially taken by a long, narrow female with flaming red hair (which is why she modeled mostly the green colors). She was called Ginette, her given name being Geneviève. During the intervals between shooting, when they changed or rearranged the lights or when Madame l'Emmerdeuse kept everybody waiting while she had a change of costume or had her hair and face repaired, I sat with Ginette, later took her out for a glass of wine, and came to like her. In contrast to the glamorous woman she pretended to be when she modeled the *créations*—making stunning entrances, swishing on and off the platform, turning abruptly to show the fall of the gowns, every step measured and planned—she was a delightful *petite bourgeoise,* the daughter of a small postal inspector in Lyons and his seamstress wife.

Her plans for life were simple and well set: to marry a good man, *"un homme bon comme pain,"* with a steady job and a good pension once he retired.

She took me into her confidence. She had a friend, Edmond, *"un monsieur sérieux,"* as she called him; he was about fifty-five, married, kind, and understanding. He visited her once or twice a week and had promised that *if and when* she found the right man to wed, he would step aside and make a generous settlement (as was then the custom in France when the relationship with a steady mistress ended).

After I had hurriedly nailed down the fact that I was not the marrying kind (no pension, no steady job, an actor working in a business with absolutely no stability and even less security), we became really good friends. She had a small flat in the Quartier, kept it spotlessly clean—she was THE most domesticated woman I have ever encountered—she loved to cook and play house. We went to the market together and she spoiled me with delicious simple meals.

When she wasn't cooking she was glued to her sewing machine, working on her trousseau for the *if and when* day.

"Sunday I will make a *coq au vin* for you, mon Waltère," she promised. That *coq au vin,* so she assured me, was a special recipe she had inherited from her aunt, who in turn had inherited it from her grandmother. "On her deathbed she gave it to me," her aunt had always said. The grandmother had proudly claimed that it had

been given to her by the *chef de cuisine de l'Empereur Napoléon!* I
believed every word!

She worked all afternoon. *"Mon amour,* we can eat in twenty
minutes," she said, and slipped into a nice little dress. One minute
later a discreet knocking could be heard at the front door, three
short and one long.

"Mon Dieu, c'est Edmond," she whispered, and without hesita-
tion pushed me into a large armoire in the kitchen, locked the door,
and took the key. All this happened in a few seconds. I was stunned
because she had been telling me that Edmond, *le monsieur sérieux,*
never called unexpectedly. I heard the front door being opened.
"Ah, chéri! Quelle belle surprise," she cried with her best silvery

laugh. Edmond apologized for arriving unannounced and asked her if it would be convenient for her to dine with him, as he had a few free hours. She was delighted, she was enchanted, and she rushed with him out of her flat.

My heart was pounding. After a while I tried to make my exit, but the armoire was a well-built old piece of furniture, the lock wouldn't give, and I hated to break down the door. So I sat on my haunches and waited. The *coq au vin* smelled delightful, but after about an hour the odor changed to one of burning chicken. Dear Ginette, I realized, had forgotten to turn off the fire on the stove.

Smell by smell I could visualize it all: the chicken getting browner and browner, the sauce thicker and blacker, the whole slow process of cremation that was taking place in that pot.

Two long hours later . . . frantic footsteps were racing up the stairs, front door thrown open, loud cries of *"Mon Dieu"* and *"Mon pauvre amour!"* She turned off the flame, tried to open my prison but couldn't find the key, kept asking *me* where it was. Finally she found it, I tumbled out. *"Mon coq au vin est complèment brûlé,"* she wailed, then took me in her arms and, tenderly and lovingly, managed to revive and console me.

Coq au Vin à la Ginette

6-pound capon
Salt and white pepper
⅓ cup butter
12 small white onions
2 cloves garlic, minced fine
1 bouquet garni made of:
  1¼ sprigs of parsley
  ½ stalk of celery, chopped

1 sprig of thyme
½ bay leaf
1¼ pounds small mushrooms
2 cups good dry red Burgundy
  wine
¼ cup brandy
1 cup leftover brown gravy

Cut the capon into 4 pieces of white meat and 4 pieces of dark meat, season with salt and pepper. In a large pan heat the butter, add the capon, onions, garlic, and bouquet garni (in a cheesecloth bag put the parsley, celery, thyme, and bay leaf tied together), and cook the capon until it is golden brown. Now remove the bird and add the mushrooms to the pan, sauté for 6 minutes. Now add the wine, brandy, and capon, simmer for ½ hour. Add the leftover gravy, stir, bring to a simmer. Season to taste. Throw away the bouquet garni! *Serves 4.*

Appetizer Besançon Style
(Hors d'oeuvres Besançon)

Butter 6 slices of whole wheat bread and cut into 2-inch squares. Mix ¼ pound of Roquefort cheese with 3 teaspoons of finely ground hazelnuts and 2 jiggers of gin. Spread dabs of this mass on the buttered squares and sprinkle with paprika and caraway seeds to taste.

Soup Burgundy Style
(Potée Bourguignonne)

1 pound lean beef	*1 teaspoon finely chopped fresh*
2 cups water	*dill*
½ teaspoon salt	

Grind the beef several times. Place in the top of a double boiler with the 2 cups of water and let simmer, with the salt added after the first half hour, for 2 hours. Strain through a fine sieve or through cheesecloth. Chill. Serve cold with chopped dill sprinkled over the top. *Serves 2.*

Crème de Paris

2 packages frozen large lima	*1 teaspoon meat stock*
beans	*2 tablespoons butter*
1 package frozen peas	*4 or 5 shallots, chopped fine*
1 pint water	*Green food coloring*
1 quart half-and-half	*Croutons (see Index)*
4 tablespoons butter	

Boil the lima beans and the peas in the pint of water till they are soft. Press them through a food mill. Boil this pulp gently in the half-and-half for a few minutes, then press the mixture through the food mill again. Add the 4 tablespoons of butter and the meat stock. Heat the 2 tablespoons of butter in a small saucepan; when it begins to bubble, add the shallots, sauté them till they are soft, run them through the food mill, and add to the soup. Add more half-and-half if you like a thinner soup. Add a few drops of green food coloring. Serve with croutons. This soup is very rich and very delicious. *Serves 8–10.*

Lobster Thermidor with Mushrooms au Gratin
(Homard Thermidor)

2 freshly boiled lobsters, 1 to 1½	*Salt*
pounds each	*Freshly ground pepper*
1 cup minced mushrooms	*Paprika*
2 tablespoons butter	*Bread crumbs*
¼ cup dry white wine	*Additional butter*
¼ cup heavy cream	*1 tablespoon grated Parmesan*
1 teaspoon cornstarch	*cheese*

Remove the meat from the lobsters and dice. Reserve the main body of the lobster shells. Sauté the mushrooms in the butter in a skillet over low heat, add the lobster meat, and simmer briefly together. Add the wine, stir, and remove from heat. Blend the cream with the cornstarch and stir into the lobster mixture. Add salt, pepper, and paprika to taste. Fill the lobster shells with the mixture, cover with bread crumbs, dots of butter, and the grated cheese. Place the stuffed shells under the broiler to form a glazed golden crust. *Serves 2.*

Fish Crêpes
(Crêpes Farcies)

Crêpes:

> 3 eggs
> 1¼ cups all-purpose flour
> ½ teaspoon salt
> 2 tablespoons melted butter

> 1 cup cold water
> 1 cup cold milk
> Cooking oil

Mix the eggs with the flour and salt, beat in the melted butter, 1 cup each of cold water and milk gradually until the mixture is smooth. Take a 6-inch skillet and brush lightly with cooking oil. Heat the skillet over moderate heat until hot, then remove from heat. Pour ¼ cup of batter into the middle of the skillet and quickly run the batter over the bottom of it. Cook for about 1 minute or until bottom side is light brown, turn the crêpe, and cook for about ½ minute more. Slide the crêpe onto a plate and repeat the operation with the rest of the batter, taking care to oil the pan between crêpes. *Serves 6.*

Fish Filling:

> 1 small onion, chopped fine
> 1 stalk celery, diced fine
> 4 tablespoons butter
> 1½ pounds fillet of sole, cut in
>   small pieces
> 1 cup water
> 1 cup milk

> 1 carrot, shredded
> 1 teaspoon salt
> ½ teaspoon white pepper
> 2 tablespoons flour
> 2 tablespoons grated Parmesan
>   cheese

In a skillet sauté the onion and celery in 2 tablespoons butter. Add the fish, 1 cup of water, milk, carrot, salt, and pepper. Simmer for about 10 minutes, when the fish should be flaky. Drain the liquid into a measuring cup and add enough milk to make 2 cups. In a small pan melt the remaining butter and blend in the flour. Add to the milk mixture. Cook this liquid mixture until thickened. Pour half the sauce into the fish and vegetable mixture and stir together lightly. Fill each crêpe with some of mixture and roll. Place the rolled fish crêpes in an ovenproof dish. Blend the grated cheese with the remaining sauce, pour the sauce over the crêpes, broil under a high flame for 1 minute, and serve immediately.

English Sole Provençale
(Sole à la Provençale)

4 small English sole	*3 tablespoons butter*
1 teaspoon salt	*1 clove garlic, chopped fine*
¼ teaspoon pepper	*1 shallot, chopped*
Juice of 1 lemon	*2 large tomatoes, peeled and*
¼ cup flour	*chopped*
2 tablespoons olive oil	

Season the fish with the salt and pepper. Sprinkle with the lemon juice. Dip the fish lightly in flour. Heat the olive oil in a skillet and cook fish until golden brown on both sides until done (about 10 minutes). Place on a heated platter and keep hot. Melt the butter in a saucepan, sauté the garlic and shallot for 2 minutes. Add the tomatoes. Stir and cook for 5 minutes. Pour over the fish. Serve immediately. *Serves 4.*

Turbot in Foil
(Turbot en Papillote)

A 2-pound turbot
2 bell peppers, sliced, membrane
  removed
2 onions, sliced
1 teaspoon paprika

2 teaspoons salt
A pinch of pepper
¼ cup lemon juice
¼ cup melted butter or
  margarine

Cut the turbot into 6 portions. Cut 6 pieces of strong aluminum foil about 12 inches square. Lightly grease the foil. Place a piece of fish, skin side down, on each piece of foil. Put slices of bell pepper and onion on top of each portion. Mix together the other ingredients and pour over the fish. Close the fish in the foil so that no sauce can escape. Place the 6 packages on a grill, about 5 inches from moderately hot coals. Cook for about 35 minutes or until the fish flakes easily when tested with a fork. (The fish packages can just as easily be placed on a cookie sheet in a preheated 350° oven and baked for 30–40 minutes. Test for doneness by opening one package and seeing whether the fish flakes. If it does, it's done; if not, close the package and cook for a while longer.) Serve immediately. *Serves 6.*

Chicken in Madeira
(Poulet au Madère)

A 4-pound chicken cut in serving
  pieces
Salt and freshly ground pepper
Garlic salt
Flour for dredging
7 tablespoons butter

A generous ½ pound
  mushrooms, cut in half
¼ cup Madeira wine
½ cup chicken bouillon
¼ cup heavy cream

Sprinkle the pieces of chicken with salt, pepper, and garlic salt, then dredge *lightly* in flour. Fry the chicken in the butter until brown. Cover the pan and simmer until the chicken is done. Now add the mushrooms and fry for 5 minutes. Remove the chicken and mushrooms from the pan and keep warm. Mix the wine with the drippings in the pan, add the bouillon, and let simmer for 1 minute. Correct the seasoning, add the cream, and return the chicken and mushrooms to the pan. Simmer, covered, for a few more minutes. Serve with buttered noodles. *Serves 4.*

Chicken in Curry with Pineapple
(Poulet Sauté au Curry et Ananas)

A 4-pound chicken cut in serving pieces
Salt and freshly ground pepper
6 tablespoons butter
1 cup dry white wine
¼ pound mushrooms, cut in half
1 medium-sized onion, chopped fine

½ teaspoon curry powder
1 tablespoon butter
2½ tablespoons flour
1 cup chicken bouillon
Small can of pineapple chunks
1 tablespoon heavy cream
Garnish: chopped parsley and maraschino cherries

Season the chicken pieces with salt and pepper, fry over a very low flame in 6 tablespoons of butter. When the chicken begins to show color, add the white wine, simmer for ½ hour. Then add the mushrooms, simmer for 5 more minutes. Add more wine if needed. In a separate pan fry the onion with the curry powder in 1 tablespoon of butter. Add the flour, bouillon, and stir until the sauce is thick. Add the liquid from the chicken pan and some pineapple juice (leave enough juice to enable you to warm the pineapple chunks just before serving). Cook for 2 minutes. Heat the pineapple chunks. Place the chicken, mushrooms, and heated pineapple chunks on a serving plate. Add the cream to the sauce, mix well, and pour over the chicken. Garnish with the chopped parsley and maraschino cherries. Serve with piping hot boiled rice and with chutney. *Serves 4.*

Veal Kidneys Mimosa
(Rognons Sauté Mimosa)

1½ pounds veal kidneys
Flour
2 tablespoons oil or butter
A pinch each of salt, pepper,
  oregano, and chopped
  parsley
1 tablespoon lemon juice

3 tablespoons heavy cream
4 large pieces of bread, toasted
Butter
2 eggs, hard-cooked, peeled, and
  chopped
Small bunch of parsley, chopped
  fine

Remove the fat and membranes from the kidneys, cut in slices, remove all white tissue, and soak in 1 cup of water and ½ tablespoon of vinegar for 1 hour, then wipe them dry. Sprinkle the kidneys liberally with flour and fry them quickly and lightly in very hot oil or butter. Add the seasonings, lemon juice, and stir. Lower the heat and add the cream, stir again. Spread the kidneys over the toast, keep warm. Melt the butter, fry together lightly the chopped egg and the parsley, add a little more salt and pepper, and garnish the kidneys with this mixture. Serve immediately. *Serves 4.*

Kidneys Flambé
(Rognons Flambés)

4 veal kidneys
2 cups water
3 tablespoons vinegar
¼ cup butter
1 small onion, chopped fine
A pinch of oregano
A pinch of sage
½ teaspoon salt

½ teaspoon pepper
½ teaspoon paprika
¼ tablespoon prepared
  mustard
1½ tablespoons heavy cream
4 tablespoons brandy
Chopped parsley

Remove the fat and membranes from the kidneys, cut them crosswise into slices, removing all the white tissue, and soak them in 2 cups of water and 3 tablespoons of vinegar for 1 hour. Remove the kidney slices and dry them. Melt the butter in a pan and sauté the onion, along with the oregano and sage, till the onion is brown. Add the kidneys and sauté for about 5 minutes. Season with the salt, pepper, and paprika, add the mustard and heavy cream. Warm the brandy, pour it over the kidneys, and ignite it by touching the edge of the pan with a lighted match. Sprinkle chopped parsley on top and serve immediately with piping hot boiled rice. *Serves 4.*

Veal Scaloppine à la Villeroy
(Escalopes de Veau à la Villeroy)

2 pounds veal scaloppine in 8 pieces, pounded thin	A pinch each of salt, pepper, nutmeg, and thyme
Freshly ground pepper	Additional flour
5 tablespoons butter	2 eggs, beaten
Additional butter	Bread crumbs
3 tablespoons flour	Crisco for frying
1 cup milk	

In a large skillet sauté the scaloppine, peppered, quickly in the 5 tablespoons of butter, let them cool. Make a white sauce out of the drippings of the veal (adding enough butter to make 3 tablespoons), the 3 tablespoons of flour, 1 cup of milk, and the seasonings. While the white sauce is still hot, spread it on the cold scaloppine, let it cool. Dredge the sauced scaloppine with flour, dip them in the beaten eggs, and then roll them in bread crumbs. Fry the scaloppine in Crisco till they are brown, about 2 minutes on each side. Serve immediately. *Serves 4.*

Chicken à la Villeroy
(Poulet à la Villeroy)

Follow the procedure for Veal Scaloppine à la Villeroy (recipe immediately preceding), but substitute boned chicken breasts for the veal scaloppine. *Serves 4.*

Calf's Tongue
(Langue de Veau Poché)

3 calf's (veal) tongues, about
    2 pounds each
Salt
2 medium-sized carrots, sliced
2 large onions, sliced

1 stalk celery, sliced
4 sprigs parsley
1 bay leaf
A pinch of thyme (less than ⅛
    teaspoon)

Soak the tongues in water for about 2 hours. Change the water, add salt and remaining ingredients, and boil for 1–1½ hours, until the hard skin will come off easily. Calf's tongue is delicious served either hot or cold with either of the two sauces given below: Caper Sauce and Salsa Verde. *Serves 6.*

Caper Sauce (Sauce aux Câpres) :

3 tablespoons butter
1 tablespoon flour
1 cup hot beef bouillon
A pinch of salt
2 egg yolks

2 tablespoons heavy cream
Juice of ¼ lemon
2 tablespoons softened butter
1½ tablespoons small capers,
    drained

In a saucepan melt the 3 tablespoons of butter, add the flour, cook, stirring steadily, for a few minutes over low heat. Then add the hot bouillon and a pinch of salt and simmer, stirring, for 5 minutes. Meanwhile, beat the egg yolks with the cream and lemon juice. Remove the saucepan from the fire and let the sauce cool a little. Spoon some of the sauce over the egg mixture and stir, then pour the mixture back into the saucepan, stirring with a whisk until the sauce thickens. Beat in, little by little, the 2 tablespoons of softened butter. Add the capers and stir. *Makes 1½ cups.*

Salsa Verde (Green Sauce) :

½ *slice white bread, soaked in*
    water and squeezed dry
1 *hard-cooked egg*
¼ *cup olive oil*
2 *teaspoons vinegar*
½ *tablespoon dry mustard*

⅛ *teaspoon each of salt and*
    pepper
1 *bunch of parsley*
½ *small yellow onion*
½ *teaspoon small capers*
Heavy cream

Put all of the ingredients except the heavy cream in a blender and blend until very smooth, then add enough cream to make the consistency of a thick sauce. *Serves 5.*

French Potato Salad

3 *pounds potatoes*
2 *cups diced celery*
1 *small onion, chopped*
2½ *teaspoons salt*
1 *cup mayonnaise*

2 *tablespoons dry mustard*
¼ *teaspoon Tabasco sauce*
½ *cup beer or ale*
2 *tablespoons chopped parsley*

Cook the potatoes in their skins till tender, peel and dice, measure 8 cups. Add the celery and onion, sprinkle with the salt. Blend together the mayonnaise, mustard, and Tabasco sauce, gradually stir in the beer. Add the parsley to the potato mixture. Mix lightly with a fork and spoon carefully so as not to break up the diced potatoes. Pour the dressing over the salad, serve on large lettuce leaves, and garnish with radish slices if you like. *Serves 8.*

Cherries Jubilee

In a chafing dish heat canned Bing cherries (count about 8 per nose), cover them with their juice, add the juice of a medium-sized lemon and 2 tablespoons of strawberry preserves, mix well. Before this mixture reaches the boiling point, add 3 tablespoons of cognac, 3 tablespoons of kirsch, and 2 tablespoons of Cointreau. (Instead of the cognac, kirsch, and Cointreau, you may use the same amount of the highest-proof rum.) Place one portion of vanilla ice cream in each fancy stemmed glass. Ignite the sauce and pour it, still flaming, over the ice cream. Serve immediately.

You have my permission to turn out the lights during this splendid flaming procedure and then sing the *Marseillaise*. *Serves 6–8.*

Crêpes Suzette

This is my own simplified version. Delicious!

16 crêpes (see Dessert Pancakes,	*Grated rind of 1 lemon*
Palatschinken, *in the Index*)	*Juice of 2 oranges*
¼ pound butter	*3 tablespoons cognac or brandy*
2 tablespoons sugar	*3 tablespoons kirsch*
Grated rind of 1 orange	*2 tablespoons Cointreau*

Prepare the crêpes as in the *Palatschinken* recipe, with a little apricot jam spread on them thinly before rolling them up. Set them aside for a short while. Melt the butter in a chafing dish, add the sugar, the grated orange and lemon rinds, and 1 tablespoon of the orange juice. Place the crêpes in this mixture. When you are ready to serve, light the flame under the chafing dish, add the rest of the orange juice. When the sauce is heated and begins to bubble, add the liquors and flame them. Then serve the crêpes, using 2 long-handled serving spoons, 2 or 3 crêpes to a person, while the liquors are still aflame. *Serves 6–8.*

Lemon Soufflé
(Soufflé de Citron)

2 eggs, separated	*Juice of 1 lemon*
2 tablespoons sugar	*Grated rind of 1 lemon*

Beat the egg yolks and sugar till fluffy, add the lemon juice and grated lemon rind. Then add the stiffly beaten egg whites, mix lightly, and pour into a buttered small soufflé dish or small casserole. Bake in a preheated 375° oven for 10–15 minutes. Serve immediately. *Serves 2.*

Mousse au Chocolat

8 1-ounce squares semisweet   A pinch of salt
    cooking chocolate   1 pint heavy cream, whipped
1 cup sugar   2 tablespoons cognac
4 eggs, separated   Additional heavy cream for
¼ cup milk   topping
1 teaspoon vanilla extract

Melt the chocolate squares in the top of a double boiler over simmering water, add the sugar, egg yolks, and milk, beat vigorously,
lift the top of the double boiler from the bottom, continue to beat
vigorously until the mousse is not quite thick. Cool. Add the vanilla
and salt, fold in the stiffly beaten egg whites, and then the pint of
whipped cream. Add the cognac. Pour into a serving dish and chill
in the refrigerator for at least 8 hours. Serve with additional
whipped cream. *Serves 6–8.*

Pineapple Parfait Cometa
(Parfait d'Ananas Cometa)

4 eggs, separated   1 tablespoon lemon juice
½ cup sugar   Grated rind of 1 lemon
1 tablespoon vanilla sugar (or 1   2 tablespoons maraschino liquor
    tablespoon sugar with 1 drop   3 slices canned pineapple, cut
    vanilla extract added)   into little pieces
½ cup milk   Juice of the pineapple slices
2 tablespoons orange juice   1 pint heavy cream, whipped

In the top of a double boiler over simmering water, cook the egg
yolks, sugar, vanilla sugar, and milk till thick. Remove the top of
the double boiler from the bottom, keep stirring the sauce till it is
cool. Add the orange juice, lemon juice and rind, maraschino liquor, and pieces of pineapple. Boil the pineapple juice down to half.
When it is cool, add it to the mixture. Pour the parfait into a

spring-form pan that is lined with aluminum foil and place in the freezer. Take out of the freezer ½ hour before serving time, remove the parfait from the pan, remove the aluminum foil, and serve. The whipped cream accompanies the parfait. *Serves 6.*

I've Never Been to China

食色性也
Mao

I do not have slanted eyes, but I suspect that hundreds of years ago some Chinese left his calling card at my ancestral home, because to me nothing beats a really good Chinese dinner.

I discovered that joy forty-nine years ago, when I was brought over for my first Broadway show. The New York papers very kindly insisted that I was the town's newest matinee idol! A greenhorn to these shores, I had to have that term explained to me.

The Wednesday afternoon performances are usually patronized by large groups of elderly ladies who sometimes take a liking (in theatrical exaggeration called "idolization") to the leading man if he is young, attractive, and charming. As I possessed these qualities *ad nauseam*, I was quickly launched on the "chicken à la king" circuit. The "idolizing" ladies bought large blocks of seats, at a discount, and often arranged a lunch before the matinee. It was a nice custom to invite the star of the show, seat him on the dais, feed him the standard luncheon menu of fruit cup, chunks of chicken hidden in a thick white sauce with peas as a side dish, and—after every mouth had been wiped clean and the napkins crumpled—to introduce him to the assembly. In return he was expected to say a few words, and if he happened to have an accent, so much the better.

At one of these matinee lunches I sat next to Anna May Wong, that lovely Chinese actress. I had met her before, in Berlin, where she worked in German films after her overnight success in Douglas

Fairbanks' *Thief of Bagdad*. It was she who opened for me the pearly gates to the heaven of Oriental cooking. She took me to Chinatown, where she knew a small restaurant that rolled out the red carpet when Anna May Wong arrived. The proprietor, Chiang How Wong (not related to Anna May Wong, so she assured me) had spent many years as chef at the Chinese Embassy in Berlin and spoke fairly good German. It was there that the actress had met him and learned that he was about to come to America to open a restaurant.

In New York I went to his little place often. Living in that city, I had no need for a car, so I went by subway to Chinatown, that strange Eastern ghetto—or, better, that city within a city. I was enchanted by its streets and its markets where there were displayed vegetables I had never seen or tasted; fascinated by the food shops with smells I couldn't identify, by the roast ducks hanging by their feet in the open; by the bewildering variety of spices for which there are no English names. It was a new world, doubly intriguing because for me Chinese food had become one of the best—if not THE best—in the world, or, at any rate, in that part of it which I knew.

Mr. Wong took kindly to me. We reminisced about Berlin, where I had spent eight years of my life, and, when business was quiet, he let me go into his kitchen and watch him work. There, for the first time, I saw a *wok*, that wonderful bowl-shaped basic cooking utensil that can be used for frying, sautéing, steaming, and deep frying. Today the wok is a universally accepted appliance that is sold all over America for use over an open fire, over electric heat, and, lately, with its own built-in electric heat.

It was here that I learned the art of not overcooking food, and especially vegetables, which should be crisp, I admired the speed with which dishes were prepared, due to the fact that almost everything is first chopped into small pieces, the oil in the wok sizzling hot, then the food is tossed into the oil, spices added, and served. The wok has a far greater heating surface than ordinary pans do, and makes quick frying so much simpler. At that time I was living in a hotel and had no private kitchen, so I could not try the simple Cantonese dishes that Mr. Wong kindly taught me.

I learned his way of preparing barbecued spareribs: they were the juiciest, most flavorful ribs. Mr. Wong began by pulling off the tough membrane from the bony side of the ribs. He loosened the membrane at the small end of the ribs on the cut side. He pushed a small knife between the meat and the membrane, then he removed the membrane from the small end to the wide end of the ribs. He told me that that technique exposed more meat to absorb the marinade and basting sauce. Then, with a heavy cleaver, he slashed part way through the bony side of the ribs. He parboiled the whole ribs for 20 to 30 minutes, depending on their thickness. He drained them and wiped them dry, then placed them in a marinade for 8 hours or, preferably, overnight:

Marinade:

6 tablespoons honey	4 tablespoons orange marmalade
8 tablespoons soy sauce	1 small can pineapple juice
1 tablespoon vinegar	1 teaspoon cinnamon
2 tablespoons brown sugar	2 tablespoons peach marmalade
2 cloves garlic, crushed	1 tablespoon sherry
½ teaspoon powdered ginger	1 tablespoon strong prepared
1 cup chicken consommé	black coffee

Thoroughly mix all the ingredients.

After 8 hours, Mr. Wong put the ribs on a grill, but first cut between them part way to make serving-size pieces. He said that approximately 5 pounds of ribs would be right for the amount of marinade.

In Chinatown, San Francisco, I got another recipe for a marinade:

2 cloves, crushed   *½ cup soy sauce*
3 slices fresh gingerroot   *1 tablespoon pepper*
½ cup sherry   *1 tablespoon monosodium*
½ cup honey   *glutamate*

Thoroughly mix all the ingredients. Personally I prefer Mr. Wong's prescription.

The honorable Huang Li-fu, a Chinese diplomat, talked about the strict ritual of attending an "official dinner" in China. He explained that custom demanded that the guest of honor rise at the end of the meal and—in flowery verbiage— praise the incomparable deliciousness of the food that had been served, a unique feast that, he promised, he would always remember and recount to his children and children's children. Whereupon the host would rise and—deeply aggrieved—admit to his shame that his miserable cook was unable to place before such illustrious guests anything better than the measly and tasteless concoctions that were not fit to be eaten. Now the guest of honor would rise again to contradict his host, assuring him that it was the very best repast he had ever tasted. Then again came the turn of the host, who would repeat his sorrow over the poor quality of the food and humbly make excuses. Then they would bow to each other and that signaled the end of the meal.

But once, the honorable Huang Li-fu recounted, he attended a formal dinner at the home of a friend. There, at the end of the meal, the guest of honor arose and—to the consternation of everyone—sadly declared that he could not remember ever having eaten such abominable and tasteless food, prepared without refinement or taste. To answer him, the host got up and exclaimed that never had he tasted such delightful food or attended a banquet of such opulence, which he would recall to the end of his days.

The honorable Huang Li-fu was quite puzzled until the host explained that his cook had suddenly taken ill and that the guest of honor had kindly lent him HIS cook!

···❯···▬▬❯◦❮▬···❮···

Barbecued Spareribs with Ginger Sauce

1 cup ketchup
1 teaspoon freshly grated ginger
4 teaspoons butter
2 tablespoons Lea & Perrins
    Worcestershire sauce
3 tablespoons lemon juice
½ teaspoon finely minced garlic
2 tablespoons honey

1 teaspoon ground coriander
4 pounds spareribs, as
    small-boned and full of flesh
    as possible
Salt and freshly ground pepper
    to taste
¼ teaspoon monosodium
    glutamate

Combine the ketchup, ginger, butter, Worcestershire sauce, lemon juice, garlic, honey, and coriander in a saucepan. Bring to a boil and blend. After boiling the sauce for several minutes, marinate the spareribs in it for a few hours. Place the spareribs on a rack with the meaty side up; add salt and pepper and sprinkle with monosodium glutamate. Bake in a preheated 350° oven for 40 minutes till brown. Brush the spareribs with the sauce, bake for 20 minutes longer. Turn the spareribs and brush with sauce. Bake for another 10 minutes, basting constantly till the rib meat is soft to the fork. *Serves 4.*

Lemon Soup

8 cups water
Grated rind and juice of 1 lemon
1 medium-sized onion, sliced
4 scallions, sliced
4 peppercorns
3 bay leaves
½ pound raw shrimp, shelled
    and deveined (reserve
    shells)

½ pound lean pork, cut into
    strips
1 fillet of sole, cut in chunks
1 chicken breast, skinned, boned,
    and cut into strips
1 cup strong court bouillon
Additional lemon juice
Salt to taste
A few anchovy fillets

Mix together the 8 cups of water, rind and juice of lemon, onion, scallions, peppercorns, bay leaves, and the shrimp shells (after rinsing them). Put the mixture in a saucepan and bring to a boil. Reduce the heat and simmer for ½ hour. Add the pork, sole, and chicken. Again bring to a boil and simmer for another 20 minutes. Remove the shrimp shells and put in the shrimp. Continue to boil until the shrimp are bright pink. Add the court bouillon, a little lemon juice, salt, and the anchovies. Remove the bay leaves. Serve the hot soup immediately. *Serves 6.*

Abalone and Chicken Soup

½ cup snow peas
4 cups chicken broth
½ cup abalone juice from can
½ cup sliced fresh mushrooms
½ teaspoon salt

¾ cup sliced boiled ham
¼ cup sliced boiled chicken
*   breast*
½ cup sliced canned abalone

Parboil the snow peas, set aside. Heat the chicken broth and the abalone juice. Add the mushrooms and salt, and let the broth boil. Then add the ham, chicken, and abalone, and when the soup begins to boil again, add the snow peas. *Serves 6.*

Fried Shrimp

1 pound raw large shrimp,
*   shelled and deveined, tails*
*   left on*
½ cup flour

2 eggs, beaten
¼ cup cooking oil
Salt to taste
White pepper to taste

Roll the shrimp in the flour, dip in the beaten eggs, and fry in the very hot oil (400°) in a skillet until the shrimp are tender. Dust with salt and white pepper. Serve immediately with a sauce made of ketchup, a little soy sauce, and a lot of dry English mustard, well mixed.

Mr. Wong's Sweet and Sour Fish

A 4-pound white fish, left whole | 6 tablespoons soy sauce
1 cup flour | 2 cups wine vinegar
Oil for deep frying | 2 tablespoons cornstarch
3 tablespoons oil | 1 medium-sized onion, sliced
1 cup sugar | 3 tablespoons chopped ginger

Clean the fish, coat it with flour, and deep-fry it in oil in a large
skillet until it is golden brown. Drain it, lay it on paper towels, and
keep it warm. Mix well the 3 tablespoons of oil, sugar, soy sauce,
vinegar, and cornstarch, boil over medium heat for 2 minutes. Then
add the onion and ginger and boil for another 4 minutes. Pour this
sauce over the fish and serve it immediately. Slice the fish in thick
pieces at the table. *Serves 4.*

Chicken with Pineapple

3 chicken breasts, boned | 2 cups pineapple chunks
3 tablespoons flour | ⅔ cup pineapple juice
1 teaspoon salt | 1½ tablespoons cornstarch
A pinch of white pepper | 3 tablespoons soy sauce
4 tablespoons cooking oil | 2 tablespoons vinegar

Cut the chicken into strips 1 inch by ½ inch, toss with a mixture of the flour, salt, and white pepper. Heat the oil in a wok, sauté the chicken in it for about 5 minutes. Add the pineapple chunks and slowly cook for another 5 minutes. In a bowl, mix the pineapple juice, cornstarch, soy sauce, and vinegar, add to the wok, and heat until the mixture is thickened. *Serves 4–6.*

Breast of Chicken with Mushrooms
(Moo Goo Gai Pan)

1 breast of chicken, skinned, boned, and cut into cubes	2 tablespoons oil
2 teaspoons and 1 tablespoon cornstarch	3 slices gingerroot, minced
	1 clove garlic, minced
¼ teaspoon salt	4-ounce can button mushrooms
¼ teaspoon freshly ground pepper	5 water chestnuts

After the chicken is cubed, blend together the 2 teaspoons of cornstarch, salt, pepper, mixing with the chicken meat until all cubes are well coated. In a wok heat the oil, mix the gingerroot and garlic together, and fry in the oil for 1 minute, stirring all the time. Now add the chicken and fry for 3 minutes, stirring all the while, until it starts to brown. Drain the juice from the mushrooms, setting aside the juice, and add the mushrooms to the chicken. Cook for 1 minute. Mix the tablespoon of cornstarch with ⅓ cup of mushroom liquid and stir into the chicken mixture until sauce thickens. Slice the water chestnuts, add to the chicken, and serve immediately. Serve over hot broiled rice and sprinkle with blanched whole almonds if you like. *Serves 4.*

Chicken with Mixed Vegetables and Almonds

2 cups diced uncooked chicken	Cornstarch
1 egg, beaten	½ cup corn oil
½ teaspoon soy sauce	¾ cup blanched whole almonds
½ teaspoon salt	2 tablespoons butter

Mix the chicken with the egg, soy sauce, and salt, dust lightly with some cornstarch. Put the corn oil in a *hot* wok, and when the oil is sizzling, add the chicken mixture, sauté until it is light brown. Remove the chicken and drain. In a small skillet, brown the almonds in the butter, set aside. Remove most of the oil from the wok and put into it the following ingredients, mixed well:

½ cup vinegar	1 cup chopped chard
½ cup sugar	½ cup canned peas
A dash of salt	½ cup shredded bell pepper
1 cup chopped celery	

Cook this mixture in the wok over medium heat, stirring all the time. Then add 1 tablespoon of cornstarch mixed with 2 tablespoons of water. When the liquid in the wok has the consistency of a thick sauce, add the browned chicken, the almonds, and toss well. *Serves 5.*

Chinese Braised Duck

A 6-pound duck	2 cups dry white wine or dry
1 teaspoon salt	sherry
½ teaspoon pepper	3 tablespoons cooking oil
½ teaspoon curry powder	½ cup chopped onions
½ teaspoon minced chives	

Cut the duck into serving-sized pieces. Combine the salt, pepper, curry, chives, and wine, and marinate the duck overnight in this marinade. Remove the duck and reserve the marinade. Heat the oil in a casserole or deep skillet, brown the pieces of duck on all sides, add the onions, and cook for 5 minutes, Pour off the fat, stir in the marinade, cover the casserole or skillet tightly, and cook over low heat for 1½ hours or until the duck is tender. Remove the duck. (The sauce may be thickened with a little cornstarch if necessary.) *Serves 4–6.*

Chinese Deep-Fried Duck

1 duck, 6–7 pounds	Oil for deep frying
2 eggs, beaten	1 cup drained canned mushrooms
¼ cup cornstarch	1 tablespoon cornstarch
1 teaspoon salt	3 tablespoons water
½ teaspoon pepper	½ cup blanched almonds,
2 tablespoons water	toasted and slivered

Disjoint the duck, put it in a saucepan with enough water to cover, and bring to a boil. Cover the saucepan and simmer for about 40 minutes. Drain but reserve the broth. Bone the duck carefully and cut the meat into 1½-inch squares, keeping the skin on the meat. Mix the beaten eggs with ¼ cup of cornstarch, salt, pepper, and 2 tablespoons water until a smooth batter results. Dip the duck squares into the batter and fry in deep hot oil a few at a time until they are browned and crisp. After you take them from the oil, drain them on absorbent paper. Skim the fat from the duck broth, reheat the broth, add the mushrooms, and add salt and pepper to taste. Mix 1 tablespoon cornstarch with 3 tablespoons water until smooth, stir into the broth, and continue to stir until the whole mixture is smooth and thick. Pour the sauce over the duck and sprinkle with the almonds. Serve immediately. *Serves 8.*

Pork, Chicken, and Vegetables

1½ pounds diced, uncooked chicken	½ teaspoon ground chili peppers
1 pound uncooked pork cut into ½-inch cubes	1 teaspoon salt
	2 teaspoons ground sesame seeds
3 tablespoons cooking oil	¾ cup beef bouillon
½ cup minced onions	2½ tablespoons soy sauce
2 cloves garlic, crushed	1 cup green peas (may be canned)
2 medium-sized tomatoes, sliced	

Sauté the chicken and pork in the oil in a wok until they are brown. Remove the meat. Sauté the onions and garlic until they are light brown. Add the tomatoes, cook over low heat for 5 minutes. Return the chicken and pork to the wok, add the chili peppers, salt, sesame seeds, bouillon, and soy sauce, cook for 35 minutes over medium heat. Toward the end of cooking time add the peas and let them simmer for another 6 minutes. *Serves 4–6.*

Pork, Bean Curd, and Mushrooms

5 ounces dried bean curd
2 medium-sized dried Chinese
    mushrooms
3 tablespoons cooking oil
2 pork chops, boned and cut into
    very thin strips

2 tablespoons sherry
1 tablespoon soy sauce
1 teaspoon salt
1 teaspoon sugar

Soak the bean curd in warm water for 15–20 minutes till soft, then drain and cut into strips. Soak the mushrooms in warm water till they are soft, drain, and slice. Heat the oil to high temperature in a wok or skillet. Add the pork strips, and stir for about 2 minutes. Add the sherry, soy sauce, salt, and sugar, mix well. (If the mixture is too thick, thin it with cold water, and then reheat it until it is good and hot.) *Serves 2–3.*

Sweet and Sour Pork with Pineapple

1½ pounds boneless pork
1½ teaspoons sherry
¾ teaspoon salt
1½ teaspoons cornstarch

3 cups oil for deep frying
Sweet and Sour Sauce (recipe
    given below)

Put the pork cubes in a bowl with the sherry, salt, and cornstarch, let them stand for ½ hour. Meanwhile prepare the sauce:

Sweet and Sour Sauce:

¾ cup canned pineapple chunks
    with juice
¼ cup mixed sweet pickles with
    juice
2½ teaspoons cornstarch
1½ tablespoons cold water

Oil (taken from the 3 cups in
    recipe above)
3 cloves garlic, crushed
3 tablespoons soy sauce
3 medium-sized tomatoes, cut in
    narrow wedges

Drain the pineapple chunks and mixed pickles, reserving the juices. Make a paste of the cornstarch and 1½ tablespoons of cold water. In a saucepan heat a little oil over a hot flame and sauté the garlic for about 1 minute, then discard the garlic. Into the saucepan put the soy sauce, juices of the pineapple and pickles, and bring to a boil. Add the pineapple chunks and pickles. When the mixture begins to boil again, add the cornstarch paste amd tomatoes, stir until well mixed and the sauce has thickened. Keep the sauce hot.

Deep-fry the pork in the remaining oil in a skillet for about 7 minutes over medium heat, drain, and pour over it the hot Sweet and Sour Sauce. *Serves 6.*

Mr. Wong's Chinese Lamb and Cabbage

3 medium-sized onions, sliced thin
1 clove garlic, minced
1 cup sliced celery
2 tablespoons oil
½ teaspoon salt
1 pound boneless leg of lamb, sliced very thin
3 cups coarsely shredded cabbage
1 beef bouillon cube
1 cup water
2 tablespoons soy sauce
1½ tablespoons cornstarch
4 cups boiled rice

Sauté the onions, garlic, and celery in the oil until the onions turn yellow. Add the salt and meat, simmer in a tightly covered large saucepan for 5 minutes. Place the cabbage on top of the lamb and cook, covered, for another 10 minutes. The cabbage should be slightly crisp. Dissolve the bouillon cube in the 1 cup of water, the soy sauce, and cornstarch, add to the lamb, stir until the mixture is thickened, cook for 5 minutes longer. Serve with piping hot boiled rice. *Serves 4–6.*

Mr. Wong's Fried Rice

4 tablespoons cooking oil
4 cups dry cooked rice
½ cup chopped, cooked shrimp
1 cup bean sprouts
¾ cup chopped scallions
¼ cup minced parsley
2 eggs, beaten
¼ cup soy sauce
Salt and freshly ground pepper to taste

Heat the oil in a wok. Fry the rice in the oil, stirring constantly, until it is slightly browned. Add the shrimp, bean sprouts, scallions, and parsley, cook for about 1½ minutes. Then add the eggs and mix well until they are almost firm. Season with the soy sauce, salt, and pepper. *Serves 4–6.*

Chinese Salad Bowl

1 large head of Chinese cabbage	Oil
2 small red onions, sliced	2 tablespoons vinegar
1 cup sour cream	Salt and freshly ground pepper
½ cup minced onions	to taste
2 tablespoons celery seeds	3 slices bacon, fried, crumbled
1½ tablespoons peanut butter	for garnish

Wash the cabbage thoroughly, shred it coarsely. Add the onion slices. Separately combine the remaining ingredients except the bacon, add to the salad, and toss well. Sprinkle the crumbled bacon over the salad before serving. *Serves 5–6.*

Rumakis

Although rumakis are not Chinese, they are included here because they are so good. They are an excellent hors d'oeuvre.

6 chicken livers, quartered	12 strips of bacon, cut in half
½ cup Kikkoman soy sauce	8 water chestnuts, sliced in 3
¼ cup sherry	pieces
½ clove garlic, crushed	½ cup brown sugar

Cover the chicken livers with a marinade made of the soy sauce, sherry, and garlic, and let stand, covered, for about 12 hours. Wrap a piece of bacon around a piece of liver and a piece of water chestnut, skewer with a toothpick. Roll them in brown sugar. Place the rumakis in a roasting pan, add the marinade, and let them stand in the refrigerator for 2–3 hours, turning once. Roast the rumakis in a preheated 400° oven for about ½ hour, pouring off the drippings occasionally and basting often with the marinade. Serve immediately. *Serves 6.*

Mr. Wong's Chinese Fruits

Into an 8-inch-high cone of shaved ice, Mr. Wong stuck preserved kumquats, canned white lichees, pineapple chunks, maraschino cherries, and sections of mandarin oranges that had all been pierced individually by toothpicks, so that one end of each toothpick was imbedded in the shaved ice and the other end was held by the fingers.

"On va les manger!"

In the spring of 1931 my employers, the Shubert brothers, decided to close *Meet My Sister,* my first Broadway show, for a summer recess. With an actor's typical optimism and the eternal hope that one's show would run on and on, that sudden closing was a nasty shock to me. *And* to my bank account. At that time I was not yet an American citizen and, as an alien, was not permitted to work in summer stock; I didn't have enough money to take a boat to Europe to spend the six-week hiatus with my parents at their summer place on the shores of the Tegernsee, and with precious little cash on hand I was afraid to face the rigors of a New York summer, living in a hotel, with no earnings coming in.

One of the stagehands in our show, a French Canadian and an avid fisherman, thought that the solution to my problem would be to go fishing! And he told me of the simple life, the back-to-nature bit—sleeping in the open on the bank of a rippling stream, living in the woods like Davy Crockett—and he happened to know just the right place for me: Lac Archambault, a hundred miles north of Montreal. Once there, I was to get in touch with a character called "Père Labin" and to bring greetings to him from Bud, his old pal! I would be received with open arms. A fellow actor, Boyd Davis, who played the butler in our show (born in London and trained at the Royal Academy of Dramatic Art), spoke the English language beautifully. When he volunteered to come along, sharing expenses, I considered that a double bonus, as I might pick up some of his British accent and lose some of my Viennese sounds. A two-week closing notice was up and we had ample time to go shopping for the great outdoors. The sporting goods department of Macy's supplied it all: clothes that would enable us to survive in the wilds of Canada, fishing rods and tackle, hunting knives, flashlights, a tropical helmet, sleeping bags (blankets and pillows I borrowed from my hotel), pots and pans, a secondhand twelve-gauge shotgun and a small-caliber rifle to protect us against the man-eating beasts of the forest. And, of course, a large supply of canned goods and dried fruit.

Loaded up as though we were planning to explore Tibet, we set out for Lac Archambault, deep in French-speaking territory. That didn't faze me. I was fluent in French because my parents had had the foresight and wisdom to supply me with a French governess while I was still at an age when I couldn't protest. Besides, I had worked in Paris, on the stage and in films.

My little maroon-colored Pontiac roadster with rumble seat took two days to take us to Montreal, where I asked a policeman to recommend an inexpensive hotel for the night. I had bragged to Boyd about my being fluent in French and I was dismayed when the policeman couldn't understand what I was saying and I couldn't understand him. The man spoke purest Canuck French and it took me a few days to get the hang of that argot.

The following morning we arrived at Lac Archambault. There was no Labin in the telephone directory, so we asked at the general store. "Oh yes," they knew him all right, they laughed. "Just go across the street to the saloon; he's bound to be there." And so he was! In a corner we saw a pile of dirty old clothes pushed up against the wall from which a hand protruded, holding onto a whiskey glass, and from the top of that smelly heap an old man's head poked out, a few yellow teeth showing as he grinned at us with bloodshot eyes.

We approached him and asked if he was Père Labin.

"*Ah oui, c'est moi,*" he assured us. We mentioned Bud, his old pal from New York, but that drew a blank, so we sat down next to him. That was a mistake. The old geezer emitted such an awful smell, such a penetrating stink, that I pitied him because he couldn't run away from himself. We explained that we were looking for a place to camp and fish. He understood, began to make sense, and promised to lead us to *the* perfect spot. "Just follow me to my car," he said, and swayed toward the door. We paid for his drink: the bartender wanted to know if we were going to pay for his whole bill, but we were inelegant and paid for just the one whiskey. Outside stood an old broken-down jalopy: he explained with a sheepish smile that the gas tank was empty, so we gave him five gallons from our canister. He led us north, on an unpaved road, for about forty-five miles. He then made an abrupt left turn: now the road stopped altogether, but he bravely drove on, through bush and

fields, into holes and over rocks until we arrived at the edge of a lake. He pulled up in front of a wooden cabin, walked to the porch, reached under a floorboard, produced a key, and opened the door. Then he went inside, threw open all the windows, came out again, and said with a flourish, *"Voilà!"*

And *"Voilà"* it was. To our great surprise it was spotlessly clean, with four bunks, table, benches, an old rocking chair, cupboard with plates, a drawer with knives and forks, large pans and two kettles, an aluminum coffee percolator, a wonderful old iron stove, and in the middle of the room, propped up on wooden blocks, a fire-engine-red Indian canoe.

Père Labin told us that he owned the whole peninsula and that, seeing what two nice gentlemen we were, he would be willing to rent us *"le bungalow"* with all the luxuries it contained. But we would have to take it for four weeks, all the rent to be paid in advance. And that the price was fifteen dollars a week.

I just looked at him: slowly I raised the middle finger of my right hand, and then pointed at his head. I walked back to our car. Boyd joined me and *le père* ran after us: *"Mais, monsieur, on va parler."* *"Pas avec un fou,"* I replied, and started the car. "You'll never find your way out of these woods," he screamed. "Oh yes, I will. My sense of direction is superb." He held onto the open window and an hour of haggling began. A few times I started the motor; he ran ahead of the car and laid himself down on the ground, daring me to run over him. Slowly, very slowly, we got together. The final deal was eight dollars a week, one week's rent in advance, and we would take the place on a week-to-week basis. He was saddened by my cruel bargaining; he called me an *"espèce de marchandeur,"* a chiseler. I fully agreed with him and we began to unload. Suddenly he remembered that the canoe didn't go with the house and for that he wanted three dollars a week. I raised my middle finger and we carried our stuff back to the car. After another twenty-five minutes at the negotiating window he agreed to take a dollar fifty, but quickly ran back and grabbed the paddle. The paddle, he insisted, did not belong to him. It was the most precious possession of a *"cher ami"* who, he was certain, would not take less than three dollars a week. I gave him fifty cents and took the paddle. Then I fished some stationery out of my bag and sat down to write a rental agreement.

Now Old Smelly was outraged: he accused me of not trusting him, of having no faith in his integrity. "In this part of the country one does not need a contract: a handshake and a man's word of honor is enough," he cried, beating his breast. *"Je suis un homme honnête!"* I ignored his shenanigans, wrote the agreement, and read it to him, slowly and loud.

"No," he screamed, "I will *not* sign it!"

"And why not?"

"Because, monsieur," he said with dignity, "I have never learned to read or write."

"That's no problem," I countered. "We will drive back to the village, and you can make your little cross on this paper in front of a public notary."

After a long pause, during which he must have considered all the possibilities, he began to laugh, and, suddenly, miraculously, he was able to read and write. We gave him a drink, which made him amiable, and he promised to come back the next day to show us where to fish and hunt.

"You will both need licenses," he said.

"My partner will not be fishing," I answered, "and neither will he hunt. He is afraid of guns. Only I shall need a permit."

He responded with a disappointed "Oh," and after another pause he snapped his fingers: he had an idea!

"But you will have to drive back to the village," he said with sadness in his voice, "because the fellow who issues these licenses insists that applicants appear in person! But," he added, "he happens to be a dear friend of mine, *un vieux copain* [an old buddy], and I am certain," and here he winked at us, "that he will make an exception. And if I take him the money he will give the permits to me. I'll bring them tomorrow morning. And," he added, "it will save you the arduous trip into the village." He stretched out his hand, "That will be eighteen dollars, please."

Bud, the stagehand in New York, had told me that fishing and hunting permits cost two dollars apiece, so I gave *le père* four dollars, added that transaction to the rental contract, and made him sign a receipt. He made one last attempt: he would have to take a bottle of Bourbon to the *vieux copain* to ease his conscience about bending the law and skipping the personal appearance.

Again I raised my middle finger.

"Alors, c'est TOUT!" (That's it!) I spoke with finality. *Le Père* sensed that he could go no further and left.

I remembered that when we had been following his car from Lac Archambault to *le bungalow,* just before he made that abrupt turn to the left that led into the roadless jungle, I had seen a small settlement. I got into my car, traced my way back, and found a small general store. There I purchased all our staples: butter, eggs, flour, salt, lard, a few vegetables, potatoes, onions, and a large canister of oil.

Boyd and I had planned to dig a deep hole next to our home to use as an impromptu ice hole, so I got a large block of ice. We had stocked up on beer, wine, and liquor in Montreal and it had been a novel experience for me, who came from Prohibition country, to be able to walk into a store and buy everything legally—no bootlegger and no guilt feelings about breaking the law. And to be able to get the real, unadulterated stuff.

Back at the house, Boyd, who had reconnoitered, informed me that there was no john on the place. It was at that moment that I discovered that I had the potential for a first-class woodsman and pioneer. I looked for and found a shovel and some tools, walked fifty yards away from the house—downwind, mind you—and dug a deep hole. From boards that were lying around and that, clever me, I had first inspected for the presence of rusty nails and splinters, I fashioned a practical sanitary commode. We pooled our initials and called the open-air retreat "The W.B."

Over a "welcome home" drink we planned our design for living. Each was to make his own bed. Boyd was to do the cleaning and washing, I the hunting, fishing, and cooking; the dishwashing was to be done together. "One more thing, my dear boy," he said (Boyd was four years older than I but persisted in calling me his dear boy), "we shall be awfully careful not to turn into sloppy bums while we are here roughing it, so let's make it a rule that we wear clean clothes for dinner, preferably with a tie!"

"Not me, dear chap," I responded, trying to sound frightfully English, "we are not on a British-led safari. I agree to wear clean clothes but refuse to wear a tie."

"Suit yourself, but *I* shall certainly wear one." And he did, all four weeks that we were there.

Early the next morning, *le père* arrived. He was cold sober, full of camaraderie, oozing goodwill.

True, he did not bring the licenses with him: he had been unable
to locate his *vieux copain,* but the next day, first thing, he would
take care of it. "I have your money right here," he said, patting his
pocket. He walked me to a meadow where he promised I would
find rabbits and quail. He pointed to a spot on the lake, quite near
the shore, where—he swore—wild duck came down to feed.

Then he inspected my fishing tackle and told me to throw it
away as it was "no good for this part of the country."

"On va les manger," he said, and walked for about a mile till we
arrived at a brook. He showed me how to bait for trout (no
artificial flies for him); instead, he took a few smelly fish eggs out of
a can, chewed some bread and rolled it all into a small ball. This he
put on the hook, approached the brook silently and let the line float
downstream. In half a minute we had a trout nine inches long and
appetizing in spite of the disgusting bait she had just swallowed.
During the next forty minutes we took five more speckled beauties,
glistening with unpolluted vigor. I was jubilant. Bud had been right
after all!

Père Labin walked along the brook to where it emptied into the
lake, and pointed to where I might have a good chance of getting
"les grandes, les vraiment grandes," the really big ones. And he
taught me how to set up a trolling rig.

As we walked back to the cabin, he tried again to get some advance rent out of me. I wanted to keep him in good humor, so I
said kiddingly, *"Mon cher père,* so far the weather has been good
and *so far* the fishing is excellent, but please consider: we are two
healthy young men and we might get lonely out here in the wilderness without female companionship."

He responded in dead earnest, "Monsieur," he said in a conspir-
atorial voice, "I have a *nièce,* a beautiful *nièce,*" and he began to
describe her enticing attributes in great detail. "Next Saturday she
will be coming to visit me, *son vieil oncle.* She is married and lives
in Montreal but she hates *son mari,* her husband, *c'est un salaud*
[an s.o.b.]. I will bring her out here. We will have a drink and I
will leave. I *know* she would love to spend some time with two such
charming young men. And believe me," he whispered, "no one will
ever know; it's our *'petit secret.'* "

And he left, plotting family pimping in order to stick us for a few
more weeks' rent and, as I figured, for a little blackmail later
should we take him up on his offer.

I had never worked with a wood stove before and approached it with reluctance and reverence. First I looked into its many openings and figured out where the fire should come out. I stacked kindling wood and logs, and lit it—and in one minute the room was so full of smoke I could barely find the windows. I soon discovered a devilishly clever little device: a small lever that, when pulled up, would permit the smoke to escape through the chimney instead of into the room.

I prepared for the gala meal!

I cooked potatoes, set up a large kettle with water, to which I added a few peppercorns, salt, and two onions, for a poor man's court bouillon. I laid the trout in a separate pan and poured boiling vinegar over them. They turned blue with joy. After the bouillon had simmered for twenty minutes, I carefully laid the fish into it. Ten seconds later I took the kettle off the fire and let it stand. The table had been set. There were no fish knives, nor lemon slices, just melted butter and a bit of chopped parsley on the potatoes. I yelled, "Come and get it." Boyd stepped up, wearing a tie, and, in honor of our French host country, we said, *"Bon appétit,"* and ate *truite au bleu.*

I had been bitten by the fishing bug. Fishermen are an insatiable bunch, they never get enough. When they catch more than they can eat, they either sell the surplus or give it away either out of kindness or because they are hungering for glory. Today, of course, all goes into the deep freeze. I decided to go after the big ones, *"les vraiment grandes."*

Early the next morning Boyd and I carried the canoe to the water. I put my fishing rod, my tackle box, the paddle, and all the rest of my gear in it, set my tropical helmet at a rakish angle on my head, stepped into the boat. And promptly overturned. I had to dive to retrieve my stuff. The tackle box had opened up and all my precious possessions had spilled to the bottom of Lac Archambault. It took me a good two hours in the water to retrieve it all. Meanwhile my tropical helmet floated on the water, bobbing around like a small life raft.

I realized that experience was needed to handle that type of watercraft, put on my bathing trunks, and spent the rest of the day practicing: getting in, getting out of that unstable little shell, paddling, and turning around. I also learned that feeling the center of gravity was helpful to the mastery of that form of locomotion.

Late in the afternoon, when we were having our predinner drink (we called it "the magic hour"), I happened to look out of the window and saw a rabbit hopping around. Very unsportsmanlike I reached for my gun and shot it. I had never before skinned a rabbit and I am afraid that I made a poor job of it, but the bunny stew the next day tasted very good.

On Saturday, Père Labin showed up to collect rent. He was oh so disappointed; his friend, the *vieux copain,* had taken sick, too ill to issue the licenses, and he was so chagrined that his *nièce* could not come up this weekend. Her husband had suddenly appeared, but she did send us her regards and wanted us to know that she was looking forward to meeting us, for sure, the following Saturday.

All this was related with great sincerity and we played along with the lying old bastard, paid him his week's rent, and turned a deaf ear to feelers for more advance.

Twice a week we drove to our "supermarket," bought freshly killed chicken, spareribs, sauerkraut, and as many spices as the limited variety they stocked permitted us to buy; life at our little place was wonderful, the weather was good, a raccoon stayed close to the house. He was enchanted with our garbage. One day we left the window open. He crawled in and stole some apples.

Boyd's impeccable laundry service kept us in clean clothes, but we had no flatiron, so all was unpressed and we looked like two vagabonds. Therefore we named the house "Bums' Rest."

I had finally mastered the art of not turning over in the canoe!

I handled it with nonchalance. I was in full command. With powerful strokes of my paddle, feeling like Big Indian Chief Chicken Feathers, I pushed it around never dreaming that any nautical problem might ever surprise me.

It happened during the second week of our residency at Bums' Rest. Morning mist was still on the lake. I was set up for trolling: about forty feet of line was out when my slow-moving craft stopped with a jerk. I thought that I had hooked onto some weeds at the bottom of the lake and began to reel in. There was another powerful jerk. I released the brake and the line began to sing, about thirty feet spun off, when I gently drew back. I HAD A FISH! It felt so powerful, so big, I was sure that I had a Canadian relative of the Loch Ness Monster on my line. My pulse was racing. "My God," I prayed, "don't let me lose this one." I tried to remember every adventure book I had read where dramatic fishing sequences had been described; aloud I repeated all the advice that pescatorial kibitzers give to a guy who is working a fish. "Stay calm," I said, "play him slowly, always keep tension on the line, never let it go slack. That will tire him out."

After about ten minutes the fish broke water; it was of a size I had seen only in fish markets. It was a *"vraiment grande."* "How will I ever get that slippery behemoth into my canoe?" I asked God. I had a light trout line on my rod. I knew it would break if I tried to lift him up. I had *no* net, and with all my newly acquired perfection as a canoeist I was certain that, if I reached over and tried to grab him by the gills, my chances of joining the monster in his element would be ninety-nine to one.

Big Indian Chief Chicken Feathers was desperate, and out of that desperation an idea was born. First, I set the brake on the wheel pretty tightly. The fish was played out and floating next to the boat. Then I tied the rod firmly to the inside of the canoe, took my shirt off, buttoned it, and knotted the neck and both sleeves. I

undressed completely, crawled to the stern of the boat, and slipped into the water, trying not to make a splash. I worked myself behind the fish, and after a few tries I managed to slip the shirt over him, then tied the shirttails together and had my leviathan in my make-shift net. I pulled the edge of the boat toward me and was able to lift the fish and roll him into the boat. I was terribly proud and completely exhausted, and the realization did not hit me until a few seconds later that, although the fish was safely in the boat, I was outside, in the water, naked and unable to get back into my canoe. The closest land was about a mile away, so I was left with no alter-native. I tied the boarding line around my neck and swam, pulling behind me the boat with the fish inside.

When I reached shore and felt firm ground under my feet, I mounted the canoe and paddled home.

In the afternoon I drove to our supermarket to get another block of ice and to show off my fish. My salmon trout tipped the scale at 18.7 pounds, not a record on the lake, I was told, but remarkable. Their admiration was without envy and showed genuine respect.

Before I cut up the fish we both photographed it. The fish alone, the fish next to a tape measure, me with the fish, Boyd with the fish, the fish looking at me, and me looking at the fish.

I had bought fresh celery, parsley, and bay leaves (they didn't have any thyme and had never even heard of dill). But with the head, tail, and fins I made a pretty good court bouillon. I filleted one side; the rest, packed in wax paper, was put into our small icehouse, covered with chunks of ice and all the newspapers the folks at the store had given me. I knew that our raccoon had an ex-cellent sense of smell, so I covered the ice hole with a wooden board weighed down with heavy stones.

The weather turned sour and so did my fisherman's luck. I spent hours trolling. In pouring rain I marched to our brook: nothing, not a nibble, and no rabbit showed his twiggly nose, and no wild duck was hungry enough to settle on the lake in range of my gun.

Out came the canned goods.

Saturday came around, and so did Père Labin, full of elaborate explanations as to why he didn't have the licenses and why his dar-ling *nièce* could not come, "But next week, I swear—on the *'croix du Seigneur'* [cross of God]—she will be here and be able to stay for a spell."

I complained about the fishing. With a disdainful expression he said: *"Mais, c'est simple,"* and walked to his car. When he returned he was carrying a large net and an empty bottle of soda water, Tied to that bottle was a heavy stone. We walked to the canoe; I was told to paddle. He sat on the floor of the boat and half filled the bottle with water. Then he reached into his filthy raincoat and produced a sack of cheesecloth that was filled with what looked like gray pebbles. This he carefully hung in the bottle. "It must not touch the water," he explained, and tied the ends of the cheesecloth sack around the bottle. The bottle had one of these rubber-tipped locking devices. He closed it firmly and wrapped wire around it. "For extra strength," he said. Then he sat back, holding the bottle upright. He pointed to where I should paddle, and when we arrived in a small cove, about seventy yards from shore, he whispered, "Let's try here," and let the weighted bottle slip into the water. All was quiet but after about a minute the lake belched. A large bubble reached the surface and after another few moments fish were floating up. *Le père* calmly collected them with his net.

I was flabbergasted. "What happened? What did you have in that cheesecloth bag?"

"Carbide, monsieur," he said, smiling, "the same stuff that coal-miners burn in their lamps." I still didn't understand. "Carbide mixed with water produces gas and that gas exploded the bottle. *Ce n'est pas légal*," he said, smiling again, but, pointing at the net, *"On va les manger!"*

Our vacation drew to a close, and when the old poacher arrived to collect his rent, needless to say without licenses and without *nièce,* I interrupted his long-winded apologies and explanations with the sad news that we were giving up *le bungalow* come next Saturday and I paid him eight dollars, the last week's rent.

He grew desperate; he swore that he had talked to his *nièce* only that morning on the phone, that she would be coming up the next

Friday and be able to stay over the weekend and she will not be coming alone—no, she will bring her girl friend with her, a beautiful woman, *une beauté extraordinaire,* "and the girls, both of them, are out for fun . . ." I cut him short to say where he would find the key and that we would leave the house in a clean and orderly condition.

A crushed man left us.

The last week was glorious, the fishing better than ever, though no *vraiment grandes* committed the folly of taking my so-expertly-handled line. I got two rabbits, one after the other—the second one only came out to see who was shooting. Even a pheasant hen showed her simple plumage as she walked past the sight of my twelve-gauge.

On Friday morning, while we were breakfasting on the porch, a small truck pulled up. Four husky men jumped out and a quartet of insults and questions rained down on us. "What the hell do you think you are doing here?" "Who, in devil's name, gave you permission?" "Who the hell are you, two burglars?" The questions were spiced with several "sons of bitches" and grave accusations of incestuous intercourse with the ladies who had given birth to us.

After a while they calmed down and I told our side of the story. Luckily I was able to produce the rental agreement. Now their wrath descended on Père Labin, "that drunken no-good bastard, that thief, that crook." I invited the gentlemen to have breakfast with us (they were four businessmen from Montreal who owned the land and the cabin). Very good coffee, fried eggs, and bacon mollified them. After they had gone through the cabin and found that two civilized housekeepers had taken good care of it, we even became quite friendly, especially after we magnanimously presented them with the contents of our icehouse. We packed our bags, stored our belongings in the car, and parted without any hard feelings.

On the way back we stopped at the grocery store to say good-by. They had been under the impression that we were friends of the owners, staying there as their guests. When I told them the story of Père Labin's *nièce,* they howled with laughter, assured us that they knew the old bugger well. He never had a niece, he was the town drunk who lived by poaching and sponging on everybody. Very kindly they said that somehow they were glad that the old crook had made a bit of money out of us and, frankly, so were we.

Beef Vegetable Soup

1 soupbone with meat (3 pounds)	1 head Savoy cabbage, chopped
5 quarts water	2 cloves garlic, crushed
2 cups chopped onions	1 bay leaf
2 cups diced carrots	½ teaspoon thyme
2 cups chopped celery	1 cup boiled rice
¼ cup diced turnips	1 tablespoon salt
	½ teaspoon pepper

Simmer the soupbone, covered, for 2 hours in the 5 quarts of water. Add the next 8 ingredients and simmer, covered, till the meat falls from the bone. Cut the meat into cubes. Strain, cool, and skim the stock. Combine the rice, meat, and soup stock, heat, and season with the salt and pepper. *Makes 10 cups.*

Sautéed Spicy Pork

3 pounds pork tenderloin, cut into 1-inch cubes	3 tablespoons soy sauce
2 tablespoons sherry	4 tablespoons sugar
3 tablespoons salt	¾ teaspoon cinnamon
	2 tablespoons oil

Place the pork cubes in a marinade of the sherry, salt, soy sauce, sugar, and cinnamon in a bowl, cover, and let stand for 2 hours. Then take out the pork with a slotted spoon and drain. Heat the oil in a wok, toss in the pork cubes, and sauté them over a medium flame until they are brown and tender. *Serves 4.*

Boiled Spareribs with Sauerkraut

4 pounds spareribs, cut into serving pieces	A pinch of thyme
Salt and freshly ground pepper	1 large can sauerkraut, drained and rinsed once
1 bay leaf	
1 large whole onion, stuck with 2 cloves	

Season the spareribs with salt and pepper, place in a deep kettle with the bay leaf, onion, and thyme, cover with water, and boil for 1 hour. Add the sauerkraut, simmer uncovered, for ¾ hour. Drain, place the spareribs on a warm platter, top with the sauerkraut. Serve with the Sour Cream-Horseradish Sauce given below:

Sour Cream-Horseradish Sauce:

1 cup sour cream	*1 tablespoon sugar*
½ cup commercial prepared	*½ teaspoon salt*
horseradish	*½ teaspoon white pepper*
¼ cup beer	

Mix all the ingredients thoroughly and serve with the spareribs and sauerkraut above. *Serves 5.*

Oxtail Stew

1½ pounds oxtails, cut into	*1 large bottle dry white wine*
equal-sized pieces	*Consommé*
4 tablespoons butter	*1 teaspoon salt*
4 tablespoons oil	*½ teaspoon pepper*
4 medium-sized onions, chopped	*1 tablespoon minced parsley*
2 medium-sized carrots, cut into	*12 whole small onions*
½-inch pieces	*½ pound whole small*
1 stalk celery (reserve top),	*mushrooms*
chopped	*Additional butter for sautéing*
2 cloves garlic, crushed	

Soak the oxtails in water for several hours, wipe them dry, then brown them in a large, heavy saucepan in the butter and oil, along with the chopped onions, the carrots, and the chopped celery. When the oxtail meat is brown, add the garlic, cook for 2 minutes. Then add the bottle of white wine and enough consommé to cover the meat. Add the salt, pepper, parsley, chopped celery tops, cook slowly, covered, for 3 hours. Meanwhile, sauté the small onions and whole mushrooms in additional butter in a skillet, add them to the stew. When the fat has risen to the surface (a few minutes), skim it off the top of the stew. Place the pot, covered, in a preheated 350° oven for 1 hour, adding some water if necessary. The meat should be soft and the sauce glossy and thick. Taste the sauce and correct the seasoning if necessary.

This stew is superb served with Polenta (see Index). *Serves 4.*

Irish Stew

1½ pounds stewing lamb, cut
    into 1½-inch cubes
2 tablespoons butter
2 cups boiling water
Salt and freshly ground pepper
2 cups potatoes, peeled and
    shaped into ovals 1½ inches
    long

6 carrots, cut into 1-inch pieces
2 cups green cabbage, shredded
    finely and barely cooked

Brown the meat in a heavy skillet in the butter. Add the 2 cups of boiling water and season with salt and pepper. Let simmer for 45 minutes. Add more water if needed, so that the liquid covers the meat completely. Add the potatoes, carrots, and cabbage and simmer, covered, for about 1 hour longer, or until the vegetables are tender. This stew is best made a day ahead, cooled, and put in the refrigerator overnight. The next day skim off the fat before reheating. *Serves 4–6.*

Roast Pheasant in Cream Sauce

2 medium-sized onions, chopped
1 stalk celery, chopped
1 medium-sized carrot, diced
1 tablespoon minced parsley, or 1
    small parsnip, diced
¼ cup shortening

4 slices bacon
1 young pheasant
Water or chicken bouillon
1 teaspoon flour
Sour cream or light cream
Salt

In a small roasting pan or Dutch oven, sauté the onions, celery, carrot, and parsley or parsnip in the shortening till the onions are transparent. Tie the bacon slices over the top and sides of the bird and place it on the sautéed vegetables. Add ¼ inch of water or bouillon in the pan and let the pheasant roast in a preheated 350°

oven for at least 1½ hours, basting frequently with the pan juices and adding more water or bouillon if necessary. When the pheasant is tender, remove it from the pan, skim the fat off the vegetables. Sprinkle 1 teaspoon of flour over the vegetables, stirring, adding more bouillon and some sour cream or light cream to make a gravy of the desired consistency. Add salt to taste. Let the gravy simmer for a while, then put it through a sieve. Serve the pheasant on a warm platter and pass the hot gravy. This is delicious served with hot cooked red cabbage. *Serves 2.*

Stuffed Cabbage

1 large head white cabbage

Stuffing (to be cooked as in the recipe for Stuffed Bell Peppers—see Index) :

2 medium-sized onions, chopped	*¼ teaspoon curry powder*
3 slices bacon, cut into small pieces	*2 eggs, beaten*
1 pound ground beef	*1 tablespoon Lea & Perrins Worcestershire sauce*
1 tablespoon chopped parsley	*Salt and freshly ground pepper to taste*
1 clove garlic, chopped	
1 teaspoon paprika	*1 cup boiled rice*

In a large pot, boil the cabbage in water to cover for 10–15 minutes. Prepare the stuffing. Cut out the core of the cabbage and loosen the leaves carefully, being sure not to break them. Fill each opened-out cabbage leaf with the stuffing, tuck in the sides, and roll up carefully. Place in a roasting pan and bake, covered with Tomato Sauce (recipe follows) or consommé, in a preheated 350° oven for 2 hours. *Makes only 4–6 servings, as only the larger leaves are used.*

Tomato Sauce

3 tablespoons flour	*1 tablespoon sugar*
3 tablespoons butter	*1 teaspoon white vinegar diluted with 1 teaspoon water*
1 small can tomato paste and 1 tomato paste can of water	*Chicken bouillon*
1½ cups tomato juice	

Brown the flour in the butter. Add the tomato paste and tomato paste can of water, cook till the mixture is thick. Add the tomato juice, stir. Add the sugar, vinegar, and enough bouillon to make the consistency of cream. *Makes about 1 quart.*

Stuffed Bell Peppers

2 medium-sized onions, chopped
3 slices bacon, cut into small
    pieces
1 pound ground beef
1 tablespoon chopped parsley
1 clove garlic, minced
1 teaspoon paprika

¼ teaspoon curry powder
2 eggs, beaten
1 tablespoon Lea & Perrins
    Worcestershire sauce
Salt and pepper to taste
1 cup boiled rice
6 large bell peppers

Sauté the onions and bacon together. Add the ground beef, parsley, garlic, paprika, and curry powder, and sauté for 3 minutes or till the meat loses it color. Add the beaten eggs, Worcestershire sauce, salt, and pepper. Mix in the boiled rice. Cut away the bottoms of the bell peppers and save the pieces as covers. Remove the stems from the peppers. Scrape out the peppers, boil them in water to cover for 10 minutes, drain, then fill them with the meat mixture. Place them in a tightly fitting casserole. Pour Tomato Sauce (see recipe above) over them and bake them in a preheated 350° oven for 1 hour. *Serves 6.*

Braised Cabbage

1 medium-sized onion, diced
2 tablespoons bacon drippings
4–5 sugar cubes
3 cups finely shredded cabbage
1 teaspoon caraway seeds

1 teaspoon salt
2 tablespoons flour
1 teaspoon vinegar diluted with 1
    teaspoon water

In a casserole sauté the onion in the bacon drippings until tender. Add the sugar, cabbage, caraway seeds, and salt. Cover and cook, stirring often, until the cabbage is golden brown. Sprinkle with the flour and season with the vinegar. Mix. Add any available broth or water if needed. *Serves 6.*

Pickelsteiner Meat
(A Casserole Dish)

½ *pound fillet of beef, sliced*	8 *tablespoons bacon drippings*
½ *pound veal, sliced*	½ *cup finely chopped parsley*
½ *pound pork, sliced*	1 *cup finely chopped celery*
1 *teaspoon salt*	1 *cup finely chopped carrots*
1 *teaspoon pepper*	2 *cups thinly shredded potatoes*

Mix the sliced beef, veal, and pork and sprinkle with salt and pepper. Grease the bottom of a heavy casserole with 4 tablespoons of the bacon drippings. Add a layer of the meat and overlay with the parsley, celery, and carrots. Add a layer of potatoes and continue to build layers of meat, parsley-celery-carrot mixture, and potatoes until the casserole is filled. Drizzle with the remaining bacon drippings. Cover the casserole and let simmer over very low heat for about 1 hour. *Serves 6.*

Czechoslovakian Sauerkraut

1 *medium-sized onion, cut fine*	1 *tablespoon sugar*
4 *slices bacon, cut into small*	1 *teaspoon caraway seeds*
pieces	1 *apple, peeled and sliced*
1 *large can sauerkraut, drained*	1 *large raw potato, grated*
and rinsed	

Sauté the onion and bacon together till the onion is golden. Add the sauerkraut, sauté a little, add the sugar, caraway seeds, apple, and water to cover. Cook, covered, for 1 hour slowly; you may have to add some water to keep the sauerkraut from drying out. Thicken the mixture with the grated raw potato. This dish tastes better the next day. Czechoslovakian sauerkraut goes well with pork sausages and hot mashed, whipped potatoes. *Serves 4.*

Excellent Fried Potatoes

6 medium-sized potatoes   1 teaspoon caraway seeds
2 medium-sized onions, chopped   Salt and freshly ground pepper
2 tablespoons Crisco or other fat   to taste

Boil the potatoes in their skins; when cooled, peel them and cut into
¼-inch slices. Sauté the onions in the fat, add the caraway seeds,
salt, and pepper, then the potato slices; turn several times carefully
over medium heat till the potatoes are golden brown. *Serves 2–3.*

Blini

I once made the acquaintance of an extremely good-looking Russian lady who was a buyer for one of New York's big department stores. But this wonderful position, she assured me when first we met, was just temporary, because very soon her high title and immense fortune would be restored to her. No one knows her secret, but she was a close relative of the Romanoffs, the dethroned imperial dynasty! She would tell fascinating stories about them, about the lavish splendor of her youth; she was able to repeat, word for word and sentence for sentence, what Nicholas, Czar of all the Russians, had said to her while she was allowed to sit on his knee—verbatim she could recall long conversations that had ominous political forebodings, which she had heard in the year 1916 at Court in Petrograd (she was then four years old). Her apartment was decorated in extremely Russian fashion. Photos of the Kremlin and the Hermitage and the flag of a Russian battleship adorned the wall. On a table lay a velvet box with medals and decorations that she claimed had belonged to her father. In a corner stood a two-foot-high samovar, an heirloom she had been able to smuggle out of Russia, that had been given to her family by Catherine the Great. Her record player emitted the music of the Don Cossacks and the strains of *"Ochichornia."* The story of her flight from Russia, through a snowstorm, pursued by wolves, was hair-raising and heartbreaking. She had made a solemn vow never to speak the Russian language again until such time as the Romanoffs had been restored to the throne of holy Mother Russia.

I believed every word she said—even though she spoke with a Hungarian accent—because she could prepare the most delicious blinis:

Five round pancakes, each four and a half inches in diameter and

one third of an inch thick, were being kept warm. The first
pancake was placed on a warm platter, buttered, and then topped
with a slice of sturgeon and some sour cream. Then the second pancake was placed on top of that, covered with red caviar and sour
cream. The third layer got sturgeon and sour cream, the fourth caviar and sour cream, and the fifth layer on that wonderful round
cake got sour cream and a sprinkling of finely chopped dill. With
that she served ice-cold vodka. The whole meal was one big ceremony, the Don Cossacks sang, we clinked glasses, and she said, *"Na
sdarowje,"* the ONLY words with which she broke her vow. Inci-
dentally, she remembered that Rasputin always ate his blinis with
black caviar.

The Lord Was Good to Me!

In 1942 I was living in Hollywood, contented to be an ingrained bachelor and smugly pleased with myself that I had successfully eluded the bonds and responsibilities of marriage for all those years, had braved the tempting siren calls of gorgeous show girls with matrimony on their minds, and the greatest perils—mothers of eligible daughters.

It was then that I made the acquaintance of the aforementioned Johanna van Rijn. That dear creature was two years old when her parents moved from Amsterdam to the Dutch East Indies. There she grew up, there she flowered into a lovely blond Dutch maiden, leading the life of the idle rich, with tutors, golf, tennis, and instruction in languages. She then discovered that she had a good singing voice. She took lessons and, shortly before World War II broke out, she came to America to finish her musical education.

The day I met her—August 8, 1:48 P.M., sunny California time, a mysterious pacemaker accelerated my heartbeat and a good fairy fitted me with rose-colored glasses. I fell in love, without reservation, without compromise. Foolishly I began blowing up my feathers, strutting and posturing grotesquely in front of and around her—a pouter pigeon off his rocker, producing guttural coos.

I must have cooed well, because she became my first, my only, and my last wife. And after I discovered that Indonesian cookery was one of her hobbies and that—as an added bonus—she spoke the Malayan language, a tongue of which I knew only two words: Mata Hari (eye of the day, or sun) and Orang Utan (man of the jungle), I felt again that the good Lord had had his eye on this old sparrow.

For our official engagement we planned a big party. The bride

volunteered a *rijsttafel*. Not knowing exactly what a rijsttafel was, I agreed, and when the guest list swelled to fifty-eight, we asked rich friends if they would kindly lend us their house for the occasion. They agreed but were slightly taken aback when my gal casually mentioned that she would have to have the exclusive use of the kitchen for four days BEFORE the party, as she planned to fix fifty-two different dishes and needed time and quiet.

Next we got hold of an importer of Indonesian specialties. A Mr. Sukarno (no relation) was the proprietor of Spices of the Far East, a store situated—of all places—in Newark, New Jersey.

Very long long-distance conversation with Mr. Sukarno—all in Malay—took place. *Tahu, daun djeruk purut, daun salam, djintan, ketchup, kentjur, ketumbar, kunjit, laos, sambal ulek, temu kuntji,* and *sereh* were ordered, and about twenty other items.

From the happy exclamations of joy which my future wife emitted, I gathered which of the spices were available for shipment and, from low mutterings and sighs of sorrow, I guessed what were not available. The only word I understood was *ketchup*. Little did I know that *their* ketchup had practically nothing to do with *our* ketchup.

A few weeks later a large package arrived from Mr. Sukarno with the thrilling news that—luckily—he had been able, after all, to get hold of three packages of *emping melindjo* and two cans of *kemiris*. Johanna van Rijn's face was bathed in happiness. Most loyally I rejoiced with her and we began planning the party. At first a Sunday was considered, but, after deep thought and earnest contemplation plus a mental countdown on all things that could possibly go wrong or be missing, we settled on a Saturday, when the stores would still be open for last-minute purchases, purchases that should be garden-, fish market-, and butcher-fresh.

Wednesday she disappeared into our friends' house, to emerge only when I picked her up for dinner, smelling deliciously of all the spices of the Far East! The next evening she was a bit tired, but a vitamin B_{12} shot fixed her up fine. The following day she was on the verge of collapsing, but *two* vitamin B_{12} shots did the job, and she even went to the beauty parlor in the evening. That night she must have slept like a geisha on a porcelain pillow because when I met her on Saturday morning every hair was still in its place.

A Hollywood "party catering service" had supplied the many dishes needed, the glasses, spoons, and forks (*no* chopsticks for *rijsttafel*). They had set up six long tables and fifty-eight chairs on the lawn of our hosts' beautiful garden. Johanna, who was by then stuck with her nickname, Kaasi, decorated the tables, banana leaves with gardenias and hibiscus in them.

I had hired film extras to work as waiters. At Western Costume, I arranged for them to be dressed as Malayan *djongos,* complete with *tjepiau* (a small turban), sarong, and the inevitable white jacket with the mandarin collar. They loved the idea of "playing waiters" instead of standing around being "crowd" as they usually were and shouted at by some second-assistant director. They were, of course, also promised an unusual meal of gigantic proportion.

Ice-cold *genever* gin was to be served, and during the meal Dutch Heineken and Amstel beer. Indonesian gamelan music, the discs supplied by Mr. Sukarno, was fed into the record player. A young man who worked for the Dutch Consulate and spoke Malay was kind enough to come and help with last-minute chores, such as put-

ting the "ready to serve dishes" in the serving bowls and handing
them to the *djongos*.

My six extras arrived, already in costume, some with make-up on
their faces. They offered to work barefoot—all for the sake of au-
thenticity. Kaasi vanished into the kitchen, not to be seen again
until the last delicacy had left the stove. I began rehearsing my
band of fellow actors.

"Each of you is assigned one table. At the sound of a gong,"
which I had borrowed from the property department of Paramount
Pictures, "you are to come out of the kitchen with a dish in each
hand, you are to walk slowly, with the natural grace of the natives
of Indonesia, a happy expression on your faces, to the head of your
table and start serving. None of that nonsense about ladies first.
Once all the guests at your table have been served—from the left
side, mind you—you are to return immediately to the kitchen, this
time NOT in a slow walk, but at a good clip. If one of the guests
should ask you what is that dish you are serving, say, 'I don't know,
sir, but it's *delicious!*' You return to the table with the new dishes
that have been handed to you, single file, with the slow natural-
grace walk, happy expression and all—and so on and on until nothing is left for you to serve. Then—ONLY then—raid the kitchen!:
a table has been set up for you."

As I walked away to greet the first arrivals, I could see that they
had begun rehearsing the graceful walk and the happy expressions.

"Where's the bride?" was everyone's question.

"In the kitchen, where she belongs," was my "funny" retort.

"Ha, ha, ha! You wouldn't dare say that in front of her."

"Ha, ha, ha!" etc., etc., and the small talk began.

The guests were given the inside dope of rijsttafel: "A festive
meal, best consumed at midday, lasting well into the afternoon and
to be followed by an extensive siesta. The CELESTIAL rijsttafel of
olden times was supposed to have contained 365 dishes, one for
each day of the year, the idea being that with every bite one should
sample a new taste. But Kaasi is serving a 'poor man's rijsttafel' of
only fifty-two different dishes, one for each *week* of the year."

I briefed them on some of the more powerful spices, like *sambal
ulek*. If you take too much of it, you might as well gargle with
Tabasco sauce. I poured *genever* gin, all the time keeping an eye on
the kitchen window for the sign when the balloon was to go up.

The signal came and I asked our friends to sit down; when the last fanny touched its chair, I struck the gong three times, feeling like Fu Manchu, the evil sorcerer.

My actors arrived in a slow motion walk, two of them overdoing the happy expressions—they were grinning from ear to ear. But they did their job well, holding in one hand a bowl of rice, in the other a cup of *sajur* (a light curry soup with chicken pieces), and when they had finished the first round they RAN back to the kitchen and out again, with a new load in both hands, slow walk, natural grace and all, bringing *krupuk* (shrimp wafers) and *kripick*, and back again, and so forth.

It was beautiful. I only wished my bride could have seen it. It was all terribly, terribly Indonesian . . . until the spell was broken by a shrill female voice asking for a Coca-Cola. I quelled the woman with a withering look.

All was served in soup plates: rice in the middle and small spoonfuls of the dishes around them, with a side plate for the overflow. Four kinds of satés, each marinated for a day in a different marinade and broiled to perfection at the last minute on charcoal (luckily our friends had a well-equipped house), fried bananas, four kinds of curry (made from scratch), pork, chicken, beef, and veal, small corn fritters, *sambal hati* (a lovely dish of chicken livers and beans), fish cakes with sweet and sour sauce, *serundung* (grilled coconut flakes), *ikan goreng* (fried fish slices), *atjar ikan* (fish in sour sauce), fried shrimp, shrimp with a thick sauce of soy beans, *gado gado* (vegetable with peanut sauce), *bebotok daging* (chopped beef with coconut milk and laurel leaves), eggs in pepper sauce and eggs in paprika sauce, with a bit of *sambal ulek; rudjak* (fresh fruit in soy sauce, many kinds of *sambalans* (condiments, if that word describes their weird, wonderful tastes, made of extracts of vegetables, fish, meats, and roots), *atjar babi* (pork ragout in sour sauce), *lombok isi* (stuffed green peppers), *besengek daging* (meat in curry sauce with radishes, coconut milk, and almonds), *sambal goreng taotgo* (a mixture of soybeans and red-hot peppers, *atjar ketimoen* (pickled cucumber relish), *sambal bubik katjang* (hot peanut relish), and on and on it went. Suddenly there was a pause. I rushed to the kitchen. The *djongos* had made their last trip, and there—slumped in a chair—was my gal.

I offered to have her brought out on a stretcher, but she bravely rose, and—she holding onto my arm—we walked into the garden.

After the applause had died down, I made a little speech, announcing what everyone knew anyway: that I would take this woman as my lawful wedded wife, that I would honor and obey her, in sickness and in health, till death did us part.

Later in the evening when I brought her to her apartment, she was so tired she could barely stand up, so I poured her through her front door and she said, "One more rijsttafel and death is going to part us pretty fast—*my* death, that is!"

Fried Shrimp
(Oedang Goreng)

1 pound raw shrimp
1 cup flour
1 egg
1 cup water
Salt and freshly ground pepper
    to taste

⅛ teaspoon nutmeg
2 teaspoons baking powder
Oil for deep frying

Wash the shrimp after removing all but the tail section of each shell. Split halfway down the backs, clean, and dry. Mix the flour, egg, water, salt, pepper, nutmeg, and baking powder into a batter. Dip the shrimp in the batter and fry in deep oil till golden brown. Drain on paper towels and serve immediately. *Serves 3–4.*

Fried Shrimp Balls
(Oedang Tjae)

1 pound raw shrimp, shelled and
    deveined
1 medium-sized onion, chopped
    fine
2 cloves garlic, chopped fine
¼ teaspoon pepper

1 dash Tabasco sauce
½ teaspoon powdered ginger
1½ teaspoons salt
1 egg
2 tablespoons butter or oil

Chop the shrimp fine. Mix together the onion, garlic, pepper, Tabasco, ginger, salt, and egg, and put through a food grinder. Mix with the shrimp, form into small balls, and fry in butter or oil till golden brown. Serve immediately. *Makes 10–12 shrimp balls.*

Shrimp Fritters
(Perkedel Oedang)

2 eggs, separated, beaten
    separately
3 slices white bread, soaked in
    water and pressed dry
1 pound shrimp, cooked, shelled,
    deveined, and chopped

1 tablespoon chopped parsley
1½ teaspoons salt
1 teaspoon pepper
¼ teaspoon nutmeg
½ cup bread crumbs
Oil for frying

Mix the beaten egg yolks, bread, shrimp, parsley, salt, pepper, and
nutmeg. Form this mixture into small 2-inch patties, dip them in
the beaten egg white, and coat them with bread crumbs. Fry the
patties in oil for 2 minutes on each side. Serve immediately. *Makes
10–12 fritters.*

Shrimp with Chinese Peas
(Oedang Masak Katjang Kapri)

1 medium-sized onion, minced
2 tablespoons oil
1 pound raw shrimp, shelled,
    split, and cleaned
2 tablespoons soy sauce

Salt and freshly ground pepper
    to taste
1 tablespoon sherry
1 cup Chinese peas, cooked until
    just crisp

Sauté the onion in the oil for a few minutes, then add the shrimp,
soy sauce, salt, pepper, and sherry. Cook for 8 minutes, and 2 minutes before serving add the peas and stir. Serve very hot. The same
can be done with fish fillets cut into bite-sized pieces. *Serves 3–4.*

Green or Red Chili Peppers Stuffed with Shrimp
(Udang Goreng Tjabe Hidjau)

12 chili peppers
2 cups finely chopped raw shrimp
2 slices white bread, soaked in
water and pressed dry
2 medium-sized onions, minced
1 leek, minced
2 eggs

Salt and freshly ground pepper
to taste
Nutmeg to taste
Butter
Bread crumbs
Oil for deep frying

Slit the peppers lengthwise, take out the seeds, and keep the stems on the peppers. Mix well the shrimp, white bread, onions, leek, eggs, salt, pepper, and nutmeg, stuff into the peppers. Butter the peppers and sprinkle them with bread crumbs. Deep-fry them in oil for 3 to 4 minutes. *Serves 4.*

Fried Fish
(Ikan Goreng)

4–6 fish fillets
2 tablespoons oil
1 medium-sized onion, chopped
2 cloves garlic, minced

1 tablespoon paprika
2 tablespoons turmeric
¼ teaspoon grated lemon rind
1 cup chicken bouillon

In a skillet sauté the fish lightly in the oil, remove fish and keep it warm. Put all the other ingredients except bouillon in the oil and sauté for 1 minute, then add the bouillon and cook till the liquid is reduced by half. Add the fish and cook for another minute. Serve immediately on warm plates. *Serves 3.*

Fish with Vegetables
(Ikan Tjha)

2 medium-sized onions, chopped
    fine
2 cloves garlic, minced
3–4 tablespoons vegetable oil
1 pound fish fillets cut into 2-inch
    pieces
½ cup ham cut into strips

Salt and freshly ground pepper
    to taste
1 cup white cabbage cut into
    small chunks
2 stalks celery, sliced
2 tablespoons soy sauce

In a large skillet brown the onions and garlic in the oil. Add the fish, ham, salt, pepper, cabbage, and celery, cook over medium heat for 15 minutes. Season with the soy sauce. Serve immediately on warm plates. *Serves 4.*

Fish with Mushrooms
(Ikan Djamur)

1 medium-sized onion, chopped
1 stalk celery, chopped
1 tablespoon vegetable oil
½ pound mushrooms, washed,
    drained, and sliced
½ tablespoon soy sauce
½ teaspoon powdered ginger

A little salt and freshly ground
    pepper
½ pound fish fillets (cod is
    excellent), cut into 1-inch
    pieces, then salted and
    peppered

Sauté the onion and celery in the oil in a skillet till they are limp. Add the mushrooms, soy sauce, ginger, salt, pepper, and fish. Stir carefully, sauté till the fish is done, about 10 minutes. *Serves 2.*

Chicken in Cabbage Leaves
(Otak Ajam)

1 chicken, 3–4 pounds
3 egg yolks
1 tablespoon ground coriander
½ tablespoon caraway seeds or
  cuminseeds
3 tablespoons minced onion
1 clove garlic, crushed

¼ teaspoon grated lemon rind
½ teaspoon salt
½ teaspoon pepper
2 tablespoons ground hazelnuts
1 large head Savoy cabbage
Chicken bouillon

Take the meat off the chicken and chop fine. Mix in the remaining ingredients except the cabbage and bouillon. Remove about 1½ inches of the hard part of the bottom of the cabbage, then boil the cabbage in salted water to cover for 10 minutes. Take the cabbage out of the water and loosen the leaves very carefully. In the center of each leaf, place 2–3 teaspoons of the chicken mixture. Fold 3 sides of the leaves toward the center, then roll. Set the rolls in a rectangular casserole in 1 layer, folded sides down. Add bouillon to half cover the rolls and bake, covered, in a preheated 350° oven for 2 hours. *Makes 10–12 rolls.*

Braised Chicken
(Ajam Doefi Hache)

*A 3-pound frying chicken, cut
    into serving pieces*
1 tablespoon salt
¼ teaspoon cayenne pepper
¼ teaspoon nutmeg
Oil for frying
2 tablespoons minced onion

5 cloves garlic, minced
1 tablespoon ground coriander
½ teaspoon powdered ginger
½ tablespoon cuminseeds
2 tablespoons soy sauce
1 tablespoon lemon juice
Chicken bouillon

Rub the chicken pieces with a mixture of the salt, cayenne, and
nutmeg, and fry them in oil till they are golden brown. Add the
remaining ingredients (enough bouillon to cover) and let simmer,
turning the chicken pieces several times, till they are done, about ½
hour. *Serves 4.*

Pineapple Chicken
(Por Ajam)

1 3-pound frying chicken
*½ teaspoon crushed dried chili
    peppers*
*¼ teaspoon shrimp or anchovy
    paste*
½ cup sliced scallions
½ cup minced onions
1 teaspoon salt

2 cloves garlic, minced
1 cup pineapple cubes
Corn oil for frying
*2 cups Coconut Cream (see
    Index)*
1 tablespoon soy sauce
1 teaspoon lime juice
1 teaspoon grated lime rind

Remove the chicken meat from the bones, cut into bite-sized
squares. Combine the chili peppers, shrimp or anchovy paste,
scallions, onions, salt, and garlic, and mix to form a smooth paste.
Mix the paste with the chicken meat so that all squares are covered.
Let them stand for 1½ hours. Sauté the chicken and pineapple
lightly in corn oil until they are light brown. Add the Coconut
Cream, stir. Then add the soy sauce and the lime juice and rind,

cook on low heat until the chicken and pineapple are tender. Serve with piping hot boiled rice. Delicious! *Serves 4.*

Chicken in Coconut Milk
(Ajam Opor)

½ cup shredded coconut
1 large onion, chopped
½ tablespoon ground coriander
1 teaspoon caraway seeds
½ teaspoon chopped dried chili
    peppers
1 teaspoon salt

½ teaspoon powdered ginger
1 clove garlic, minced
1 tablespoon lemon juice
A 2-pound frying chicken, cut
    into small pieces
4 tablespoons butter
1 cup Coconut Milk (see Index)

Mix together thoroughly all the ingredients except the chicken, butter, and Coconut Milk. Coat the chicken pieces with the mixture and let them stand for 2 hours. Melt the butter in a saucepan with a cover, brown the chicken pieces in it, add the Coconut Milk, and cook, covered, over low heat for 25–30 minutes, till the chicken is tender. *Serves 2.*

Chicken Liver Sambal Goreng

½ cup water
2 large onions, chopped
2 cloves garlic, chopped
½ bell pepper, chopped
1 teaspoon turmeric
1 teaspoon salt

2 teaspoons brown sugar
1 pound chicken livers, cut in
    half
1 bay leaf
2 packages frozen string beans,
    cooked

In a large skillet mix together the water, onions, garlic, bell pepper, turmeric, salt, and brown sugar. Pour this mixture over the livers, add the bay leaf, and simmer for ¾ hour. (If the sauce is too thick, add some consommé.) Add the string beans and cook for another 15 minutes. Serve with piping hot boiled rice. *Serves 3–4.*

Pork with Bamboo Shoots
(Babi Rebung)

1 medium-sized onion, sliced	1 teaspoon powdered ginger
2 cloves garlic, crushed	1 cup sliced bamboo shoots
1 tablespoon oil	3 tablespoons soy sauce
1 pound pork, cut into strips 1	½ tablespoon sugar
inch long	1 teaspoon cornstarch dissolved
Salt and freshly ground pepper	in 2 tablespoons consommé

Sauté the onion and garlic in the oil. Add the pork, which has been coated with salt, pepper, and ginger. Add the bamboo shoots, soy sauce, and sugar, stir, and simmer for 20 minutes. Before serving, thicken with cornstarch mixed with the consommé. Serve topped with Fried Onion Rings (see Index). *Serves 4.*

Pork in Soy Sauce
(Babi Ketjup)

1 pound pork, cubed	2 cloves garlic, minced
½ cup chicken bouillon	½ tablespoon sugar
3 tablespoons soy sauce	1 tablespoon sherry

Place the pork in a saucepan, add the other ingredients, bring to a boil, and simmer for 20 minutes, till the meat is tender. *Serves 4.*

Braised Pork
(Babi Tjha)

1 pound lean pork, cubed	2 tablespoons oil
1 teaspoon salt	2 tablespoons minced leek
1 teaspoon powdered ginger	2 tablespoons Chinese peas
2 tablespoons minced onion	Chicken bouillon
2 cloves garlic, minced	

Coat the pork with salt and ginger with your fingers. Sauté the onion and garlic in the oil. When they are golden, add the meat

and sauté till brown. Add the leek, peas, and bouillon to barely cover, and let simmer till done, about ½ hour. *Serves 4.*

Nasi Goreng
Nasi goreng literally means fried rice.

4 slices bacon, chopped
2 large onions, coarsely chopped
2 cloves garlic, coarsely chopped
1 bell pepper, coarsely chopped
¾ pound leftover roast or any
    other cooked meat, cut into
    small pieces
1 teaspoon paprika
½ pound ham, coarsely chopped

1 tablespoon Lea & Perrins
    Worcestershire sauce
Salt and freshly ground pepper
    to taste
2 cups boiled rice, cooked the
    day before
1 egg, beaten
Cooking oil

Fry the bacon with the onions, garlic, and bell pepper. When they are limp, add the meat and fry a little longer. Add the paprika, ham, Worcestershire sauce, salt, and pepper. Add the rice last. Mix thoroughly. This is best made a day ahead, then heated in a covered, buttered ovenproof dish and poured over the omelette (next paragraph).

Make an omelette of the beaten egg and a little salt, fry in a little oil, cut into julienne strips, and place on the *nasi goreng. Serves 4.*

Palembang Curry
(Kerrie Palembang)

1 pound beef, cut into short, thin slices
Salt and freshly ground pepper
1 teaspoon nutmeg
3 cups water or bouillon
2 tablespoons oil
½ medium-sized onion, chopped fine
1 clove garlic, chopped fine
1 teaspoon paprika
3 dashes of Tabasco sauce

1 teaspoon ground coriander
1 teaspoon ground cuminseed
1 teaspoon powdered ginger
2 tablespoons curry powder
1 bay leaf
2 cups Coconut Milk (see Index)
2 teaspoons grated lemon rind
2 medium-sized potatoes, cubed
1 medium-sized onion, chopped and fried in oil till brown

Season the beef with salt, pepper, and the nutmeg, and boil in the 3 cups of water or bouillon till the meat is half done. Put it aside. In a large skillet heat the oil, add the onion, garlic, all the spices and the bay leaf, sauté for 3 minutes. Add the Coconut Milk, the meat with its liquid, then add the lemon rind, stirring while bringing to a boil. Before the meat is done, add the potatoes, cook for 15 minutes. Remove the bay leaf. Just before serving, top with the fried onions. *Serves 4.*

Mixed Vegetables in Curry Sauce
(Sajur Kerrie)

3 medium-sized onions, chopped
1 clove garlic, minced
½ bell pepper, minced
4 tablespoons oil
1 bay leaf
1 teaspoon ground ginger
1 teaspoon ground coriander
1 teaspoon ground cuminseed
1 tablespoon curry powder
Grated rind of ½ lemon
1 pound chicken wings

1 cup chicken bouillon
1 cup water
1 small head of cabbage,
    chopped
1 large potato, cut into small
    cubes
¾ cup vermicelli
Salt and freshly ground pepper
    to taste
½ cup Coconut Milk (see
    Index)

In a large skillet, sauté the onions, garlic, and bell pepper in the oil till they are soft. Add the bay leaf, ginger, coriander, cuminseed, curry powder, and lemon rind, and sauté for another minute. Add the chicken wings, sauté them till they are completely coated and golden brown. Add the bouillon, 1 cup of water, and cabbage, cook covered for ½ hour. Add the potato cubes to the *sajur,* together with the vermicelli. Cook till the potatoes are tender and the chicken wings are done. Remove the bay leaf. Season with salt and pepper. Add the Coconut Milk just before serving. The *sajur kerrie* is served on top of piping hot boiled rice. *Serves 6.*

Kaasi Curry Sauce

This curry sauce can be added to any leftover meat, cut into ½-inch cubes, or to whole shrimp, boiled, shelled, and deveined.

3 medium-sized onions, cut into chunks
1 clove garlic, chopped fine
1 stalk celery, chopped fine
½ bell pepper, chopped
2 tablespoons oil
1 medium-sized apple, chopped
2 tablespoons peanut butter
2 tablespoons flour
½ teaspoon turmeric
¼ teaspoon pepper
¼ teaspoon ground coriander
¼ teaspoon ground cuminseed
¼ teaspoon powdered cardamom
¼ teaspoon powdered ginger
3 tablespoons curry powder
3 cups chicken bouillon
1 cup Coconut Milk (see Index)
2 eggs, hard-cooked, peeled, and cut in half lengthwise

In a large skillet sauté the onions, garlic, celery, and bell pepper in the oil till they are limp. Add the chopped apple, sauté for another minute, stirring. Add the peanut butter, flour, and all of the spices, cook for another minute, stirring. Then add the bouillon, cover the skillet, and let the sauce simmer for 20 minutes, let it cool. Then put it in a blender and blend till it is very smooth. Return it to the skillet and add the Coconut Milk, stirring. Add the meat or shrimp. Let the curry dish stand for a few hours before serving. When you are ready to serve, place the hard-cooked eggs on top of the curry. *Makes 3 cups.*

Curry Side Dishes

Here are a few of the frequently served accompanying dishes for curry.

Chutney
Peanuts
Raisins
Mandarin oranges (drained)
Peeled cucumber sticks

Small slices of melon
Small slices of pineapple
Fried bananas or banana chunks rolled in shredded coconut
Coconut chips

Braised Lamb
(Kambing Opor)

*3 pounds boneless lamb, cut into
½-inch cubes
½ cup cider vinegar
½ cup water
2 cloves garlic, minced
2 teaspoons salt
½ teaspoon dried crushed chili
peppers*

*½ cup minced onions
½ teaspoon powdered saffron
1 teaspoon ground cuminseed
2 teaspoons ground coriander
1 teaspoon powdered ginger
4 tablespoons corn oil*

Marinate the lamb cubes in the vinegar and ½ cup of water for 30 minutes. Remove the lamb from the marinade, set the meat aside. Mix the garlic, salt, chili peppers, onions, saffron, cuminseed, coriander, ginger, and the marinade, and in a blender make a smooth paste. Roll the lamb cubes in the paste. Fry the cubes in the oil until they are brown. Add the water, cover the pan, and cook over low heat until tender, about ½ hour. *Serves 4–6.*

Pork Saté
(Saté Babi)

*2 pounds boneless lean pork
¼ cup smooth peanut butter
1½ teaspoons ground coriander
1½ teaspoons salt
1 teaspoon ground cuminseed
½ teaspoon freshly ground
pepper*

*3 medium-sized onions, grated
1 clove garlic, minced
1½ teaspoons lemon juice
1 tablespoon brown sugar
3 tablespoons soy sauce*

Cut the pork into 1½-inch cubes. Separately mix the peanut butter with all the other ingredients in a medium-sized bowl. Add the pork cubes and stir until the cubes are well-coated on all sides. Cover and let stand in the refrigerator for several hours. When ready to broil, stick the cubes of pork on 6 skewers and broil them over charcoal or under the broiler for about 15 minutes, turning frequently. Serve with Saté Sauce (recipe follows). *Serves 6.*

Saté Sauce

1 clove garlic	½ teaspoon salt
1 small onion	½ teaspoon powdered turmeric
1 cup peanuts	Juice of ½ lemon
3 dried hot chili peppers	1 cup water
2 pieces candied ginger	

Put all ingredients in a blender and run at medium speed for about 30 seconds. Then place the mixture in the top of a double boiler and cook over simmering water for 30 minutes. If desired, thin with Coconut Milk (see Index). *Makes 1½–2 cups.*

Indian Spiced Rice
(Nasi Kebuli)

1 large boiling chicken, cut in serving pieces	5 cups water
	½ teaspoon nutmeg
1 quart chicken bouillon	2 cloves
Oil for frying	Salt to taste
3 medium-sized onions, chopped	2 small onions, chopped and
2 cloves garlic, chopped	fried, for garnish
3 cups rice	

Let the chicken pieces simmer for 1½ hours in the bouillon. Remove the chicken from the bouillon, dry, and fry the pieces in hot oil until they are slightly brown. Set aside. Sauté the chopped onions and garlic until brown. Add the rice, stir for a few minutes, add the 5 cups of water, and let the rice cook till half done. Add the nutmeg, cloves, and salt. Mix the fried chicken pieces with the rice and let the mixture boil until the rice is cooked. Before serving, sprinkle with the fried onions. *Serves 4–6.*

Mixed Vegetables
(Sajur Asam)

1 small eggplant, cut in cubes	1 cup cubed cabbage
1 small can creamed corn	2 tablespoons sugar
½ cup cut-up green beans	1 bay leaf
1 onion, sliced	½ teaspoon lemon juice
⅛ cup peanut butter	2 cups chicken bouillon

Put all ingredients in a saucepan and simmer for 25 minutes. *Serves 4.*

Fried Onion Rings
(Bawang Goreng)

Cut the desired number of onions into very thin slices, separate the slices into rings, and fry them in deep hot oil until they are crisp and golden brown.

Vegetable Salad
(Gado Gado)

2 cloves garlic, minced	¾ cup water
½ cup chopped onions	Shredded lettuce
2 tablespoons oil	1 cup cooked green beans
½ cup smooth peanut butter	1 cup bean sprouts
1 teaspoon salt	1 cup precooked shredded
1 teaspoon sugar	cabbage
¼ teaspoon powdered dried chili	2 tomatoes, diced
peppers	2 hard-cooked eggs, sliced
2 teaspoons grated lemon rind	1 large cucumber, sliced
¾ cup Coconut Milk (see	
Index)	

Sauté the garlic and onions together in the oil for 3–4 minutes. Add the peanut butter, salt, sugar, chili peppers, lemon rind, and slowly add the Coconut Milk, which has been mixed with the ¾ cup of water. Cook over low heat for 5 minutes, then let it cool. On a foundation of shredded lettuce, lay the green beans, bean sprouts, cabbage, tomatoes, eggs, and cucumber slices. Pour the sauce over the vegetables. Chill well and serve. *Serves 8–10.*

Fried Noodles
(Bahmi Goreng)

Although this superb dish is called Fried Noodles, the noodles are not actually fried. They are boiled and set aside, then they are added at the last moment and gently folded over.

4 pork chops
2 tablespoons cooking oil
5 slices bacon, cut up
6 cloves garlic, chopped
½ pound raw shrimp, shelled, deveined
4 medium-sized onions, sliced
4 stalks celery, sliced
1 bunch scallions, sliced
½ head cabbage, cut in small pieces
1 head romaine lettuce, cut in pieces

1 small can peas, drained
1 can bean sprouts, drained
¼ pound boiled ham, cut in small cubes
4 nests of Chinese noodles, boiled, then rinsed in cold water
1 teaspoon salt
½ teaspoon pepper
½ teaspoon powdered ginger
¼ teaspoon Tabasco
2 tablespoons soy sauce
Juice of ½ lemon

Fry the pork chops in the oil until brown and done, then cut the meat into small pieces, set aside. Add 2 tablespoons of water to the pan drippings and set aside. In a large saucepan with a cover render the chopped bacon, add the chopped garlic and the shrimp. When the shrimp are pink, remove them from the saucepan. In the bacon fat quickly sauté the onions, celery, and scallions till they are soft. Add the cabbage, cover the saucepan, and steam for a few minutes. Uncover the pan, add the romaine lettuce, and steam it until it is wilted, stirring carefully. Add the cut-up pork, and the conserved pan drippings, the peas, bean sprouts, ham, and noodles. Fold over with 2 wooden spoons. Add the seasonings and the lemon juice. Correct the seasonings to taste. *Serves 4.*

Potato Sticks
(Sambal Goreng Kentang Kering)

4 medium-sized potatoes, cut
  julienne style
2 tablespoons oil
1 tablespoon chopped onion
1–2 tablespoons ground chili
  peppers (or paprika)

¼ teaspoon lemon juice
1 tablespoon sugar
¼ teaspoon grated lemon rind
½–1 cup Coconut Milk (see
  Index)
Salt to taste

In a skillet sauté the potatoes in the oil till they are golden brown, remove them from the skillet. In the oil simmer the remaining ingredients till the mixture is thick, remove from the fire, and carefully mix with the potato sticks.

Corn Fritters
(Perkedel Djagung)

These fritters are served, one per person, as an accompaniment to rijsttafel.

1 cup sweet corn kernels
½ stalk celery, chopped
1 shallot, chopped fine
1 clove garlic, minced
1 tablespoon chopped parsley
½ teaspoon salt

¼ teaspoon freshly ground
  pepper
1 egg, beaten
2 tablespoons flour
Oil for frying

Combine all ingredients except oil to make a batter. Drop tablespoonfuls of the batter into sizzling oil in a skillet. Fry on both sides until golden brown, then remove to paper toweling for a few seconds. Serve hot. *Makes 6–8 fritters.*

Banana Fritters
(Pisang Goreng)

2 eggs   1 teaspoon oil
½ cup milk   4 bananas
1 cup flour   3 cups vegetable oil
1 teaspoon baking powder   Cinnamon and powdered sugar,
1 teaspoon salt   mixed

For the batter, beat the eggs, stir in the milk. Sift the flour, baking powder, and salt together, and beat into the eggs and milk. Beat in the 1 teaspoon of oil. Peel the bananas and cut them diagonally into 1-inch pieces. Dip them into the batter, coating them heavily, and deep-fry them in the very hot vegetable oil until they are golden brown. Sprinkle the cinnamon and powdered sugar over them and serve immediately. *Makes 12–16 small fritters or 6–8 dessert fritters.*

Fried Bananas
(Pisang Goreng)

6 large bananas   ⅓ cup oil
½ cup brown sugar, spread out
    on a dish

Only bananas that are fresh and not too ripe should be used. Peel them, cut them in half lengthwise, then in half vertically, giving you 24 pieces. Roll the pieces in the brown sugar. Fry them over medium heat in the oil until they are golden brown. Serve them immediately. *Serves 6.*

Spicy Sauce
(Rudjak Manis)

10 chili peppers
1 tablespoon sugar
2 teaspoons grated lemon rind
¼ teaspoon shrimp paste or
    anchovy paste

1 teaspoon salt
Soy sauce to make the
    consistency of a thick sauce

Mix all ingredients in a food processor or blender. This sauce is
eaten as an accompaniment to raw fruits. *Makes ½ cup of very hot
sauce.*

Hot Peanut Relish
(Sambal Katjang)

2 cups ground peanuts
1 teaspoon shrimp paste or
    anchovy paste

3 squirts of Tabasco sauce
1 tablespoon sugar
1 tablespoon soy sauce

Mix all ingredients thoroughly. *Makes 2 cups.*

Pineapple Relish
(Sambal Nanas)

1 tablespoon vegetable oil
1 small onion, sliced
1 small hot pepper, chopped
1 fresh pineapple, cut into small
    cubes, or a scant 2 cups
    canned pineapple chunks,
    drained (reserve juice)

½ cup pineapple juice
½ teaspoon powdered cinnamon

In a skillet, heat the oil, sauté the onion and pepper in it for 2 minutes, add the remaining ingredients, and cook for 10 minutes. *Makes 2 cups.*

Coconut Milk
(Santan)

This recipe is not to be confused with Coconut Cream, the recipe following.

2 cups hot milk
1 cup grated coconut

Add the hot milk to the coconut, let stand for 40 minutes, then press through a sieve. *Makes 2¼ cups.*

Coconut Cream
(Santan)

This recipe is not to be confused with Coconut Milk, the recipe above.

1 cup grated coconut
2 cups hot heavy cream

Add the hot cream to the coconut, let stand for 35 minutes, then press through a sieve. If you then want to whip the Coconut Cream, chill it first. *Makes 2¼ cups.*

The Poor Goose

It happened during the last year of World War II in Aschaffen-burg, Germany. A dentist who lived with his two teen-age daughters had been given a goose for their holiday dinner. The goose, which came fresh from a farm, was alive and noisy. As it was ten days before Christmas, she was kept in a small crate in the kitchen, but as the day of the feast approached, the good doctor and his girls became very anxious—none of them had ever killed or plucked a goose. They couldn't even figure out that it might be easier to pluck

the goose after she had met her maker, and they didn't dare to ask anyone for advice for fear that they would be denounced as hoarders or dealers on the black market.

So the dentist—ever the professional man—said, "It's easy. I'll put her to sleep with a small dose of anesthetic and she won't feel anything when we pluck her." Which they did. Then they went to the living room to rest from their labors and held an earnest conference as to which method should be used to put her out of her misery. Suddenly out of the kitchen waddled, barely able to stand or balance, their prematurely awakened goose, picked clean down to the last fluffy feather.

This appearance the family took for a sign from heaven! The bird was reprieved and named Lazarus because he too had risen from the dead, and when Lazarus refused to grow back her plumage, the girls knitted her a sweater. It was light green.

Roast Goose
(Gebratene Gans)

A 6-pound goose	3 medium-sized apples, peeled
Salt	and cored
Marjoram	½ cup pitted prunes
Powdered caraway seeds	½ cup water

Remove all loose fat from the cavity of the goose. Rub the skin and the cavity with salt, marjoram, and caraway. Fill the cavity with the apples and the prunes, close it with skewers. Prick the skin well with a sharp fork so that much of the fat will drain off during roasting. Put the ½ cup of water in a roasting pan, place the goose, breast side down, on a rack in the roasting pan, and roast, uncovered, for 1 hour in a preheated 325° oven. Then turn the goose over, removing all fat from the pan, and roast for 2 more hours. For a crisp skin, during the last 25 minutes turn the oven up to 400° and pour ½ cup of water over the bird. Let the goose rest for ½ hour, covered with aluminum foil, before carving. (The fruit stuffing is not usually served. The goose fat is highly prized as a seasoning for vegetables. It is also spread on dark bread and eaten as a delicacy.) *Serves 6.*

Help Wanted

With great admiration and genuine envy of their knowledge I have read various books by Dionne Lucas, Julia Child, James Beard, Craig Claiborne, and other famous cooks. But I feel that our society has bypassed that leisured age, that time of complacent luxury for the patient attention to refined details that their great recipes demand. I know very few hostesses who have the time or the inclination to stand for hours in the kitchen preparing complicated dishes, dishes that require very special ingredients.

Except in the homes of a few hobby cooks who are proud to serve intricate menus, you will find these gastronomical delights only in very exclusive restaurants, and there, of course, the kitchen help does the nasty work: cleaning and preparing, slicing and chopping the vegetables, trimming the meats and trussing the fowl, scaling and drawing the fish and cracking the lobsters. And after the meal is all over, served and eaten, *they* clean up the kitchen and even carry out the garbage.

Futurologists promise us a new life, one that will make domestic help superfluous. No more need to push the vacuum cleaner around the house; dusting will be taken care of by ducts in the walls that will electrically attract and remove dust before it has a chance to settle. Culinary needs will be satisfied by a centrally located huge computer that will offer an infinite variety of preprepared goodies. All *you* will need to do is to dial a set of numbers and the meal of your choice will drop from a chute in your feeding machine, complete with glasses, cutlery, salt and pepper packs, and roll in front of your seat. You will dial another set of numbers for your beverages, which will fall out of a spout, and after you are satisfied and have wiped your mouth (*that* you may have to do yourself), you'll press a button and the tray will be retracted and disappear.

Washbowls, bathtubs, toilets, and bidets will be self-cleaning and self-rinsing; making beds and changing linen will also be unnecessary. *HOW* that will be accomplished the futurologists have not yet figured out, but, rest assured, they are working on it. Any paintings you like will instantly be projected onto your walls, there to stay and be enjoyed until you get sick and tired of them and dial for a different wall decoration.

Oh, happy, happy future! No more cleaning ladies will appear early at your door expecting breakfast and lunch with special consideration for their dietary habits, stay for seven hours or so in order to slowly transfer the dirt from one corner of the room to another, every few weeks to break a piece of your valuable china and carelessly let a few knives and forks drop into the garbage can. You will not be constrained to laugh it off with a cheery, "Oh, that's perfectly all right, dear Anna," so as to ward off their feeling hurt or threatening to quit. Neither will you be obliged to pretend not to notice their sneaking into your laundry room in order to wash *their* family's dirty clothes in your washing machine, and turn a blind eye to the liquor and wine that have been siphoned off your bottles, not daring to lock the liquor closet for fear of offending. Nor to pay them for these chores more money than a university professor with a family of four is earning. Oh, happy future!

When I was still a bachelor I had a Chinese houseboy working for me. He was my dresser in the theatre and otherwise took care of my apartment. The telephone, and the fact that he was supposed to answer it when I was not home, amused him no end. The messages he wrote down in what he thought was English created problems, and the time required to decipher them I called "the riddle hour." Even when finally I assigned numbers to those of my friends who called often, he wrote down the numbers in his own peculiar way so that an 8 looked like a 5 and a 3 like a 9. But he was honest, jolly, and loved to take care of my wardrobe. He was very small and my wardrobe very large. Once I came home and caught him parading in my clothes in front of the mirror laughing himself sick. The l's and the r's of the English language were a big hurdle for him, and so were the p's and f's. One day a friend who occupied my apartment for a while complained of dirt behind the radiators: "De lady

is too farticular," was his only reaction. And when I told him to get my tuxedo out for the evening, he carefully brushed it and asked, "Boss, you gonna go to a farty?"

After 1943, when I married, we found that due to the war all the professional help had been absorbed by the factories and that houseboys had almost completely disappeared. It was tough to find someone able and trustworthy in a town like Hollywood. A parade of women of all colors passed through our home; the pretty ones wanted to be in pictures, and if you asked for a reference you were called a dirty capitalist.

And then we found Mattie—a huge woman who stayed for many years until she got married. She was a nice and willing helper but went completely to pieces with stage fright when we had company. She dropped more food onto and in front of our guests than I care to remember.

One evening, before a dinner party, my wife asked her to put a dinner roll at each place. That's exactly what she did; when we entered the dining room there was a dinner roll on the seat of each chair.

But could she prepare Southern food!

Canapés à la Mattie

1 tablespoon butter
1¼ tablespoons flour
¼ cup milk
¼ cup chicken bouillon
2 scallions, chopped fine
1 tablespoon oil
½ pound cooked, shelled,
    deveined shrimp, chopped
    fine

1 tablespoon dry white wine
Salt and freshly ground pepper
    to taste
1 tablespoon finely chopped
    parsley
1 teaspoon chopped fresh dill
3 slices white bread trimmed of
    crusts

To make a white sauce: In a medium-sized saucepan, over low heat, melt the butter, add the flour, milk, and bouillon, and stir till you have a thick sauce. Sauté the scallions in the oil, add to the white sauce, add the shrimp, wine, salt, pepper, parsley, and dill, then allow the sauce to cool. Toast the bread, then spread the sauce over the slices, and bake in a moderate oven till the canapés are hot. Cut each slice of toast into 4 pieces, serve immediately. *Makes 12 canapés.*

Frog's Legs à la Mattie

Count 6 frog's legs per person. Soak them for 1 hour in milk. Dry
them and dredge them in flour. Dip them in beaten egg, then roll
them in unseasoned bread crumbs. Deep-fry them in a half-and-half
mixture of oil and butter. Place them on paper towels to drain, and
keep them hot. Serve with lemon wedges. Some people like tartar
sauce with the frog's legs.

Fish Slices in Beer Dough

1 pound fish filets cut in pieces 1
    by 3 inches
Salt
Lemon juice
1 egg, separated
⅓ cup flour

⅓ cup beer
½ teaspoon salt
A generous pinch of Lawry's
    seasoned salt
Oil for deep frying

Season the pieces of fish with salt and lemon juice. Beat the egg
yolk slightly, blend in the flour, beer, salt, and Lawry's seasoned
salt. Beat the egg white till very stiff, then fold it into the batter.
Coat the pieces of fish lightly with additional flour, dip into the batter, and fry them quickly in deep hot oil till they are golden brown.
Drain on paper towels briefly and serve very hot. *Serves 2.*

Seafood Gumbo

2–3 tablespoons bacon fat
1 medium-sized onion, chopped
1 clove garlic, minced
2 cups sliced okra
1 stalk celery, sliced
2 cups canned tomatoes

1 bay leaf
A pinch of thyme
½ pound raw shrimp, shelled
    and deveined
Salt and freshly ground pepper
    to taste

Place the bacon fat in a heavy skillet, add the onion and garlic,
sauté till they are light brown. Add the remaining ingredients,

cook, covered, for 15 minutes. Uncover and cook slowly till the sauce is thick. Remove the bay leaf. Serve over piping hot boiled rice. *Serves 4.*

Deviled Crab

½ pound fresh crab meat
½ cup minced scallions
1 tablespoon chopped parsley
1 egg, beaten
1 teaspoon mayonnaise
1 teaspoon Lea & Perrins
    Worcestershire sauce
¼ cup grated Parmesan cheese
½ cup unseasoned bread crumbs
    tossed with melted butter
½ teaspoon salt
⅛ teaspoon pepper
Extra bread crumbs

Mix the crab meat with all the remaining ingredients except the extra bread crumbs. Divide the mixture in 4 ramekins, sprinkle the tops with bread crumbs, and bake in a preheated 350° oven for 15–20 minutes, or till the tops are brown. *Serves 4.*

Clam Croquettes—Canapés

1½ tablespoons butter
1½ tablespoons flour
½ cup milk
A pinch of nutmeg
A pinch of thyme
Salt and pepper to taste
Worcestershire sauce to taste
1 small can minced clams,
    drained
Flour
1 egg, beaten
Unseasoned bread crumbs
Oil for deep frying

To make a white sauce: In a medium-sized saucepan, melt the butter over low heat, add the flour, stirring steadily, the milk, nutmeg, and thyme, then add salt, pepper, and Worcestershire sauce, stirring constantly until you have a very thick sauce. Stir in the minced clams. Spread the mixture on a platter and put in the refrigerator for 1 hour, then mold into small croquettes ½ inch wide and 1 inch long. Dredge them in flour, egg, and roll them in bread crumbs. Fry the croquettes in deep oil till they are golden brown, drain them on paper towels. These croquettes are delicious served with cocktails. *Makes 8–10 croquettes.*

Baked Rice

2 tablespoons butter	2 sprigs parsley
2 tablespoons minced onion	1 sprig fresh thyme or ¼
¼ teaspoon minced garlic	teaspoon dried
1 cup uncooked rice	½ bay leaf
1½ cups chicken stock	⅛ teaspoon cayenne pepper

Melt 1 tablespoon of the butter in a heavy ovenproof saucepan with a close-fitting cover, and sauté the onion and garlic in it till they are translucent. Add the rice and stir briefly over low heat till all the grains are coated with butter. Pour in the stock and stir, making sure that there are no lumps in the rice. Add the parsley, thyme, bay leaf, and cayenne. Cover, and place in a preheated 400° oven for exactly 17 minutes. Remove the sprigs of parsley, the sprig of thyme, and the bay leaf. Stir in the remaining tablespoon of butter with a two-pronged fork. *Serves 3–4.*

Shrimp Jambalaya

2 medium-sized onions, chopped	¼ teaspoon cloves
1 stalk celery, chopped	1 pound boiled ham cut into
½ bell pepper, chopped	¼-inch cubes
4 tablespoons butter	2 pounds raw shrimp, boiled,
4 cups canned tomatoes	shelled, and deveined
2 cloves garlic, minced	3 cups cooked rice
1 teaspoon chopped parsley	Salt, freshly ground pepper, and
½ teaspoon thyme	cayenne pepper to taste

Sauté the onions, celery, and bell pepper in the butter till they are tender. Add the tomatoes and cook for 5 minutes, stirring constantly. Add the garlic, parsley, thyme, and cloves, cook for 30 minutes, stirring frequently. Stir in the ham and cook for 4 minutes, then add the shrimp and cook for 3 minutes. Stir in the rice and season to taste. *Serves 6.*

Mattie's Southern Fried Chicken

1 cup flour
1 teaspoon baking powder
A pinch of salt
1 egg, separated
1 tablespoon sugar

1 cup milk
1 tablespoon melted butter
A 4-pound chicken, cut into 8
    pieces
Oil for deep frying

First make a batter: Sift the flour with the baking powder and salt.
Beat the egg white till very stiff and add the sugar, mix well. Then
beat the egg yolk with the milk and butter, mixing well, pour into
the flour mixture, and mix thoroughly. Fold in the egg white and
blend. Do not make the batter too thick. Dip the chicken pieces in
the batter. In a large iron skillet, pour oil about ¾ inch deep, heat
it almost to the boiling point. Fry the chicken pieces, only 3 at a
time, on both sides till golden brown. Place briefly on paper towels
and serve very hot! *Serves 2–3.*

Barbecued Spareribs Lohmann

Sparerib Sauce:

½ cup minced onions
2 teaspoons dry mustard
½ teaspoon garlic powder
1 cup ketchup
2 tablespoons Lea & Perrins
    Worcestershire sauce

½ cup vinegar
3 tablespoons sugar
⅛ teaspoon pepper
1 cup water

Mix all ingredients thoroughly and cook until thick.

Spareribs:

2 pounds spareribs
Salt

Freshly ground pepper
Garlic salt

Sprinkle salt, pepper, and garlic salt on both sides of the ribs, put on a rack in a roasting pan, and bake in a preheated 350° oven for 1 hour. At the end of the hour spread the sauce on the ribs and bake for another 30 minutes. *Serves 3.*

Breaded Rabbit

A 3-pound rabbit, cut into serving-size pieces

Prepare the rabbit exactly as you would Viennese Breaded Fried Chicken (see Index). *Serves 4.*

Cooked Coleslaw Dressing à la Bob

¾ cup sugar	1 heaping teaspoon black pepper
2 tablespoons butter	1 tablespoon dry mustard
1 generous tablespoon salad oil	2 eggs, well beaten
⅓ cup cider	1 small head of cabbage,
1 heaping teaspoon salt	shredded fine

Into a saucepan put the sugar, butter, oil, cider, salt, pepper, and mustard, bring to a slow boil. Turn off the heat, add the eggs slowly, mix well. Pour the dressing over the cabbage in a large bowl and allow it to cool before serving. (Optional: sprinkle 1 teaspoon of celery salt over the cabbage before the dressing is added.) *Serves 4–6.*

Fresh Cranberry Sauce

4 cups fresh cranberries	2 cups sugar
1 cup orange juice	½ cup coarsely grated walnuts

Mix the cranberries and orange juice in a saucepan, cook, tightly covered, for 8 minutes. Add the sugar and mix well. Cool, chill, and serve after the walnuts have been stirred in. *Makes about 2 cups.*

Southern Pecan Pie

It is rich!

3 eggs
⅔ cup sugar
A dash of salt
1 cup dark corn syrup

⅓ cup butter, melted
1 cup pecan halves
An unbaked 9-inch pie shell

Beat the eggs thoroughly with the sugar, a dash of salt, the corn syrup, and melted butter. Add the pecans, stir. Pour the mixture into the pie shell and bake in a preheated 350° oven for 50 minutes till a sharp knife inserted halfway between the outside and the center of the filling comes out clean. Cool before serving. *Serves 6.*

Crispy Chocolate Cookies

½ cup and 3 tablespoons shelled almonds
1¼ cups flour
½ cup and 3 tablespoons sugar

5 tablespoons bitter cocoa
½ cup and 3 tablespoons butter
2 tablespoons rum
1 egg, beaten

Peel the almonds (put them in boiling water for a minute to make peeling easier), then chop them fine. In a large bowl, put the flour, sugar, and cocoa, mix well. Make a well in the center and put in nearly all of the butter, then add the rum and the beaten egg. Mix thoroughly *by hand* until you have a smooth dough. Line the inside of a large square pan with well-buttered aluminum foil, put the mixture into the pan and spread evenly. Bake in a preheated 300° oven for 35 to 40 minutes. When the cookies are done, let them cool for a while, then invert the baking pan on a board, pull off the aluminum foil carefully, and cut the results into squares. *Makes about 3 dozen cookies.*

After our children were born, a Mexican lady entered our household . . . and our hearts. Maria Zincuinegui is the dear creature's name: she was the most reliable nurse that parents could wish for. Knowing that Maria was in charge, we could leave for long or short trips without worry.

She introduced us to Mexican cooking. She is a very devout lady: when I had to get up very early and didn't want to trust my temperamental alarm clock, I used to ask Maria to awaken me. She didn't possess a clock but she prayed to the poor souls in purgatory, and they awakened her in time. She cooked eggs by reciting Hail Marys, and they were always done right. She now lives happy and content in her enviably wonderful faith in Southern California, and has remained a true friend.

Maria's Arroz con Pollo

A 4-pound chicken, cut into 8 pieces	2 cups water
1½ teaspoons salt	1 12-ounce can tomatoes
⅛ teaspoon pepper	2 chicken bouillon cubes
¾ teaspoon paprika	¼ teaspoon powdered saffron
4 tablespoons cooking oil	1 bay leaf
1 medium-sized onion, chopped	½ teaspoon oregano
1 clove garlic, minced	1 cup frozen peas, defrosted
1 cup uncooked rice	4 pimientos, cut up

Season the chicken pieces with the salt, pepper, and paprika. Brown the chicken in the oil in a large skillet. When the pieces are brown, put them in a large casserole. In the same skillet, sauté the onion, garlic, and rice till the onion is soft. Loosen any particles on the bottom of the skillet, add the 2 cups of water, the tomatoes, bouillon cubes, saffron, bay leaf, and oregano, bring to a boil. Pour this sauce over the chicken in the casserole, cover it tightly, and bake in a preheated 350° oven for 30 minutes. Uncover, stir in the peas, and put the pimiento pieces on top. Cook for another 10 minutes or until the rice is done. *Serves 8.*

Mexican Fish Soup

¼ cup salad oil
1 large onion, chopped
1 clove garlic, crushed
2 tablespoons chopped parsley
½ cup chopped celery
2 tablespoons chopped bell
   pepper
4 tomatoes, peeled and cut up
1 6-ounce can tomato paste
1 teaspoon paprika
2 teaspoons salt
⅔ cup dry sherry
4 cups water

¼ teaspoon basil
A pinch of rosemary
½ teaspoon oregano
1 teaspoon Lea & Perrins
   Worcestershire sauce
1½ pounds of a white fish,
   boned and cut into 1-inch
   pieces
2 lobster tails and 2 claws, cut
   into 1½-inch pieces
6 sea scallops (large) or 15 bay
   scallops (small)
2 crab legs, halved

In a large kettle heat the oil, add the onion, garlic, parsley, celery, and bell pepper, and sauté till the vegetables are soft. Add the tomatoes, tomato paste, paprika, salt, and sherry, simmer for about 20 minutes, stirring occasionally. Add the 4 cups of water, the rest of the seasonings, cook slowly for 1 hour. About 15 minutes before serving, add the fish pieces. After another 10 minutes, add the shellfish. Cook slowly for another 5 minutes. Serve in deep bowls accompanied by French bread. *Serves 6–8.*

Ensalada Maria

Lettuce leaves to line the bottom
   of a bowl
1 medium-sized can asparagus
   tips
½ pound string beans, canned or
   cooked
½ head of cauliflower, separated
   into flowerets cooked al
   dente

1 medium-sized cucumber,
   unpeeled, sliced
1 bunch radishes, sliced
1 leek, sliced
1 medium-sized onion, sliced
1 bunch watercress
2 hard-cooked eggs, chopped

Sauce Vinaigrette:

½ cup white wine vinegar   ½ teaspoon tarragon
½ teaspoon salt   1 teaspoon capers
¼ teaspoon pepper   2 teaspoons pickle relish
1½ cups olive oil

Mix the sauce ingredients well and allow to stand for 1 hour before using. Line the bottom of a bowl with lettuce leaves, place all the vegetables on them, and pour on the Sauce Vinaigrette. Toss lightly and serve immediately. *Serves 6–8.*

Ensalada Olé

1 large can asparagus, cut into   ¼ teaspoon dry mustard
   small pieces (reserve liquid)   1 tablespoon gin
½ cup mayonnaise   1 pound medium-sized raw
½ cup sour cream   shrimp, boiled, shelled,
¼ teaspoon lemon juice   deveined

Make a dressing of the asparagus juice, mayonnaise, sour cream, lemon juice, mustard, and gin, mix thoroughly. Place the shrimp and asparagus in a bowl, add the dressing, toss carefully, and let the salad stand, covered, in the refrigerator for at least 6 hours. *Serves 4.*

···✦──━▶◉◀━──✦···

When our children were small we tried to teach them that in a restaurant there were dishes one could order other than spaghetti with meat balls, hamburgers with French fries, and peanut butter and jelly sandwiches. We made it a rule that after their ninth birthday each could choose his or her birthday dinner.

When Leo, our youngest, had his birthday, it took him a long time to make up his mind. At last he said earnestly, "First, I would like to have snails; then vichyssoise; after that filet menon [he didn't quite make the word "mignon"] with string beans and almonds and Lyonnaise potatoes." Our faces were bathed in proud delight. "And for dessert?" we asked. He gave it a lot of thought, then his little face lit up and he blurted out, "Twinkies" (a cupcake with some sort of white cream inside that the kids bought at school at two for a nickel).

He went to Riverdale, New York, and after he had been there for a week his worried mother called to find out how he liked school. Among her many questions she asked him how the food was in school. Very matter-of-factly he answered, "Oh, I guess it's okay, but so far we haven't had crêpes Suzette ONCE!"

What Richard the Lion-Hearted Started

Quite a few years ago—in 1190 to be exact—Richard the Lion-Hearted, son of Henry II, out of Eleanor of Aquitaine, felt the urge to liberate the Holy Land. Like most such attempts, the underlying motives were noble, filled with a burning desire to bring Christianity to the poor heathens who were living, happy in their ignorance of the true faith, under the cruel yoke of the evil Saladin.

Richard was joined in that expensive and elaborate undertaking by several other groups of liberators. History has not handed down to us whether these groups were then known, as they would be today, by their capitalized initials: such as PLO, ILO, MPL, FNLA, etc.

During the long journey and the siege of Jerusalem, Richard (an unpleasant and arrogant character) managed to insult all the other liberators; so, when the enterprise failed and he wanted to return home, none of the countries he had to cross in order to get back to England would give him a safe-conduct. Being lion-hearted, he traveled in disguise and got as far as Vienna. There, on the banks of the beautiful blue Danube, he was caught by the sleuths of Leopold of Austria, whom he had also insulted. Leopold imprisoned him and then sent ransom notes to England. He was in a good bargaining position because Richard's whereabouts had been kept secret. Not even Richard's erstwhile traveling companion, a beautiful young minstrel who answered to the name of Blondel, knew where his master was hidden, but, being a courtier, he was aware that captives of royal blood were always given the VIP treatment at some fortress.

And so, lute in hand, he set out, strolling from castle to castle, singing "their song." One day his grand tour of castle-hopping reaped its reward: from a window high up in a turret he heard a familiar voice picking up the second verse of "their song." Blondel

was a bright little minstrel and sent word back to England that Richard the Lion-Hearted was being held captive at Burg Dürnstein, thirty kilometers west of Vienna.

Postal communications were then nonexistent and messengers were often waylaid, so it took some time for the ransom negotiations to be concluded. The loot, 150,000 marks, was partly delivered, partly promised, and finally Richard was able to return to his loved ones.

Later on, Dürnstein became a cloister and housed the Sisters of St. Claire, but there must have been some scandal because Joseph II abruptly closed and dissolved that pious community. It was then bought by a Frenchman, a Monsieur Thiery, whose descendants still own it. Old M. Thiery first used it as a relay station for changing the horses that pulled the barges upstream. The bargemen and their master were so exhausted from watching the horses pull so hard that they too had to stop for refreshments, so M. Thiery developed the relay station into a restaurant, the Richard Löwenherz. The wine in that part of Austria, called the Wachau, was very famous and the restaurant prospered, and when the invention of the steam engine made the horses obsolete the restaurant remained, and is today one of the glories of the Wachau. I have eaten memorable meals in this fine, beautifully kept place.

Roast Saddle of Venison
(Rehrücken)

The best way to roast a saddle of venison is to marinate it beforehand. Choose either of the marinades given below.

Marinade 1

3 cups red wine	2 stalks celery, sliced
1 cup chicken bouillon	1 bay leaf
1 clove garlic, minced	¼ teaspoon thyme
8 juniper berries, crushed	¼ teaspoon powdered ginger
1 medium-sized parsnip, sliced	¼ teaspoon nutmeg

Bring all ingredients to a boil, let simmer for 5 minutes, let cool. Place the venison in a container that will allow the marinade to cover the meat; cover the container. Leave the meat in the marinade in the refrigerator for 4 days, turning twice daily.

Marinade 2

>   *1 quart buttermilk*

If you use Marinade 2, place the venison in a deep container, cover with the buttermilk, and leave in the refrigerator for 4 days, turning twice daily.

Roasting the venison

A rack of venison, 5–7 pounds	*2 stalks celery, sliced*
¼ pound salt pork, cut into	*1 small parsnip, sliced*
strips ¼ inch by 2 inches for	*1 bay leaf*
larding	*2 cloves*
Salt	*1 cup Burgundy wine*
8 juniper berries, crushed	*½ cup chicken bouillon*
3 tablespoons oil	*1½ tablespoons flour*
1 medium-sized onion, chopped	*1 tablespoon currant jelly*
1 carrot, sliced	*4 tablespoons sour cream*

Before roasting the venison, remove it from the marinade and wipe it dry. Lard the meat with the salt pork. Rub the rack with salt and the crushed juniper berries, brush it with 1 tablespoon of the oil. (If the rack if not going to be larded, rub it with salt and the juniper berries, rub the meat with oil, and *tie* the salt pork over it.) Heat the remaining oil in a roasting pan, sauté the onion, carrot, celery, and parsnip, along with the bay leaf and cloves, till the onion is limp. Place the venison, round side down, in the roasting pan, roast in a preheated 350° oven for 45–60 minutes, turning once and basting often with wine and bouillon. Remove the rack from the pan and keep it warm. Remove the fat from the pan, mix it with the 1½ tablespoons flour, the rest of the bouillon, the pan vegetables, and the pan drippings, and cook, stirring constantly, till the gravy is made. Strain the gravy. Add the currant jelly and the sour cream, mix well. To serve the venison, with a very sharp 6-inch knife

blade cut out the whole fillet from each side of the saddle, cut each
fillet into serving slices that are cut on the bias—that is, at a slight
angle—replace them in the saddle just as they were before. Pour a
little gravy over the meat and serve the rest separately. Wonderful
to see as it is brought to the table. *Serves 6.*

Rabbit in White Wine
(Kaninchen in Weisswein Sosse)

*1 young rabbit, skinned, cut into
    serving pieces*
Salt and freshly ground pepper
3 slices bacon, cut in half
1 large onion, chopped

1 tablespoon butter
1 tablespoon oil
1 cup chicken bouillon
1 cup dry white wine
5 peppercorns

Sprinkle each piece of rabbit with salt and pepper, wrap each in a
half slice of bacon. In a skillet sauté the onion in the butter and oil
till the onion is transparent. Add the rabbit and brown lightly on all
sides. Add the bouillon, white wine, and peppercorns, cover the skillet tightly, and let simmer for at least an hour till tender. This is
delectable. *Serves 4.*

Roast Hare
(Hasenbraten)

A 4- to 5-pound hare
*Buttermilk, approximately a
    quart*
Salt and crushed peppercorns
6 juniper berries, crushed
5 strips bacon
1 medium-sized onion, chopped
2 carrots, sliced
1 stalk celery, sliced
1 small parsnip, sliced
½ cup oil

1 tablespoon flour
½ cup red wine
½ cup chicken bouillon
A few whole peppercorns
A pinch of nutmeg
A pinch of powdered ginger
1 bay leaf
¼ cup heavy cream
1 tablespoon lemon juice
1 tablespoon currant jelly

Skin and clean the hare thoroughly, set it in buttermilk to cover for
8 hours, then remove it from the buttermilk and dry it well. Rub it

with salt, crushed peppercorns, and juniper berries, cover with the strips of bacon. In a roasting pan sauté the onion, carrots, celery, and parsnip in the oil for 4–5 minutes. Place the hare on top of the vegetables and roast, covered, basting frequently, in a preheated 350° oven for 45 minutes. Remove the hare from the pan and keep it warm. To prepare the sauce: Skim the fat from the pan drippings and discard it. Blend in the flour, wine, bouillon, some whole peppercorns, the nutmeg, ginger, and bay leaf, boil gently for a few minutes. Return the hare to the sauce in the pan and continue roasting for another 45 minutes, basting with more bouillon if necessary. Before serving, remove the hare from the sauce, add the heavy cream, lemon juice, and currant jelly, simmer for 2 minutes, then strain the sauce. Place the hare on a heated platter, pour some of the sauce over it, and serve the rest separately. Best served with hot boiled noodles or potatoes. *Serves 4.*

P.S. Rabbit and wild duck can be prepared the same way.

Roast Pheasant

1 pheasant	1 egg
Salt	1 small can liver pâté, preferably
1 medium-sized onion, chopped	goose liver
¾ cup sliced mushrooms	1–1½ tablespoons butter
5 tablespoons lard	¾ cup Madeira wine
2 slices white bread, soaked in	1 teaspoon flour
water and pressed dry	
Salt and freshly ground pepper	
to taste	

Clean the bird and rub it inside and out with salt. To prepare the stuffing: sauté the onion and mushrooms in the lard till the onions are transparent. Add the bread, salt, and pepper, mix well, and let cool. Mix in the egg and liver pâté. Stuff the pheasant and rub it with cold butter. Place the bird on a large sheet of foil, edges folded upward, add the wine, make a tight-fitting bag so the wine won't run out, place the bag in a buttered casserole, cover tightly, and cook in a preheated 350° oven for at least 2 hours. Remove the pheasant from the casserole, add the flour to the liquid and the vegetables, and cook over low heat till the sauce thickens. Pour it over the bird and serve. This is delectable. *Serves 2.*

Bavarian Red Cabbage
(Bayrisches Rot Kraut)

This is very satisfying served with sausages and whipped mashed potatoes.

2 tablespoons goose drippings or duck fat or chicken fat
6 cups shredded red cabbage
Salt and freshly ground pepper to taste
3 whole cloves
2 sour apples, peeled, cored, and chopped

1 cup boiling water or chicken bouillon
2 tablespoons flour
⅛ teaspoon cinnamon
4 tablespoons brown sugar
2 tablespoons vinegar

Heat the drippings or fat in a large skillet, add the cabbage, salt, pepper, cloves, and apples. Sauté for a few minutes. Pour the 1 cup of boiling water over them and cook slowly for about 15 minutes. Combine the flour, cinnamon, sugar, and vinegar, and more water if necessary, cook for a few more minutes, then add to the cabbage. *Serves about 4.*

Sweet and Sour Cabbage Ilona
(Paradeiser Kraut)

1 firm cabbage, 4–6 pounds
4 level tablespoons salt without iodine
5 tablespoons lard or margarine
2 medium-sized onions, chopped
Rind of ½ lemon
2 tablespoons salad oil
2 16-ounce cans good quality tomato juice

1 small can tomato paste
1 teaspoon Lea & Perrins Worcestershire sauce
2 teaspoons oregano
1 teaspoon thyme
4 tablespoons sugar
4 tablespoons white vinegar

Remove the hard outer leaves of the cabbage. Cut the head in half and cut out the central cores. Place the 2 halves, cut side down, on a chopping board and slice into long, narrow strips (no shredding). Put a thick layer of cabbage in a large bowl, add 1 tablespoon of salt, and repeat till you have 4 layers. Now mix the cabbage and salt with your hands, make a high mound of cabbage, put a heavy plate upside down on the mound, and press down. Place a heavy object on top of the plate and let the cabbage sweat for at least 30 minutes. In the meantime, put the lard or margarine in a large, heavy skillet, sauté the onions in it till limp. Add all the other ingredients except the sugar, vinegar, and cabbage, simmer slowly while stirring for 15 minutes. Take handfuls of cabbage and squeeze the juice out, add to the skillet, and cook for 5 minutes. Then add the sugar and vinegar, simmer for about 20 minutes, till the cabbage is done. This dish has great zest! *Serves 8.*

Palffy Dumpling
(Palffy Knoedel)

10 one-day-old rolls
1 cup milk
¼ pound plus 1 tablespoon
    butter, melted

10 egg yolks
10 egg whites, stiffly beaten
½ cup grated Parmesan cheese

Cut the rolls into ⅜-inch cubes, pour the milk over them. Mix the butter with the egg yolks, add to the bread cubes. Mix the beaten egg whites and the Parmesan cheese, add to the bread mixture. Butter a wet large cloth napkin, place the mixture on it, wrap it securely in a loaf form. Boil it in plenty of salted water for 45 minutes. Let it cool for a bit, then slice it. *Serves 6.*

Rice with Peas
(Risi Bisi)

3 quarts rapidly boiling water
2 cups fine-grain rice
A large pat of butter
Onion salt to taste
Salt to taste

1 10-ounce package frozen tiny peas
2 tablespoons grated Parmesan cheese

Into the boiling water put the rice, let it cook for about 20 minutes until the rice is al dente—*do not overcook it*. Drain the rice in a colander and rinse with very hot water. After the water has completely drained off, put the large pat of butter onto the rice, and some onion salt (not too much), salt to taste, and keep the rice warm in the oven. Cook the peas according to package instructions, drain the liquid from them, season to taste, and mix into the rice carefully. Sprinkle the grated Parmesan on top of the *risi bisi*. *Serves 4–6.*

Tomato Salad

1 medium-sized ripe tomato per person

Dressing:

2 hard-cooked eggs, mashed
1 small onion, chopped
¼ teaspoon pepper
¼ teaspoon salt
½ teaspoon sugar

1 tablespoon vinegar
½ teaspoon dry mustard
4–5 tablespoons salad oil
Chopped parsley or chives

Spear the tomatoes with a sharp fork and immerse in boiling water for a moment. Allow them to cool, peel them, slice in thick slices, and arrange them, overlapping slightly, on a platter. For the dressing, mix together thoroughly the remaining ingredients except the chopped parsley. Put a little dressing on each tomato slice, and sprinkle with chopped parsley or chives. Let the salad stand for ½ hour before serving. *Makes enough dressing for 4 tomatoes.*

Cucumber Salad
(Gurkensalat)

2 pounds cucumbers	Salt to taste
¼ cup salad oil	White pepper to taste
¼ cup white vinegar mixed with	½–1 cup sour cream
¼ cup water	1 tablespoon snipped dill
2 tablespoons sugar	

Peel the cucumbers and slice them lengthwise, remove the seeds
with a spoon. Slice the cucumbers thinly and place in a glass or
plastic bowl. Add the oil, vinegar, sugar, salt, and pepper. Cover the
bowl tightly and let stand in the refrigerator overnight. Just before
serving, drain the cucumbers in a colander, pressing them slowly

down with a wooden spoon to remove as much liquid as possible. Mix with the sour cream and dill.

The architecture, the historic and artistic traditions, the music, the exhilarating air, and—last but not least—the wines and food

of lovely Salzburg sometimes affect my bride of many years and
me like a powerful magnet, and we rush to the garage of our
small chalet in Switzerland (where we now live in contented retirement) to check gas, oil, water, and tire pressure on our 1968
Mercedes. We load our aged silver-gray poodle, Amos, seventeen
of my dear little wife's bags, without which she cannot do, and
two bags of mine into the car. Then to the *autostrado:* Chiasso,
Milano, Verona, Brenner, Innsbruck, and on to Salzburg to enjoy
the festivals and to eat *Salzburger Nockerln,* a dessert so light, so
lovely, it defies description.

There at the Peterskeller, *Salzburger Nockerln* are always on
the menu. The Peterskeller used to be part of a monastery that is
now open to the public as a restaurant. Unfortunately, they did
not have professional waiters, and lay brothers served the guests.
I am convinced that these good brothers were pious, God-fearing
men, saintly in their devotion to Our Lord, and paragons of obe-
dience to their abbot. But as waiters they were a miserable lot.
The one we drew must have had years of special training and experience in ignoring guests. He was thin as a coatrack, his cassock
floating around his frame like a brown spinnaker. Again and
again he swished past our table, the spinnaker brushing our
chairs, face uplifted, looking far away, preoccupied, and unap-
proachable. Calling, snapping fingers, waving, even whistling, we
could not make him stop long enough to wait on us. Finally, one
in our group got up and, with hands folded as in prayer, blocked
the good lay brother's path and said, *"Herr Ober, Beichten,"*
meaning that he wanted the lay brother to hear confession. The
request startled him. He stopped and informed us that he was not
an ordained priest and, therefore, not empowered to hear confession, a statement that greatly strengthened my trust in the Catho-
lic Church. Touched by the devout attitude of our group, he
stayed long enough to take our orders and even volunteered advice on what to eat and what to avoid that day. When we left he
showed us to the portal and we promised to pray for him.

••◦•▸◦◂•◦••

Salzburger Nockerln are served in most good restaurants in
Austria. The very best I have eaten were at the Goldener Hirsch,
in Salzburg, that famous old hotel close to the Festspielhaus. It is

owned by Countess Walderdorf and her son and caters to the elite of the beautiful people who populate Salzburg during the season. And it's expensive as hell!

Salzburg Soufflé
(Salzburger Nockerln)

6 egg whites	1 tablespoon granulated sugar
5 tablespoons powdered sugar	3 egg yolks
3 tablespoons unsalted butter, softened	1 tablespoon vanilla sugar
	Grated rind of ½ lemon
2 tablespoons milk	Additional powdered sugar

You will need an oval ovenproof dish (not Pyrex) about 10 inches long. Beat the egg whites till they are very stiff. Gradually fold in the powdered sugar and beat till well mixed. In the oval dish put the softened butter, the milk (do not use skim milk), and the granulated sugar, heat over a very low flame till the sugar is melted. Beat the egg yolks and fold them into the egg whites. Add the vanilla sugar and the grated lemon rind. With a large spoon or spatula transfer one third of the mixture to one end of the baking dish, a second third to the middle, and the last third to the other end. Place in a preheated 375° oven, and after 10 minutes the top of the mixture should turn light brown. Before serving, sprinkle a lavish amount of powdered sugar on top and rush the *Nockerln* to the table, where expectant faces and drooling mouths will await the feast. You will be surprised how fast it disappears. After all, it's really nothing but sweet air! As with most good things in life, so with *Salzburger Nockerln*—there are many variations. *Serves 3.* Here is another delicious recipe:

Variation

½ cup butter	10 egg whites
1 cup granulated sugar	¼ cup hot milk
10 egg yolks	2 tablespoons powdered sugar
3 tablespoons flour	

Beat together the butter, sugar, and egg yolks till the mixture is fluffy. Add the flour and mix well. Beat the egg whites till very stiff, then fold them into the egg yolk mixture. Cover the bottom of the oval ovenproof dish with the hot milk, pour in the mixture, and bake in a preheated 350° oven for 10 minutes. Dust the top lavishly with powdered sugar. Serve immediately. *Serves 6.*

His Name Was J.P.

When I first went to Hollywood, it was impressed upon me that the surest and best way on the road to success was with a staff of specialists.

"Let a professional attend to your needs," they kept telling me. "For instance, it's bad form to talk to the studio bosses yourself. They won't respect you if you do. Hire yourself an agent. All you pay him is ten per cent of what you make and he does all your worrying for you.

"Don't attend to all the little business details yourself," they kept harping. "Don't write your own checks and pay the rent and grocery bills yourself. Nobody will respect you if you do. Hire a business manager. All you pay him is five per cent of what you make and you'll never be in trouble.

"And by no means," they implored me, "ever have any personal contact with the press. They despise you if you do. Hire yourself a go-between, a publicity agent."

"How much will he get?" I inquired.

"He will take you for whatever the traffic will bear, and no holds barred."

So I asked around and listened; I wrote down the names of about fifteen publicity agents; I put them all in a hat, closed my eyes, and reached in.

I drew a honey. The name was J.P. I called him on the telephone. He happened *not* to be in conference at that moment, and not tied up during the next hour or so—which was very unusual, he assured me. So he came right over.

"Glad to meet you, Mr. Slo . . . Sla . . . Slu . . . Sli . . . What was that name again?"

"Slezak," I answered. "Walter Slezak."

"Never heard of him," he said with a blank look. "Never ever heard of him. That oughta show you. That name ought to be publicized."

I agreed.

"But don't you worry," he continued. "I am going to take care of that for you. You certainly got yourself the right boy." He slapped me on the back and asked me if I liked scotch. While I fixed him a drink he surveyed the house, made a quick estimate of my financial potentialities, and decided on a direct full-blast frontal attack.

"If I handle you, it won't be cheap," he suddenly yelled. "No, sir-r-r. It'll cost you a potful of gold, but brother, it'll be worth it. It'll be the best investment you ever made. You see, my boy," he laid his hand on my shoulder and assumed a fatherly air, "I'll make your name a household word. Something nobody will be able to do without. Something like Sinatra or Serutan. It's really quite simple if you know the answers, and *brother,* do I know them. Tell me," he challenged, "what would Garbo, Roosevelt, G. B. Shaw, yes, *even* Liberace be without publicity?" He paused to let that thought sink in, but before I had the chance to venture what they would possibly be, he went on. "Tell you what I'll do for you. You sign a contract with me for three years. Yes, sir, two years at least. It takes that long for them to get used to a name like Slezak. By the way . . . Slezak . . . that sounds like a sneeze. You wouldn't consider changing your name, would you?"

I said, "No, I wouldn't."

"Well, then, we'll just have to make the best of it. Now you pay me in advance, but don't expect to see any results for at least three or four months. It takes a long time to get the ball rolling. But once it rolls, brother, do I kick it along."

He jumped to his feet. "We'll have to start our campaign with a bang. With something that will make them sit up and take notice. With something that hits them right between the eyes. Something that spreads your name in headlines across every newspaper in the country."

For a moment he stood still, deep in thought. Then he wheeled around. "I've got it!" he exclaimed. "I'll get you arrested for drunken driving. Wonderful!"

I didn't get the point.

"We'll get a swell picture layout," he continued enthusiastically.

"The officer smelling your breath. You walking the line, arms out-stretched, balancing on one foot. Then a picture of you behind bars. You cry. Yes, sir, you cry like a baby. That ought to get you a lot of sympathy—a big fat guy like you crying. Then we'll photograph you with the judge and mention him by name; he'll like that. He takes away your driver's license. Now you are stuck. You are a pe-destrian. You try to hire a chauffeur, but no dice. They're all in the Army; so what do you do . . . ? You drive to the studio on a bicy-cle. Yes, sir, an old prewar bicycle. We'll get a picture of you from the rear. That ought to make a good comedy shot. And a few days later—while the people are still thinking of you on a bicycle—you get it stolen from right under you. Another headline! And you know who is going to steal it? A kid. A nice, wholesome, freckle-faced kid. You face the kid in court. 'Why did you do it?' you ask him. 'Don't you know it's a sin to steal?' And then again, you cry. Yes, sir, you cry like a baby. As a payoff you let the kid have the bi-cycle so as not to make a thief of him. That ought to get you a lot of sympathy."

J.P. finished his drink and poured himself another one.

"The next thing you know, we'll send you to a swank nightclub. You'll smash a photographer's camera and pick a fight with some celebrity. Maybe Humphrey Bogart, so we'll be sure to make head-lines."

"But I like Humphrey Bogart," I replied.

"What do you want? You want friends or good publicity?"

Ignoring my attempt to argue that point he rolled on. . . . "You'll get knocked down. We'll take a picture of you on the floor surrounded by waiters and a pretty checkroom girl in a low-cut dress leaning over you."

"Is that the right kind of publicity?" I asked carefully.

"My dear boy," he answered rather pompously, "there is only one right kind of publicity, and that's the kind that gets in print and spells out your name again and again and again. It's the constant repetition that does the trick."

It so happened that I, who am and always have been non-belligerent, mild-mannered, and overall lovable, got mixed up in a brouhaha at the Mocambo one night, and—when trying to escape the melee—got socked by the bodyguard of F.S., whose public rela-tions outfit worked faster than J.P., my agent. The next day, while I

was still in bed with an icepack on my head and a half pound of
filet over my left eye, J.P. walked in. His manner was jubilant.
"Brother," he yelled, "brother, what a break we got!"

He threw the morning paper on my bed. I switched on the light,
peeled the filet from my eye, and read:

> *Today's Puzzle: What foreign actor got pinched while driving
> pickled and got socked by F.S. for his obnoxious behavior at the
> Mocambo?*

I have inherited frugality, so that the same evening I put the filet
to good use; I ground it up and prepared a beefsteak tartare.

Beefsteak Tartare

Dry mustard	Capers
Salt	Worcestershire sauce
Freshly ground pepper	Tabasco sauce
1 tablespoon oil	Lawry's seasoned salt
Yolk of 1 egg	Lemon juice
1 or 2 anchovy fillets, mashed	1 pound finely ground filet of
Paprika	beef
Chopped onion	1 teaspoon cognac

Mix the mustard, salt, pepper, oil, and egg yolk well, then add the
remaining ingredients except the beef and the cognac, mix very
well. Then add the beef and mix. Add the cognac and serve on a
dish. *Serves 1 or 2.*

Caviar

In the fall of 1954, I opened in a new musical on Broadway. It was called *Fanny,* and the unforgettable Ezio Pinza was my co-star. At the end of the play I had to die onstage, lying in a bed and wearing a long white nightshirt, and while I was dying Ezio held my hand —and sang. I often thought, What a wonderful way to go—with the timbre of that glorious voice in my ear.

One of the most pleasant aspects of being in a hit show is that one's friends, famous colleagues, and celebrities came backstage after the performance to offer praise, massage one's ego, and spread the kind of sunshine that actors love and need. One evening the Shah of Iran attended a performance with his empress—then it was Soraya—and they were escorted backstage, where photographers, secret service men, and newspapermen were swarming around. Suddenly a man from the State Department, pale and horrified, rushed up to me.

"Mr. Slezak," he gasped, "it is impossible for you, *wearing a nightshirt,* to have your picture taken with the Empress of Persia!"

I turned to the Empress and asked her—in German—if she could possibly survive such a horrifying breach of Etiquette. She laughed, took my arm, and we posed with the rest of the company.

The following evening a small package arrived at my dressing room. It was cold to the touch, weighed about two pounds, and a hot wave of hope flowed instantly through my gastric system. After the last curtain call I rushed home, clutching the package like Rodolfo in Puccini's *La Bohème* held onto Mimi's ice-cold hand, holding it as if it was the Hope Diamond. (I had danced with the Hope Diamond several years before in Denver, Colorado; it was then attached to the narrow breast of Mrs. Evalyn Walsh McLean and is now in the Smithsonian Institution in Washington.)

With trembling hands Kaasi and I opened the present—two
pounds of the finest silver-gray Iranian caviar! We broke open a
bottle of champagne, got some vodka from the freezer, and toasted
the Shah, his empress, the Peacock Throne, the Caspian Sea, and
the sturgeons who had given this delicacy. We did not toast Iranian
oil, because at that time neither of us realized how important it was.

In a serious discussion we toyed with the idea of waking the children and letting them partake of the meal, but we successfully
fought down that rash generous impulse, deciding that they were
still too young to appreciate small fish eggs without shells.

Caviar should be served COLD: thin slices of toasted white
bread, crusts trimmed—topped with spoonfuls of caviar and a few
drops of lemon juice. Then, dear people, close your eyes, fold back
your ears, stop making conversation, concentrate, and gently kiss
every fish egg with your tongue.

There are some people—ill-advised people, I would say—who
consume caviar covered with chopped hard-boiled egg or with
finely chopped onions, some even with capers or with baked potatoes and sour cream. But not I! Give me the simple life: a slice of
toast, a few drops of lemon juice, and LOTS of caviar.

A Yankee in Japan

By a strange piece of luck I got hold of the diary of one B. F. Pinkerton, Lieutenant, U. S. Navy, assigned to participate in the maiden voyage of the cruiser U.S.S. *Abraham Lincoln*. Destination: Nagasaki, Japan. Mission: to spread goodwill!

On March 19 at eight bells the cruiser left the San Francisco naval yard—weather cloudy, wind eighteen miles SSE, sea rough. The diary recalls in dreary nautical language the life on board, with many petty complaints about the food, about standing watch at ungodly hours, and about the nuisance of having to stand up in the officers' mess every time the captain walked in.

On arrival in Nagasaki, Lieutenant Pinkerton put in for extended shore leave. Aware that he cut a handsome figure in his white uniform, he saw himself as a roving Yankee who ventured forth, boldly expecting the fairest of every land to be his reward. He came from a rich family, was not strapped for cash, and so headed for the best, the most exclusive, geisha house. For his companion of the evening he picked an exquisitely painted seventeen-year-old doll who—so the proprietor explained in broken English—was called Cio-Cio-San but answered to the name "Butterfly." Lieutenant Pinkerton was enchanted with her, but the rigors of sitting cross-legged all evening and the complete lack of communication imposed by the language barrier left him unsatisfied.

Tiny Butterfly had a little drum that she tapped gently. She sang little songs in a high-pitched canary voice, making every effort to please. But her ideas of pleasing him were somewhat different from his conception of pleasure. After two hours of drinking tea, nodding approval to her dancing, her drum tapping, her fan waving, and her high-pitched singsong conversation, he left—rather stiff-legged and much slowed down in his roving. In elaborate sign language he indicated that he would return the following evening.

Next day he got in touch with the American Consul, who straightened him out about the instant availability of geishas. They were not, he explained, prostitutes. Being a geisha was an honored profession. At the age of seven they entered a special school where they learned to dance, to play several instruments, to sing and learn a large repertoire of traditional airs, sad ones and ditties full of gaiety, according to the mood of the guest. They were instructed in the art of conversation and learned to perform the intricate tea ceremonies. They were regarded as persons of pleasing accomplishment, and when they reached maturity the geisha house proprietors put them under contract (and mostly managed to keep them in perpetual bondage). Their only escape was marriage.

Lieutenant Pinkerton—that despicable heel—figured that if there were no other way to possess that eighty-seven pounds of luscious delight he would marry the gal, knowing full well that such a union would be meaningless in the United States and that his ship would sail for home port in five weeks *with him on board!*

He returned to the geisha house for three more frustrating evenings, hoping that his desires might be satisfied without the bother of a marriage ceremony. But every time his pantomime became too explicit and his groping hands reached out, little Butterfly managed to flutter away, leaving him sitting cross-legged on the floor. She smiled, she giggled, with dainty fingers she tapped her little drums, and sang and danced from a safe distance.

The American Consul, who regarded the whole thing as a lark, put him in touch with Mr. Goro, a *nakodo* (marriage broker), who promised to make all the arrangements. Lieutenant Pinkerton's diary does not mention what sums of money changed hands in that transaction, but it does note that Mr. Goro was a splendid fellow, helpful, that he also dabbled in real estate and was thus in a position to provide a lovely bungalow, high up on a hill with a breathtaking view of the harbor and completely furnished. Mr. Goro could also provide a maid in residence, a Ms. Suzuki, who had worked only in the best houses, was renowned for being impeccably clean, an outstanding cook, and able to understand and talk the English language.

On the day of the marriage the bride appeared with a large retinue of relatives, including an uncle who conveniently happened to be a Buddhist bonze. He married them in a short ceremony, tea was served to all, the honorable Mr. Goro ushered out the guests, and Lieutenant Pinkerton's long-awaited moment was about to arrive when Ms. Suzuki announced dinner. She had prepared a sumptuous meal.

The next few weeks passed harmoniously. Cio-Cio-San and her new husband mostly kept to their room—honeymooning—and Ms. Suzuki to her cooking. During respites in honeymooning the groom visited Ms. Suzuki's kitchen, making copious notes.

The U.S.S. *Abraham Lincoln* left at its appointed time *with* Lieutenant Pinkerton, who bragged endlessly about his conquest and in his diary he recounted all the details of his brief marital life in disgustingly explicit detail, but—lucky for me—he also noted in equally precise detail the preparation of many of Ms. Suzuki's dishes.

About a year after his return to the States he received a long, newsy letter from the American Consul in Nagasaki: "Little Madame Butterfly," he wrote, "mourned your sudden departure for a full week and then took up with a rich merchant prince, one honorable Mr. Yamadori, who set her up in business. She now owns a restaurant, Chez Butterfly, with Ms. Suzuki as *chef de cuisine*.

The *Guide Michelin* gives Chez Butterfly two and a half stars.

Raw Fish as an Appetizer
(Sashimi)

Any kind of fresh fish fillets—no bones—tuna, flounder, bass, even eel
Soy sauce
Tabasco sauce
Japanese vinegar
Prepared mustard
Horseradish

The fish fillets must be cold. Cut them into strips about 1 inch long and ⅛ to ¼ inch thick. Arrange them on a plate. Place each of the remaining ingredients in its own saucedish. Serve the fish and side dishes so that your guests can dip the fish strip into the accompaniments of their choice. Refreshing and tasty!

Japanese Soup

2 pounds pork tenderloin   3 bunches watercress, coarsely
1½ cups soy sauce   chopped
2½ quarts water

Grind the meat and marinate in the soy sauce 2 hours. Bring
the 2½ quarts of water to a boil, add the marinade and meat, boil
for 3 minutes. Add the watercress and boil at high heat for another
6 minutes. *Serves 8–10.*

Soup with Shrimp

1¼ pounds raw shrimp, shelled   2 tablespoons cornstarch
   and deveined   4 cups beef broth
1 teaspoon salt   4 cups clam juice
¾ tablespoon sugar   ⅓ cup finely sliced mushrooms
1 tablespoon sake   ½ cup green peas
2 cups water

Grind the shrimp in a food mill to a fine paste. Mix that paste with
the salt, sugar, sake, water, and cornstarch. Shape the mixture into
small balls. Now combine the beef broth and clam juice and bring
to a boil. Carefully lay the shrimp balls into the liquid and cook for
10–12 minutes over a very low fire. Then add the mushrooms and
peas and cook for another 5 minutes. *Serves about 8.*

Tempura—A Main Dish

20 medium-sized raw shrimp
7 sea scallops
20 string beans

1 quart corn oil in a deep fryer
Batter (recipe given below)

Shell the shrimp, leaving on the tails, then devein them, rinse, and *dry* them on paper towels. Rinse and *dry* the scallops and string beans. Dip the shrimp, scallops, and string beans individually in the batter, set them gently in the hot oil (it should not be too hot, about 325°, constant heat). When they are golden brown, remove them from the oil and serve piping hot with Tempura Sauce (recipe given below). *Serves 6.*

Tempura Batter

2½ cups flour
3 egg yolks

2 cups cold water

Sift the flour twice. Beat the egg yolks and water together, then gradually add the flour, mix lightly.

Tempura Sauce

1 cup clam juice
⅓ cup soy sauce
⅓ cup sake

3½ teaspoons sugar
4 tablespoons grated white radish
1½ teaspoons powdered ginger

Mix together the clam juice, soy sauce, sake, and sugar. Divide the sauce among 6 small bowls. Just before serving, put a little radish and ginger into each bowl. *Makes 6 small bowls of sauce.*

Celestial Tempura—An Accompaniment

This tempura can be served along with other tempuras; for example, Shrimp Tempura, the recipe immediately below this one.

1 egg yolk	½ cup flour
½ cup ice-cold water	Corn oil for deep frying
1 teaspoon Japanese vinegar	1 medium-sized can mandarin
½ teaspoon salt	orange sections, drained
1 egg white, beaten stiff	

To make a batter, combine the egg yolk, the ½ cup of ice-cold water, vinegar, and salt. Add the beaten egg white and mix. Sift in the flour and stir well with a spoon. Almost fill a deep-frying skillet with corn oil. Dip the oranges one at a time into the batter and drop into the hot oil (about 325°). Never deep-fry more than 4 pieces at a time. Fry until slightly brown. Serve immediately.

Shrimp Tempura

2 eggs, separated	1 cup flour
¾ cup beer	2 pounds raw shrimp, shelled and
1 tablespoon olive oil	deveined
1 tablespoon soy sauce	Corn oil for deep frying
1 teaspoon dry mustard	

Make a batter of the egg yolks, beer, olive oil, soy sauce, mustard, and flour. Then beat the egg whites till they are stiff and fold into the batter. Dip the shrimp individually into the batter and deep-fry in the hot oil (about 325°) for about 4 minutes. Serve immediately. *Serves 8–10.*

Eels on Skewers

3 medium-sized eels   1 tablespoon powdered ginger
Sake   (optional)
Soy sauce

Skin the eels, bone them, and flatten them. Then cut them into
1-inch pieces and skewer them. Marinate them in a mixture of the
sake and soy sauce (add the ginger to the marinade if you wish).
Marinate the eels for 1½ hours, turning them occasionally. Then
broil them at high heat for no more than 5 minutes. Serve immediately with piping hot boiled rice. *Serves 6.*

Japanese Clams

This dish is served as a soup.

30 medium-sized clams   Flour
1 cup sake   Cooking oil
1 cup sweet sherry

Clean the clams thoroughly, place them in a colander, put the colander in a kettle, and over simmering water steam them open,
about 10 minutes. Remove them from the kettle and reserve the
clam broth. Take the clams from the shells, and reserve the shells.
Marinate the clams in a mixture of the sake and sherry for about 2
hours, then strain the marinade into the clam broth. Dredge the
clams in flour, then sauté them lightly in a little cooking oil in a
skillet until they are golden brown on both sides. Add the broth
mixture to the clams and simmer for another 12 minutes. You may
serve the clams in their shells on a dish, or without the shells in a
bowl. *Serves 4–6.*

Sukiyaki

1 pound sirloin
1 soybean cake (optional)
2 cups sliced onions
2 stalks celery, chopped
1 cup chopped Chinese cabbage
1 cup chopped spinach
10 scallions, sliced
1 cup sliced bamboo shoots
1 cup sliced mushrooms
½ cup soy sauce
3 tablespoons light brown sugar

¼ cup sake
½ cup dry sherry
¾ teaspoon monosodium
    glutamate
½ teaspoon pepper
½ cup beef or chicken stock or
    bouillon
Beef suet
¼ cup uncooked vermicelli or
    Japanese noodles
4 eggs

Preparation in the Kitchen:

Cut the sirloin into paper-thin slices against the grain and arrange neatly on a platter. Cut the soybean cake into 1-inch squares and arrange on a large platter with the onions, celery, cabbage, spinach, scallions, bamboo shoots, and mushrooms. Combine the soy sauce, brown sugar, sake, sherry, monosodium glutamate, pepper, and stock and bring to a boil. *Serves 4.*

At the Table:

Use a very large skillet, a large chafing dish, or an electric hibachi. When the skillet is hot, render the suet for a few minutes, quickly fry the meat slices until they are light brown on both sides. Remove them and keep them warm. Pour the sauce into the skillet and bring to a boil. Add all the vegetables except the spinach, and after 2 minutes return the meat to the skillet. Add the spinach last. (Use only a third of these ingredients at a time so that the cooked food will always be fresh and crisp.) Cook for 4–5 minutes, and 3 minutes before serving add the vermicelli. Break each egg into a small bowl, stir with a fork, and dip the pieces of meat into the egg for a second before you eat them. Serve with piping hot dry rice and drink hot sake.

Teriyaki of Beef

1½ pounds filet of beef, sliced
    thin
4 tablespoons soy sauce
4 tablespoons dry sherry

2 teaspoons sake
⅔ tablespoon powdered ginger
2½ tablespoons cooking oil

Marinate the beef slices for 3 hours in a marinade of the soy sauce, sherry, sake, and ginger. Dry the beef with a paper towel, fry on all sides until it is light brown. Serve immediately with hot boiled rice. *Serves 2.*

Pork Cio-Cio-San

1 pound pork tenderloin
Salt and freshly ground pepper
    to taste
2 tablespoons cornstarch
2 eggs

1 teaspoon sake
¾ cup finely ground almonds
¾ cup finely ground peanuts
Oil for frying, about 1–1½ cups

Cut the pork into 2-inch-long strips, salt and pepper them, and sprinkle with cornstarch. In a small bowl, beat the eggs with the sake, then dip the pieces of pork in the eggs. Mix the ground almonds and peanuts together thoroughly, and roll each piece of pork in them. In a skillet, fry the pork *slowly* (so that the nuts won't burn) in the oil. This dish is delicious with a salad or green vegetables. *Serves 2.*

Suzuki's Delight—A Dessert

1 6-ounce can frozen
concentrated pineapple juice
1 6-ounce can frozen
concentrated tangerine juice
2 tablespoons powdered ginger
3 cups water
¾ cup sugar
⅛ teaspoon salt
⅓ cup cornstarch
2½ teaspoons grated lemon rind

3½ teaspoons lemon juice
1 tablespoon butter
1 small can water chestnuts, cut
very fine
Fresh fruit—apples, peaches,
pears, nectarines, or
plums—peeled and sliced or
cut up, or served as a
compote

Mix the juice concentrates with the ginger and the 3 cups of water in a saucepan and bring to a boil. Mix the sugar, salt, and cornstarch in a bowl and slowly add the hot juice mixture, stir. Return the mixture to the saucepan and cook slowly for 3–4 minutes, stirring constantly. Mix in the grated lemon rind, lemon juice, and butter, place in the refrigerator and chill. Then add the water chestnuts, stir. Pour the well-chilled sauce over the prepared fruit. *Makes enough sauce to serve several people.*

Hunting in America

One of the wisest laws ever passed by the government of our two-hundred-and-three-year-old Republic is the law that prohibits game to be sold commercially.

But for *that* law every doe, every buck, every elk, bear, and all our winged friends would have been shot into extinction long ago.

When I hunted game, twenty-five to thirty years ago, there were very few legal requirements for becoming a hunter. In many of the states, the law merely said that you had to be over eighteen years of age and have two dollars for a hunting license. If you fulfilled these prerequisites, you could enter, loaded gun in hand, lands that were not posted and you could aim and shoot at any game that happened to be in season. (Being dressed up in the regalia of a bright red coat and a bright red shirt and a bright red cap would not really prevent, but would merely diminish, the very good chances that you would be shot at.)

In those days, and in most of the states, I believe, you did not have to receive any instruction on how to handle a gun, or have to pass any examination to prove that you knew how to shoot it, or whether you were an accurate shot, or whether you could judge the distances that your bullets could still be dangerous, or whether you could estimate the width of spray of your shotgun pellets.

The law didn't usually ask whether you had been taught and guided by a knowledgeable and experienced sportsman or had just graduated from the shooting gallery in the town's amusement park.

And the law wasn't interested in whether you were the kind of person who could be trusted with a lethal weapon.

Carrying a high-powered gun often changes the personality of men: their dormant cave man instincts awaken and their lust for bringing home a dead deer, strapped to the fender of the car for all the world to see, makes them ignore the rules of conduct our society has developed.

I have noticed that intelligent and cultivated men who would never use swearwords or obscenities change abruptly once they are on a hunting trip. Here they overflow with four-letter words, everything is, "That goddamned THIS and the fucking THAT," and that was twenty to thirty years ago, when these nondescriptive adjectives were not so freely used as they are now, when they confront us daily on the screen, TV, radio, and the other media of communication.

All in all I have wonderful hunting memories. I have met up with some real sportsmen, hunters who would rather pass up a shot than take a chance and cripple the animal. Complete strangers have welcomed me to their camp, and one offered me half his game because I had been skunked that day and had to return home.

But I have also had some unpleasant experiences with meat hunters and armed riffraff.

We were once staying at our farm in Bucks County, Pennsylvania. It was the first day of the deer season. I was out early and got a buck with a clean shot, tied the tag to its antlers, and was about to gut him when three men—two whites and a black—walked up to me and pointed their guns at me.

"Wadda ya doin' with our buck?" the black man asked. "We shot that here bastard an he jes' run over here and fall down."

I stayed calm. "You know that isn't true," I said. "You heard the shot and you came here. Besides," I added, "the land is posted!"

"We see no sign, mista, some son-of-a-bitch musta taken the sign down." They laughed uproariously. I asked them for their hunting licenses. "We left 'em back at the car," he said, grinning, "might lose them here." After a pause he said evenly, "Them woods is mighty dangerous, mista."

I knew I had lost the game *and* the deer but made one last attempt: "What are your names?" I asked.

"Mine's Joe Smith," the black man said, laughing. One of the other two broke in, "And mine's also Joe Smith, and so is my brudder's here. You see, mista," they were now fully enjoying themselves, "we is triplets and our mudder she couldn' think of no udder names," and while he said that he put the finger on the trigger of his gun, still pointing it at me.

The only names I could think of were the dear names of my wife and of my three children. I picked up my gun and walked away, hoping that they wouldn't shoot me in the back. It would have been a "hunting accident"!

Because of lax control meat hunters often get away with murder. They will kill a doe, lay the animal on the luggage rack of their car, then strap an old pair of antlers to the head of the doe, and thus pass the controls of game wardens who are too busy or do not care to check more thoroughly. And later these poachers brag about their cleverness.

While I was playing the Broadway show *My Three Angels* at the Morosco Theatre in New York, in 1953, I spent a Sunday and Monday morning hunting in Connecticut. I was lucky and brought home a large buck.

I named him "Max." I had names for all the deer I shot. Three weeks later, on a Saturday afternoon between the matinee and the evening performances, tables were set up in the basement of our theatre. Our whole cast, the stagehands, electricians, doormen, box office personnel, and ushers stood around, drink in hand, waiting for Max.

At 5:30 P.M. a procession of waiters hurried across the Shubert Alley to our theatre, pushing large service wagons filled with exquisite delicacies. Behind that procession walked, like a pleased mourner, my beloved spouse.

Vincent Sardi, the owner and wonderful host of New York's most famous theatrical restaurant, had given permission to my wife to prepare and roast, in her own inimitable way, my deer in the kitchen of his restaurant, and he catered the rest of the meal.

Word of that culinary event had spread to the other theatres of the district, and soon the curious and the hungry began dropping in. When the bell rang for the evening performance, there was no more Max, just his antlers decorating my dressing room.

My late friend Tom Knudsen, the head of one of California's biggest creameries (Knudsen's velvet cream cheese), owned duck ponds near Bakersfield. His regular shooting companion was Lauritz Melchior, the undisputed greatest Wagnerian tenor of his time. I was often invited to go along.

One morning shortly before dawn we were already crouching in the blinds. The first ducks began to fly over and the hunt was on. Later in the morning they must have realized that unfriendly beings were down below in those camouflaged bushes and they stayed away.

Out came the duck calls!

I reached into my pocket. No duck call. Forgotten in Hollywood. I grew ashamed, despondent, desperate, the only hunter without a duck call! And I began to analyze that call. Soon my lips and my tongue were forming rude sounds: loud and offensive Bronx cheers were floating up in the morning air. They proved to be a powerful attraction for the birds, who, hearing such passionate and novel love calls, flew down toward my blind, sex on their minds.

Even my shooting didn't scare them away. And one by one the other hunters stuck their heads up, looking in my direction and wondering, "What's he using?"

I have since tried to patent this invention, but my lawyer, L. Arnold Weissberger, informed me that the sound was already in public domain.

We usually set the ducks overnight in buttermilk, and they responded gratefully by being extra mild and tender.

Spoiled by frequent good hunts, I became overconfident and invited three friends and their wives to a venison dinner. My wife, more prudent than I, thought that a very rash thing to do, but I grandly set out for the woods, sure that the goddess Diana would be with me again. Well, she must have been busy somewhere else, because I got skunked; rain, rain . . . and when the rain stopped the mosquitoes came out in swarms, finding me delectable. "Venison" avoided me as if someone had given them advance notice where I would be at a given time. After two fruitless and disappointing days I had to return empty-handed to RKO Studios to earn an honest living. But because my gal had a bright idea we didn't call off the dinner.

She figured that, if buttermilk worked with ducks, why not try it on a large leg of lamb, lay it for five days in buttermilk, lard and prepare it like a leg of venison.

Before we sat down to dinner, there was one critical moment, when, forgetting that one of our friends spoke German, I said to my wife, *"Hast Du das Lampl noch begossen?"* ("Did you baste the little lamb?"), but it went unnoticed; and unnoticed went the fact that they ate and enjoyed young mutton. Of course, we never told them.

The Plump Jacques Cousteau

In my study are a few framed mementos of some accomplishments of which I am proud:

1. My Tony Award, for the best star performance in a musical (1954).
2. My pilot's license, which kept me safely in the air for 1,334 hours.
3. Two certificates of occupancy for additions to our house in Hollywood, for which I had drawn the plans and then built with my own fat little hands.
4. My permit to rent or buy and operate scuba diving equipment.

It was during a three-week engagement in San Diego that I met a few divers who raved about the glories that can be experienced underwater. Being of a methodical mind, I looked around for a teacher and found one at the Marine base. He was a diving instructor, a huge tough guy used to shouting commands at his recruits. Once he yelled at me, "Pick up your gear!" and—suddenly remembering that I was a private pupil—added, "Sir."

"Okay. Get into that pool and let's see if you can swim." In my boyhood, when I had learned to swim, the Australian crawl was unknown. "You swim like a frog!" was his disgusted reaction. "I guess I could teach you how to crawl," he said condescendingly, "but with an old fellow like you it would take six months of hard work and then you might only swim ten per cent faster." He looked at my shape and added, "You displace too much water!"

The lessons began with my having to swim the length of the pool *underwater,* carrying twelve pounds of extra weight. "That took you fifty-one seconds," he commented in a disappointed voice. I was then dressed in a wetsuit, with oxygen bottle, mask, and mouth-piece, and tested for buoyancy. It took twenty-seven pounds of weights to keep me floating underwater, which added to his disappointment. "If you should ever have to throw off your weights, you'll shoot up like a cork!" Then he shook his head. "Are you sure you want to learn how to dive?" I was sure!

After two weeks of training, getting to know and respect the equipment, I was allowed out into the ocean. This time he had another fellow with him, also a Marine instructor. We swam fifteen feet underwater, then suddenly I could get no more air; they had cut off my oxygen supply. Then my mask was ripped off, my fins removed, and my weight belt snatched off. He had been right: I did shoot up like a cork, but I had passed the test. "Good thing you don't panic," was his only reaction. I was proud when he said in a patronizing manner, "I guess you're okay." I begged him to go out with me once more because I wanted to learn how to shoot fish. We swam to a cove where there was an abundance of fish around us. I aimed at one below me, shot off my spear . . . right through my instructor's fin. "For that I'd have washed you out!" he snarled later. But he gave me good advice: in shark-infested waters NEVER hang the fish you shoot on your belt. And to demonstrate the danger, he had brought with him a hundred-foot line. On the end he hung freshly shot mackerel and we watched small sharks go for the bleeding fish—ignoring us. After a few tries I gave up shooting fish. It's too easy. They swim up to your mask and all but nuzzle you (maybe they thought I was just another overgrown jellyfish).

Most of my diving was done around Santa Catalina Island. There I found a small cove with just a few sport boats lying at anchor. In California the catching of lobsters by any means other than by hand is illegal. These clever crustaceans will hide in crevices under rocks, and many a fisherman who has reached into those hollows has had his hands mauled by moray eels that also inhabit these vacuities. But the lawbreakers are inventive. They have constructed a device for grabbing lobsters: a two-foot-long clutch hook, very practical and highly illegal. When swimming under sport boats you can see these hooks hanging down in the water, the lines cut when a patrol boat arrives and later picked up again from the bottom.

The sport I liked best was gathering abalone. These delicious shelled creatures rest on rocks, their camouflage making them hard to see. They have to be approached with caution, because if *they* see you first they will clamp tightly to the rock, almost impossible to break loose. Their suction power is fantastic, and one has to slip the knife quickly between the shell and the rock and lift them off. After that you just place them against your wet-suit and they will stick to your body.

The most beautiful part of diving was to sit quietly twenty feet below on the ground, watch the sunlight break, playing through the huge weaving kelp trees, and admire the fish.

In California there is a beautiful species called the garibaldi perch: it is the color of pure gold (not red, like most goldfish). They swim in company with six-inch-long, light blue, completely transparent fish. They are tame and curious, an unforgettable sight. And a beautiful memory, because at my age I no longer fly or dive.

Clam Chowder

¼ pound salt pork, cut into
  small cubes
3 medium-sized onions, sliced
  thin
8 medium-sized potatoes, sliced
  thin
1 teaspoon salt

Freshly ground pepper to taste
1 pint clam juice
1 quart shucked clams (measured
  after shucking), chopped
  fine
1 quart HEATED milk (do
  NOT boil)

Fry the salt pork in a large kettle over low flame until it is brown
and crisp and all fat is cooked out. Remove the pieces of salt pork.
Add the onions, fry until golden, then add the potatoes, salt, and
pepper, and mix gently. Add the clam juice and enough water to
barely cover. Add the clams and cook the mixture until the potatoes
are tender—NOT mushy. Add the quart of rich hot milk. Use only
a wooden spoon to stir. *Serves 8–10.*

Sautéed Abalone Steaks

6 abalone muscles
Butter
Salt and freshly ground pepper to taste

Slice and pound 6 abalone muscles into thin steaks (best use a
wooden mallet); they should be about ¼ inch thick. Sauté them in
a large skillet in a generous amount of butter for less than a minute
on each side. Add salt and pepper to taste. Serve immediately on
warmed plates. *Serves 6.*

Breaded Abalone Steaks

6 abalone muscles
Flour
1–2 eggs, beaten

Salt
Bread crumbs
Butter or oil

Slice and pound the 6 abalone muscles into thin steaks (best use a wooden mallet); they should be ¼ inch thick. Drag the pounded steaks through flour, then through the beaten eggs, to which have been added a few drops of water and some salt. Then coat the steaks with bread crumbs, patting the crumbs deeply into the steaks. Sauté the steaks in an ample amount of butter or oil for no more than a minute on each side. Serve immediately on heated plates. *Serves 6.*

Baked Bluefish

A 4–6-pound bluefish
Generous sprinklings of garlic
   powder and onion powder
Salt and freshly ground pepper
   to taste

1 stick of butter
Finely chopped parsley
Lemon wedges for garnish

Clean and split the fish, rub it well with garlic and onion powders, salt, and pepper, and place it in an oiled pan. Put lots of squares of butter on top of the fish, bake it in a preheated oven at high heat—about 425° to 450°—till tender, about 25 minutes. Sprinkle generously with the parsley. Serve immediately on a heated plate with lemon wedges. If you have small bluefish, do not split them, but place them next to each other in the pan, covered with lots of butter. Baking time will be shorter. *Serves 4.*

Striped Bass in Foil

1 5-pound bass
Salt and white pepper
Onion powder
2 carrots, sliced
3 stalks celery, sliced
1 medium-sized onion, sliced
3 sprigs parsley

1 bay leaf
¼ teaspoon thyme
1 teaspoon salt
10 peppercorns
½ cup chicken bouillon
½ cup dry white wine
Mayonnaise

Rub the fish with salt, white pepper, and onion powder. Make a court bouillon by simmering, tightly covered, the remaining ingredients except the mayonnaise, for 15–20 minutes. Spread out a large piece of aluminum foil and place half the vegetables on it. Place the bass on the vegetables, cover with the rest of the vegetables and all the liquid. Close the foil into a neat package, and try to make it air-tight. Bake in a preheated 350° oven for 30 minutes. Remove the fish from the foil and place it on a warm platter. Discard the vegetables. Serve it immediately with a bowl of mayonnaise. *Serves 4.*

On the Chicken à la King Circuit

I was laid up with a broken ankle, my right leg encased in tons of plaster of Paris, when one of our neighbors in Larchmont, New York, dropped in to console me in my enforced idleness.

"Why don't you put your gift of gab," as she ironically called my loquacity, "to work and write a lecture? It would keep your mind occupied, you could do it on crutches, and it might bring in some money!"

The last thought sparked the creation of a discourse named "Show Business Is No Business" (title: courtesy of the wonderful Al Hirschfeld).

In it I followed the progress of a new play from the moment it came out of the author's typewriter. He had taken two years to write it, did seventeen rewrites, and now felt that it was fit to be seen and heard by the world at large. He handed the manuscript to a play broker who peddled it around producers' offices. It was finally optioned, bought, the angels were asked to finance it; then came the casting, the rehearsals, the usual horrors of the out-of-town tryout. And at last the New York premiere and the opening-night party at Sardi's. It was a story I knew well (having been in a few flops), and luckily I was able to try out my talk in New Jersey. It was well received, an agent began booking me, I became a traveling salesman in lecturing. I enjoyed it tremendously, met many interesting and nice people, and soon learned some of the pitfalls of that profession.

First, NEVER go to a cocktail party before your talk! You might have one, or two, or too many and your speech would get blurred. In a small town in the Middle West a lady who was president of the women's club that had hired me insisted that I go to a cocktail

party. She, the poor dear, had drunk a little more than I. When she stepped onto the platform to introduce me, she was stoned. She weaved onto that stage, held onto the lectern, and began, "Walter Slezak was born at an early age," then she smiled uncertainly and slowly slid to the floor. I walked onto the stage, picked her up, dragged her off, returned, and assured the audience that she had indeed told the truth: I WAS born at an early age.

The second taboo is never to accept the kind invitation of the sponsors to pick you up at the station and take you to your hotel. Invariably a sweet old lady will meet you, and a detour to her house will be arranged "to meet the folks for a friendly chat," and there goes the rest you need after your trip, because lecturing is hard work. A lot of concentration is needed to keep a large audience of strangers quiet and entertained while you are standing on a platform all by your lonely self, with no props, no scenery, and no costumes.

Whenever I had time between shows, TV, or films I went on the road for a spell. In October 1962 I was booked for two sessions in Hawaii. My wife wanted to come along, so we met in Honolulu at the airport, arriving in two different planes. Several years earlier we had made our wills and our lawyer had asked, "You two are always flying around in your small plane; if both of you should perish, do you want your three children to go to one family or will you split them up in three different homes?" That day we grew up. I sold the plane and we never flew together again, not even in a commercial carrier.

My first lecture in Hawaii was on Saturday the twentieth of October. The next day friends of ours who own pineapple plantations gave a luau for us, which was a fabulous and indescribable feast. And on Monday the twenty-second we were privileged to use the Admiral's launch to see Pearl Harbor.

"Want to hear the President's speech?" the pilot of the launch

asked. He turned on the radio: we heard John Kennedy's voice warning the Russians that unless they respected the blockade of Cuba and removed their ballistic missiles, atomic war might break out. We listened, mute with shock and fear; all we could think of was to get home to the children in Larchmont. We begged the pilot to call the airport on his radio and find out if we could get on an afternoon flight back to the mainland. We were in luck and drove directly to the airport, leaving all our luggage at the hotel. We had just enough time to call my sponsor, cancel my next lecture, and make the flight.

In the plane we were sitting together, holding on to each other's hands, when the stewardess leaned over: "The folks in Row 7 would like to know if you two are newlyweds."

"No," my wife answered, "just happy to be together—and very scared."

The Fat Nureyev

I must confess to a deplorable cultural shortcoming: I am not—repeat, NOT—a balletomane. I am fully aware that this admission stamps me as an uncivilized, boorish clod, but I cannot help it. Boys in tights with padded jockstraps leave me as cold as thin, muscular women do, especially when they are prancing about on their toes, wearing starched tutus.

I do admire their acrobatic feats, their high leaps, their passionate dedication, their great discipline, and their eternal hope. But of all the performing arts, classical ballet does not turn me on.

True, I have been moved by individual performances such as that of Pavlova as the Dying Swan, and of Serge Lifar in *The Afternoon of a Faun*, but I look at ballet as a realist. When the premier danseur, with great hesitancy, dares to touch the hand of the prima ballerina and she retreats with trembling reluctance, with fluttering hands, in shock at that manly presence, and then half a minute later he reaches up her crotch, lifts her high into the air, and carries her around the stage like the Olympic messenger bringing the lighted torch into the stadium, that is when hilarity overcomes me.

About twelve years ago my wife dragged me to a performance of a Russian dance troupe; it was a poor road company—the prima ballerina, still wearing braces on her teeth, was unsure of what she was doing, and it brought to my mind the Players Restaurant in Hollywood. There, much to the annoyance of the customers, every evening a young man tapped away at a cembalo. I complained to the maître and learned that, as the young man did not have a cembalo of his own, his uncle, who was the proprietor of the place, let him practice in the restaurant.

In Berlin—the year was 1924—when I was still a very young and a very *thin* leading man, an independent film company approached me to play the lead in their forthcoming production, and they wanted to know if I had ever studied ballet.

I needed the job badly, so I quickly arranged my feet in the second position, made a few graceful movements with my hands, held my head high, and, with a haughty expression, informed them that I had studied at the ballet school of the Vienna Opera.

They were thrilled! Before signing the contract I took the precaution of asking for the schedule. I was in luck: all the outdoor shots would be filmed first, then all the scenes in the studio with the ballet sequences last. I knew that by then they would have so much film on me that they couldn't replace me and reshoot all my scenes. So I promptly signed, knocked on wood, and prayed to my guardian angel to be near when the big éclat came.

The day before the ballet rehearsals were to begin, I arranged a "bad fall," resulting in "strained muscles and pain in my back." After the first wave of dismay had rolled over the producers, they decided to have my dancing done by a double, a professional ballet dancer, about the same build as mine, wearing identical costume and blond wig! He danced all the long shots, and a few times the camera picked up my face in a close-up, usually after some great terpsichorean feat, a pirouette or a spectacular entrechat, and there was I, looking triumphant, my eyes radiant with accomplishment brilliantly executed, and so on and on through the whole ballet. At the end I took the curtain calls, throwing kisses at an unseen audience, accepting roses with faked surprise and overdone modesty.

That was my first brush with ballet. The second came forty years later. I was invited to "dance" the part of Dr. Coppelius in a ballet film that was to be shot in Madrid. I then weighed about 265 pounds, a benign hippopotamus hiding the graceful dancer that was underneath. I danced it for comedy, parodied all positions, and had great fun. The film was an outstanding flop but for being an outrageous ham I got great notices.

But the most memorable thing was that Dr. Coppelius introduced me to Madrid.

I still drool when I think of the food we had there. We were living in a hotel, unable to cook ourselves, but I collected recipes, came back with a whole folder, and tried them out after we got home. There was only one dish I could not reproduce: suckling pig as they prepare it in Spain, because in our economy-minded society

they do not slaughter a pig that is only a few weeks old, whereas in Spain they slit it lengthwise, break it open, and lay it on the grill.

The best restaurant in Madrid is Horcher's. There food is regarded as a religion. I used to know old man Horcher from my days in Berlin before I came to America in 1930. It was a great restaurant then and is even greater today.

"The proof of a dish is its memory," he used to say.

Avocado Appetizer

3 ripe avocados
1 cup plain yogurt
2 tablespoons dry sherry
Salt and white pepper to taste
A dash of cayenne pepper
Juice of ½ lemon

2 tablespoons ketchup
¾ cup cubed cooked ham
¾ cup canned peas
2 red peppers, sliced julienne
Heavy cream
1½ dozen shelled pistachio nuts

Cut the avocados in half lengthwise, remove the pits, carefully cut out the meat, cube it in small pieces, and mix well with the next 6 ingredients. Mince the ham, peas, and peppers and add enough heavy cream to make a smooth mixture, then add to the avocado mixture. Fill the empty shells, garnish with the pistachios, and serve very cold. *Serves 6.*

Avocado Soup

4 ripe medium-sized avocados
4 cups milk or bouillon
Salt and freshly ground pepper
    to taste

½ teaspoon curry powder

Peel the avocados and purée the meat in a blender; chill. Mix well with the remaining ingredients. Be sure to prepare the soup just before serving, or it will turn brown. Serve this delicious soup very cold in chilled soup plates. *Serves 4.*

Gazpacho

3 medium-sized ripe tomatoes,
  peeled and chopped
1 stalk celery, chopped
1 bell pepper, seeded and
  chopped
1 cucumber, peeled and diced
2 cloves garlic, crushed
1 tablespoon chopped parsley
2 tablespoons mayonnaise
1 cup tomato juice

2 cups chicken stock
Juice of 1 lemon
1/4 teaspoon hot pepper sauce
Salt and freshly ground pepper
  to taste
Garnish made of additional
  cucumbers, tomatoes, onions,
  and bell peppers—all
  chopped
Croutons

Run all of the vegetables and the mayonnaise in a blender. Stir in the tomato juice, chicken stock, lemon juice, hot pepper sauce, salt, and pepper. Chill until VERY cold. Pour into chilled cups, serve immediately, and accompany with any of the vegetables given in the list of ingredients as garnish. Serve with croutons. *Makes about 9 cups.*

David's Paella

This recipe should be done in five stages in order to avoid the three cardinal sins in the preparation of paella: soggy rice, mushy vegetables, and dry, rubbery meat or seafood. By sautéing the rice first and then cooking it carefully, it remains *al dente*. The vegetables, if they are cooked properly, remain colorful and crisp, and because the pork is not boiled with the rice, it also retains its flavor. Finally, it is clearly impossible to cook shrimp and lobster simultaneously for the same length of time and not have the shrimp overcooked and the lobster raw. *Serves 12.*

First Stage: Rice
This step should be done 3 hours ahead of time.

1/2 cup Mazola oil
6 cups long-grained rice
5 cups boiling water

10 cubes chicken bouillon
3 mussels, carefully cleaned
A pinch of powdered saffron

Using a large cast-iron skillet, heat the oil on high heat and brown the rice quickly (using 2 cups of rice at a time). Add all the browned rice to a large saucepan containing the 5 cups of boiling water and the dissolved bouillon cubes, the mussels, and the saffron. Lower the heat to a simmer, cover, and check the rice after 7 minutes; it has to be *al dente* (it cooked fast because it was sautéed first). Drain off any excess liquid. Set aside.

Second Stage: Meat
This step should also be done 3 hours ahead of time.

¼ cup oil	A pinch of powdered saffron
12 medium-sized onions, chopped	3 pounds pork fillets, cut into
2 hot peppers, chopped	strips ½ by 1½ inches
5 cloves garlic, chopped fine	3 whole chicken breasts, cut in
Salt and freshly ground pepper	half
to taste	2 tablespoons butter

Heat the oil in a large skillet, add the onions, hot peppers, garlic, salt, pepper, and saffron. Sauté till onions are transparent. Add the pork, which should be browned but not boiled in the onion juices (using high heat avoids this). Do not cover. In a separate skillet fry the chicken breasts in the butter till they are golden brown on each side. Bone the breasts, cube the meat, and set it aside.

Third Stage: Seafood

6 cups boiling water	2 pounds lobster tails, shelled
9 mussels, carefully cleaned	3 pounds jumbo shrimp, shelled
12 clams, carefully cleaned	and deveined

Pour the boiling water into a kettle, place a colander over it, add the mussels and clams, cover the kettle, and steam for 5 minutes. Add the lobster, each tail cut into 3 pieces, and after 10 minutes add the shrimp, letting them steam for 3 to 4 minutes or till the shrimp turn pink. Set aside and keep warm.

Fourth Stage: Hot Sauce

Make this sauce—for brave ones—5 hours ahead of time.

1 pork chop, diced	*3 hot peppers*
2 clams, shelled	*2 cloves garlic*
1 mussel, shelled	*Salt and freshly ground pepper*
3 cubes chicken bouillon	*to taste*
½ cup V-8 juice	

Put all the ingredients in a medium-sized saucepan, simmer for 20 minutes, set aside, covered.

Fifth Stage: Vegetables

2 pounds whole mushrooms	*12 green peppers, cut into strips*
½ cup olive oil	*Salt to taste and lots of freshly*
3 bunches scallions, cut into	*ground pepper*
2-inch lengths, including the	*3 hot peppers*
green parts	*3 cloves garlic, peeled*
12 red sweet peppers, cut into	
strips	

Clean the mushrooms and leave whole. Heat the olive oil in a large paella pan, add the scallions, red sweet peppers, green peppers, salt, and pepper. Now squeeze the hot peppers and the garlic through a garlic press and add to the vegetables. Place the paella pan in a preheated 400° oven for about 30 minutes, stirring frequently (the point is to keep the vegetables crisp). This should be done just before serving. Now add the rice, pork, chicken, and seafood to the vegetables, mix well, and place in a hot oven till heated through. Serve the hot sauce separately.

Sangría

1½ bottles of good red wine,	*3 plums, halved*
preferably Burgundy	*1–2 ounces brandy*
2 limes, sliced	*¾ cup berries*
2 oranges, sliced	*Sugar to taste*
2 peaches, quartered	*1 small bottle soda water*

Mix the wine, limes, oranges, peaches, plums, and brandy. Leave them in the refrigerator for 4 hours. Then add the berries and sugar to taste. Add the small bottle of soda water. Serve very cold. *Serves about 8.*

Touring by Bus

"Wouldn't it be wonderful if we could take a trip someday, just the two of us, without arriving in a different town every afternoon, without checking in and unpacking in a strange hotel, without your having to put on make-up every night, worrying about business at the box office and about giving a good performance? Without our sleeping in unfamiliar beds and seeing the face of a new waiter every morning when he pushes in the breakfast table?"

This deep heartfelt sigh was emitted by my wife toward the end of our long road tour with William Goldman's beautiful play *The Lion in Winter*. We had crisscrossed the United States from New York to Maine, Florida to Wisconsin, Louisiana to Texas, from California to Canada. It was hard work, mostly one-night stands. For the longer stretches we went by air; for the short hops (under 250 miles a day) we traveled in our own bus with a special compartment for myself, my wife, and our silver-gray poodle Amos. We performed in all sorts of halls and theaters, in anything that had a large enough seating capacity and sufficient space for our elaborate set, which was mounted on a revolving platform.

Nevertheless, it was a wonderful way to discover America. We played at many of this country's great universities, some with theaters with up-to-date technical equipment that would put to shame many a Broadway playhouse. The huge number of students these schools can house, teach, and graduate into the pool of our intellectual and economic society is incredible; the wealth of these institutions—acquired by endowments and bequests—is amazing, and the student bodies are marvelous audiences, quick on the uptake and highly critical. During the tour we had some anxious moments: the turntable, a construction with a will of its own, refused to turn;

our bus got stuck for two hours on the highway because a truck and trailer had overturned, thereby blocking the road and endangering our evening's performance.

In Denver I was walking our dog in front of our hotel, the dog off the leash, when he saw a Greyhound bus and, thinking that it was our bus, jumped in. The doors closed and, disregarding my agonized screams, the bus pulled out. I threw myself into a taxi, it took us over three miles to catch up with the bus and—after much pointing and yelling—to bring him to a stop. I retrieved our four-legged friend, raced back to town just in time for the rising curtain!

In Montreal our tour came to an end and we flew back to our home in Switzerland. In many of the cities and towns we had visited I was able to get a few recipes.

Hot Crab Spread Eleonore

8 ounces cream cheese
1 tablespoon milk
2 tablespoons Lea & Perrins
    Worcestershire sauce
1 7½-ounce can crab meat,
    drained and flaked

2 tablespoons chopped scallion
2 tablespoons slivered almonds
Chopped parsley for garnish

Mix the first 3 ingredients well, then add the crab meat and the chopped scallion. Place in an 8-inch pie plate, sprinkle the slivered almonds around the edge of the pie plate. Bake in a preheated 350° oven for 15 minutes. At serving time sprinkle chopped parsley around the center. Keep the spread warm after serving. *Serves 8–10.*

Meat Ball Appetizers

2 pounds ground beef
1 large onion, grated

1 egg, lightly beaten
Oil for frying

Mix the first 3 ingredients and shape them into small balls, brown them all over in the oil, and then drop them into the sauce:

Sauce:

1½ cups chili sauce
Juice of 1 lemon

1 cup grape jelly

Combine the ingredients, place over low heat, and let meat balls simmer till they are hot. Serve immediately and keep hot. *Makes about 50 small meat balls.*

Sweet and Sour Cocktail Sausages

¼ cup prepared mustard
1 cup currant jelly
1 pound frankfurters, sliced
    diagonally, or Vienna
    sausages, whole or halved

Mix the mustard and jelly in a chafing dish, add the sausages, heat, and serve. *Recipe yields about 1¼ cups cocktail sauce.*

Curried Seafood Dip

2 8-ounce packages cream
    cheese
¼ pound sharp Cheddar cheese,
    grated
1 small wedge Roquefort cheese
1 teaspoon garlic salt
½ teaspoon curry powder
2 tablespoons Lea & Perrins
    Worcestershire sauce

1 teaspoon paprika
1 tablespoon mayonnaise
1 tablespoon lemon juice
1 7½-ounce can lobster or
    shrimp, chopped
Light cream

Combine all ingredients except the seafood and cream, mix well until smooth, mix in the seafood, adding cream if necessary for the right consistency for a dip. Chill for several hours or overnight. *Makes about 2½ cups.*

Avocado Dip

2 8-ounce packages cream cheese,
    softened
2 ripe, soft avocados, peeled and
    mashed
1 small ripe tomato, chopped fine

1 tablespoon minced scallion
1 tablespoon lemon juice
Salt and freshly ground pepper
    to taste

Mix all the ingredients well, cover tightly so as to prevent avocado from darkening, refrigerate till well chilled. *Makes 2 cups.*

Dill Dip for Vegetables

1 cup mayonnaise
1 cup sour cream
1 tablespoon minced onion
1 tablespoon minced parsley

1 teaspoon dried dill
1 teaspoon Spice Islands Beau
Monde seasoning

Mix all the ingredients thoroughly, refrigerate for several hours before serving. *Makes a generous 2 cups of dip.*

With this dip you can use such raw vegetables as:

Carrot strips
Cucumbers, peeled and cut in strips
Cherry tomatoes
Zucchini, raw, sliced
Broccoli, raw, cut into flowerets
Cauliflower, raw, cut into flowerets
Radishes
Mushroom caps
Celery stalks
Scallions

Another Dip for Vegetables

1 hard-cooked egg, chopped
4–5 scallions, chopped
1 cup mayonnaise
2 teaspoons lemon juice

1 scant teaspoon curry powder
1 scant teaspoon powdered ginger
½ teaspoon salt

Place all the ingredients in a blender and blend at high speed till very smooth. Serve with cut-up raw vegetables such as cauliflower, zucchini, turnips, celery, carrots. Delicious! *Makes 1½ cups.*

Beet Hors d'Oeuvres

Using a small-sized melon ball cutter, scoop out small depressions in the tops of small canned beets. Pat the shells dry with paper towels. Fill with a mixture made of:

Sour cream   Chopped sweet or dill pickles
Minced chives

Kaasi Lobster Soup

⅓ cup oil   1 cup dry Sauterne
2 medium-sized onions, chopped   6 cups chicken bouillon
1 medium-sized leek, carefully   ½ teaspoon paprika
    washed, chopped fine   2 tablespoons minced parsley
1 clove garlic, chopped fine   ½ pound canned lobster meat
4 large ripe tomatoes, chopped   ½ pound cooked, shelled,
    fine   deveined shrimp
A pinch of powdered saffron   Salt and freshly ground pepper
1 bay leaf   to taste

Heat the oil in a large, heavy kettle, sauté the onions, leek, and garlic in it till soft. Add the tomatoes, saffron, bay leaf, and wine, let cook till the tomatoes are soft, constantly adding bouillon. Add the paprika, parsley, lobster meat (including its liquid), and shrimp. Let stand in the refrigerator for 12 hours. Remove the bay leaf. Before serving, heat the soup well and add salt and pepper to taste. Serves 6.

Kaasi Borscht

2½–3 cups canned beets   ½ teaspoon salt
⅓ cup chopped onion   3 tablespoons cider vinegar
1 medium-sized cucumber, peeled   Buttermilk
    and chopped   ½ cup sour cream
2½ cups chicken bouillon   Chopped fresh dill

Drain the beets, reserving the liquid. Put into a blender the beets, onion, cucumber, and beet juice, remove from the blender. Add the bouillon, heat thoroughly, but do not boil. Add the salt and vinegar and allow to cool. Let this stand overnight in the refrigerator. Add enough buttermilk to give the consistency of a creamed soup. Serve well chilled in cups, top with a tablespoonful of sour cream, sprinkled with a little chopped dill. This delicious soup is even better served with Ham Crescents (see Index). *Serves 8–10.*

Vichyssoise

3 medium-sized leeks, washed very carefully and chopped fine	4 stalks celery plus greens, chopped fine
1 medium-sized onion, chopped fine	4 cups chicken bouillon
	1 pint light cream
2 tablespoons butter or margarine	Salt and freshly ground pepper to taste
4 medium-sized potatoes, sliced thin	A dash of nutmeg
	Minced chives for garnish

Sauté the leeks and onion in the butter till they are soft; do NOT brown them. Add the potatoes, celery, and bouillon, simmer, covered, till the vegetables are tender, about 30 minutes. Put the mixture in a blender and process at low speed for about 1 minute. Remove from the blender, add the cream, salt, pepper, and nutmeg to taste. This superb soup should be served very cold in very cold cups or soup bowls. Sprinkle with minced chives for flavor and garnish. *Serves 8–10.*

Lobster Adi

6 quarts water	1 bunch of dill with stems
4 tablespoons sea salt or kosher salt	4 live lobsters, each 1–1½ pounds
2 bottles light beer	

Put the 6 quarts of water, salt, beer, and dill in a large kettle, bring to a boil, and cook over a medium flame for 20–25 minutes. Bring

the water to a rolling boil, add the lobsters—*their backs down*—
cover the kettle. When the water boils again, cook the lobsters over
a medium flame for 8 minutes. Take the kettle off the flame,
remove the lobsters, and break off the claws. Clean each lobster by
splitting it in half lengthwise and taking out the stomach. Serve immediately with hot lemon butter or dill mayonnaise, each given
below:

Hot Lemon Butter

> ¾ cup melted butter
> Juice of 1 lemon

Mix the ingredients and serve hot.

Dill Mayonnaise

1 cup mayonnaise	A small bunch of fresh dill,
2 tablespoons sour cream	chopped fine
Juice of ½ lemon	

Mix the ingredients thoroughly. Make this mayonnaise well ahead
of time. *Serves 4.*

Roast Duck

1 duck, 4–5 pounds	2½ teaspoons sherry
4 tablespoons chopped onion	¾ cup soy sauce
4 tablespoons chopped celery	1 tablespoon salt
½ teaspoon cinnamon	1 teaspoon white pepper
½ cup Sambuca (Italian liqueur	Paprika
available in the U.S.)	⅔ cup warmed honey
½ teaspoon honey	2 tablespoons vinegar
2½ teaspoons sugar	

This is quite an undertaking! First have a needle and strong thread
ready. Clean the bird, removing as much fat as possible from the inside and end. Tie the neck securely. Put in a saucepan the onion,
celery, cinnamon, Sambuca, the ½ teaspoon honey, sugar, sherry,
and all but 1 tablespoon of the soy sauce, and bring mixture to a
boil. Pour the sauce into the rear opening of the duck and sew up.

Rub the outside of the duck with the salt, white pepper, and a little paprika. Place the duck, breast up, on a rack in a roasting pan, roast in a preheated 500° oven for ½ hour. Pour off the fat. Mix the warmed honey, vinegar, and remaining soy sauce, pour this over the duck so that it is covered with sauce. Continue to roast the duck at 350° now, for 2 hours, basting and brushing frequently with the honey mixture. Before serving, remove the thread. Pour the juices into a gravy boat as sauce. This is very good served with piping hot boiled rice and with Plum Sauce (recipe follows). *Serves 3–4.*

Plum Sauce

1 cup mango chutney   2 teaspoons light brown sugar
2 cups red plum jelly   2 teaspoons dry red wine

Strain the chutney and chop the chunks into fine pieces. Mix the jelly with the brown sugar and wine, add to the chutney. Cover and let stand at room temperature for at least an hour. For an easy sauce: Put all the ingredients in a blender and blend at high speed till the sauce is smooth. *Makes 3 cups.*

Roast Chicken with Stuffing

This roast chicken has fine rich flavor.

A 3½-pound roasting chicken   Paprika
Salt and freshly ground pepper   ½ tablespoon dried onion
Onion salt   1 tablespoon butter or margarine

Rub the chicken with salt, pepper, onion salt, and paprika. Into the
cavity put the minced dried onion, rub the outside well with the
butter. Wrap the bird in aluminum foil and let it rest in the refrigerator for 6 hours. Let it stand at room temperature for 2 hours. At
the end of that time prepare the stuffing:

1 large onion, chopped fine   1 egg, beaten
1 tablespoon margarine   Salt and freshly ground pepper
½ pound chicken livers, chopped   to taste
4 slices white bread, soaked in   ¼ cup minced parsley
    water and pressed dry   Chicken bouillon

Sauté the onion in the margarine till golden brown. Add the livers
and cook for another ½ minute. Tear the bread into tiny pieces and
add, along with the egg, salt, pepper, and parsley, mix well. Fill the
cavity of the bird with this mixture, place it in a roasting pan,
breast up, in a preheated 350° oven. The first ½ hour of roasting
should be done uncovered; baste frequently, adding a little water if
necessary. Then roast, covered, for 1–1½ hours until done. Make a
rich gravy from the drippings, adding a little bouillon or water for
the right consistency. Serves 3–4.

Chicken with Cheese Sauce

3 whole chicken breasts, cut in   4 tablespoons butter
    half   1 cup milk
1½ teaspoons salt   3 tablespoons grated Parmesan
¼ teaspoon white pepper   cheese
3 tablespoons flour   2 tablespoons grated Swiss cheese

Bone the chicken breasts, place each half between 2 pieces of wax paper, and pound very thin. Rub each half with a mixture of the salt, white pepper, and 2 tablespoons of the flour. Melt 3 tablespoons of the butter in a large skillet and brown the chicken in it, skin side first. Transfer it to a large shallow baking dish. Melt the remaining tablespoon of butter in a saucepan, blend in the rest of the flour. Gradually add the milk, stirring steadily to the boiling point, cook over low heat for 5 minutes. Mix in the cheeses until they are melted, pour over the chicken breasts. Bake in a preheated 350° oven till the top is golden brown. *Serves 6.*

Chicken on the Spit

2 whole broiling chickens
¼ cup water
¼ pound butter

2 tablespoons A.1. sauce
4 squirts of Tabasco sauce

Place the birds on the spit of a rotisserie, making sure that they are well balanced. Do not salt them. Let them turn over charcoal heat, preferably, for ½ hour. Meanwhile make the sauce: Bring to a boil the water, butter, A.1. sauce, and Tabasco sauce. Baste the chicken frequently with the sauce after they have turned for that first ½ hour, and roast them till they are done—about 1 to 1¼ hours. *Serves 4–6.*

Cherry Sauce to Glacé a Pork Roast

This will make enough sauce to glacé a 3- to 4-pound boned pork rib roast, with some sauce left over for serving with the roast at the table.

1½ cups cherry preserves	2 tablespoons light corn syrup
3 tablespoons finely chopped	1 tablespoon white vinegar
toasted almonds	1 tablespoon water

Combine the ingredients in a saucepan and simmer for 15 minutes. Thirty minutes before the roast is done, baste it with cherry sauce, and repeat 10 to 15 minutes. At the table serve the remaining sauce hot. *Serves about 8.*

Filets Mignons with Ginger Rice

2 filets mignons, each ½ inch	1 cup raw rice
thick	4 cups boiling salted water
¼ teaspoon salt	Salt
¼ teaspoon nutmeg	Onion salt
1 egg, lightly beaten with ½	2 tablespoons butter
teaspoon water	½ teaspoon curry powder
3 tablespoons finely chopped,	1 tablespoon ginger preserves
unpeeled almonds	¼ cup butter

Into the filet mignons rub the salt and nutmeg. Dip them in the egg, then coat them with the shredded almonds. Pound the filets lightly with the flat side of a large knife so that the almonds will stick to them. Set them aside while preparing the rice. Cook the rice in the 4 cups of boiling water for about 20 minutes. Place it in a colander, rinse with hot water, shake the water out completely, and let the rice dry out. Season it with salt and onion salt to taste. Melt the 2 tablespoons of butter in a saucepan, add the curry powder, and stir. Add the rice and mix well. Add the ginger preserves and mix well again. Cover tightly and keep the rice warm. Melt the ¼ cup of butter in a skillet and fry the filets at medium heat for 3 minutes on each side. Place the rice on a heated platter, set the filets on the rice, and serve immediately. (Instead of ginger preserves, you can use a tablespoon of chutney. In that case the dish is called Filets Mignons with Chutney Rice.) The dish is excellent. *Serves 2.*

Lore's Veal Schnitzel

6 slices cooked ham	*Vegetable shortening or butter*
6 thin slices veal	*for sautéing*
Flour	*6 tablespoons tomato purée*
2 eggs, beaten	*Grated Parmesan cheese*
Bread crumbs	

Place a slice of ham on each veal slice, bread each double slice by dipping in flour, egg, then bread crumbs. Sauté the double slices lightly on each side in a generous amount of shortening or butter. Place these cutlets next to each other (not on top of) in a shallow square casserole. Spread a tablespoon of tomato purée on each cutlet, cover each with grated cheese, and bake in a preheated medium oven for 20 minutes or till the cheese has melted completely. Serve immediately on heated plates. *Serves 6.*

Roast Leg of Lamb

1 6-pound leg of lamb	*Garlic cloves, peeled and cut into*
Salt	*little spikes*
Pepper	*1 cup apple juice*
Onion powder	*Flour*
Paprika	*Chicken bouillon*
Worcestershire sauce	

Rub the lamb with salt, pepper, onion powder, paprika, and Worcestershire sauce. Insert the garlic spikes into vertical slits in the meat. Wrap the leg in wax paper and set aside for 8 hours. Place in a roasting pan, pour over it a cup of apple juice, and roast for 1½ to 2 hours in a preheated 350° oven, basting frequently. When the roast is done, remove it from the pan to make the gravy, pour off as much of the apple juice as possible, discard it. Thicken the drippings with a little flour and add enough bouillon to give desired consistency. Cook and stir over a low flame. Let the lamb stand for 15 minutes before slicing. *Serves 6.*

Swedish Meat Balls

1 pound lean beef	*1 medium-sized onion, chopped*
¾ pound veal	*fine*
¼ pound pork	*2 tablespoons butter*
¼ teaspoon each of pepper,	*1 cup bread crumbs*
powdered ginger, allspice,	*1 cup milk*
and nutmeg	*2 eggs*

Grind together the beef, veal, and pork 3 times, using the fine blade of the grinder. Add the pepper, ginger, allspice, and nutmeg, mix lightly. Sauté the onions in the butter till they are soft, mix well with the bread crumbs, milk, and eggs. Combine the meat and bread-crumb mixtures, mix well, shape into small balls about 1½ inches in diameter (about 50 balls), place in a single layer in a lightly greased baking pan. Bake in a preheated 350° oven for 20 minutes, turning the balls once so as to brown on both sides. Remove the meat balls to a serving dish and keep them warm. Meanwhile prepare a brown gravy:

For the gravy:

¼ cup butter	*Salt and freshly ground pepper*
¼ cup flour	*to taste*
4 cups chicken bouillon	

Melt the butter in the pan in which the meat balls were baked, stir and mix with the drippings. Blend in the flour to make a smooth paste, then stir in the bouillon. Cook over medium heat, stirring, till the gravy thickens and comes to a boil, then strain the gravy. Season to taste and pour over the meat balls. *Serves 6–8.*

Veal Cutlets Oscar Scandia

4 veal cutlets (top leg of veal)	*Béarnaise sauce (recipe given*
2 tablespoons butter	*below)*
12 cooked asparagus	*Paprika*
½ cup crab meat	*¼ cup grated Parmesan cheese*

Sauté the cutlets in the butter, place them side by side in a baking dish. Cover each one with 3 cooked asparagus. On top of them place a spoonful of crab meat and top with about 3 tablespoons of béarnaise sauce on each cutlet. Dust with paprika, sprinkle the cutlets with the grated Parmesan, and heat for a few minutes under the broiler. Serve immediately. *Serves 4.*

Béarnaise sauce:

4 egg yolks	*2 teaspoons minced shallots*
¾ cup chicken bouillon	*¼ teaspoon pepper*
1 teaspoon cornstarch	*Lemon juice to taste*
Salt to taste	
4 tablespoons melted butter	
2 teaspoons chopped fresh	
tarragon or 1 teaspoon dried	
tarragon	

Put in a blender the egg yolks, bouillon, cornstarch, and salt, blend at low speed for 1 minute. Then pour into the top of a double boiler over barely simmering water, heat while beating and add the 4 tablespoons of butter bit by bit. After the sauce has thickened, return it to the blender and add the tarragon, shallots, pepper, and lemon juice to taste. Blend for a few seconds. Return the sauce to the double boiler, cover, and place over warm water till serving time.

Sweet and Sour Frankfurters

1 large can pineapple chunks in
    unsweetened juice
¼ cup light brown sugar, firmly
    packed
2 tablespoons cornstarch
¼ cup vinegar
4 green onions (tops included),
    cut in julienne strips
1 tablespoon soy sauce

½ tablespoon salt
1 pound frankfurters cut in
    quarters lengthwise(!)
1 small can water chestnuts, cut
    in half
2 tablespoons minced bell pepper
2 medium-sized tomatoes, cut in
    wedges

Drain the pineapple chunks, reserving the juice. Combine the brown sugar and the cornstarch, stir in the pineapple juice, vinegar, onions, soy sauce, and salt, cook over low heat, stirring constantly, until the sauce is thick. Boil for 2 minutes, then carefully stir in the frankfurters, water chestnuts, and bell pepper. Top with the tomato wedges. Heat to serving temperature. Serve over piping hot rice. *Serves 6.*

Ham Crescents

¾ cup chopped boiled ham
¼ cup grated Parmesan cheese
Enough butter to hold chopped
    ham and Parmesan cheese
    together

1 cup flour
¼ cup butter
¼ cup cream cheese

Mix the ham, Parmesan cheese, and butter to make a paste. Set aside. Make a dough from the flour, ¼ cup butter, and cream cheese, chill for 1 hour. Roll out the dough thinly on a heavily floured board, cut out 3-inch triangles, and place a heaping teaspoonful of the paste in each triangle. Roll each triangle, starting at a broad side, and bend into a crescent. Place them on a buttered cookie sheet and bake in a preheated 350° oven for 15–20 minutes.

You may brush the crescents with beaten egg yolk before baking to give them a glaze finish. *Makes 12–15 crescents.*

Welsh Rabbit

2 tablespoons Lea & Perrins
　　Worcestershire sauce
½ teaspoon dry mustard
A dash of cayenne pepper
A dash of paprika

½ cup beer or ale
¾ pound sharp Cheddar cheese,
　　grated
4 pieces of freshly made toast

Mix the first 4 ingredients in a skillet and turn on low heat. Slowly add the beer. DO NOT BOIL IT. Add the cheese gradually and stir till it is melted. Serve very hot on toast. Very tasty. *Serves 4.*

Noodle Pudding

½ pound wide noodles
2 sticks butter, melted
4 eggs
½ teaspoon salt
3 tablespoons light brown sugar
1 pint sour cream

3 teaspoons vanilla extract
1 large can fruit cocktail, drained
1 cup raisins
1 cup grated coconut
1½ cups Raisin Bran

Cook the noodles in plenty of boiling salted water till they are done. Mix half the butter with the eggs, salt, brown sugar, sour cream, vanilla, fruit cocktail, and raisins. Add this mixture to the noodles, put into a baking dish. Put the remaining butter in a saucepan and add the coconut and Raisin Bran, brown them slightly, and spoon them over the noodles. Bake in a preheated 350° oven for 45 minutes. This pudding goes extremely well with baked or boiled ham. *Serves 4–6.*

Rice Pilaf

1 quart water
2 tablespoons pickling spices
A dash of powdered saffron
1 small onion, chopped
1 cup butter or margarine

1 teaspoon salt
2 cups uncooked rice
½ cup almonds, blanched
½ cup raisins

Combine the water and pickling spices in a large saucepan, bring to a boil and cook, covered, for 1 hour. Remove the pickling spices, add the saffron to the water, and let boil for another minute. Sauté the onion in the butter till it is soft. Add the salt and rice and cook slowly, stirring, till the rice is lightly browned. Add the rice to the saffron water and bring to a boil. Add the almonds and raisins. Cover tightly and cook over a low flame till the rice is done —about 20 minutes. Serve it immediately. *Serves 4–6.*

Fried Zucchini

2 medium-sized zucchini
1 egg, beaten with a little water
   till foamy

Bread crumbs
Crisco for frying

Wash and scrub the zucchini and cut them into ½-inch slices. Dip the slices into the egg, then the bread crumbs, patting the crumbs well into the zucchini slices. Fry them in Crisco, turning them once. Drain them on paper towels and serve immediately. Delicious! Underripe tomatoes can be prepared the same way and are equally good. *Serves 4.*

Churchill Salad

1 pound beets without tops
1½ teaspoons salt
2 tablespoons prepared French
    mustard
1 teaspoon wine vinegar
Salt to taste

½ teaspoon freshly ground white
    (or black) pepper
½ cup olive oil
¾ cup heavy cream
Parsley for garnish

Place the beets in a heavy saucepan with enough water to cover, add the salt, and bring to a boil, simmer for 45 minutes or till the beets are tender. Drain them and let cool. Skin them and slice about ¼ inch thick. Combine the mustard, vinegar, salt, and pepper, and mix together with a whip. Slowly add the olive oil, beating constantly till fairly thick, then mix the cream in well. Pour this dressing over the beets and toss very carefully so as not to break up the slices. Garnish with parsley. *Serves 6.*

Curried Macaroni Salad

1 cup mayonnaise
3 teaspoons curry powder
2 tablespoons lemon juice
½ cup chopped radishes
1 medium-sized cucumber
    (unpeeled), chopped

¼ cup chopped bell pepper
¼ cup chopped celery
1½ cups cooked macaroni shells

Blend the first 3 ingredients well. Mix the remaining ingredients, add the dressing, mix well, chill, and serve. *Serves about 4.*

Greek Salad

1 clove garlic, peeled
Shredded salad greens
Tomato slices
Cucumber slices
Bell peppers, cut julienne
Chopped scallions
Chopped parsley

Small pieces of celery stalks
Chopped celery leaves
Goat cheese (feta)
Vinegar
Corn oil
A sprinkle of sugar

Run the garlic around the inside of a salad bowl, toss in the vegetables, crumble some goat cheese into the bowl, add vinegar to taste, corn oil, and a sprinkle of sugar. Toss well.

Honolulu Salad with Ham

½ cup mayonnaise
2 tablespoons sweet pickle relish
1 tablespoon prepared
    horseradish
1 tablespoon prepared mustard
1½ cups diced ham

1 medium-sized can pineapple
    chunks, well drained
Salad greens torn into bite-sized
    pieces
¼ cup chopped bell peppers

For the dressing, combine the first 4 ingredients, chill well. Separately chill the ham, pineapple, salad greens, and chopped bell pepper. At serving time add the dressing, toss well. *Serves 2–4.*

Hawaiian Cucumber

¼ cup rice wine vinegar if
    available (or other wine
    vinegar)
2 tablespoons water
½ teaspoon sugar

2 tablespoons freshly grated
    gingerroot
2 cups diced cucumbers (not
    peeled)

Into a salad bowl put the vinegar, water, sugar, and gingerroot, mix well. Add the cucumbers and toss. Serve well chilled. *Serves about 4.*

Jackie's Salad with Ham

5 medium-sized potatoes, peeled,
    boiled, and diced
1 bunch scallions, chopped
1 small can beets, chopped
4 small sour pickles, sliced thin
½ pound boiled ham, chopped
1 cup mayonnaise

Salt and freshly ground pepper
    to taste
10 hard-cooked eggs coarsely
    chopped, except 2, which
    are sliced and used as
    garnish
Paprika

Mix the first 8 ingredients very carefully. Garnish the salad with the
2 sliced hard-cooked eggs, sprinkled with a little more salt and
pepper and with paprika. Make the salad at least 8 hours (better a
full day) before serving time. *Serves 6.*

Hawaiian Punch

⅓ cup lemon juice
⅓ cup pineapple juice
⅓ cup orange juice

2 ounces Bacardi rum
1 ounce cognac

Mix the ingredients in a cocktail shaker and serve with or without
ice cubes. Very refreshing and cooling. *Serves 1–2.*

Guardian Angels

I really believe in guardian angels. With the hectic life we have led, our dear angel must have worked overtime many a day. But faithfully he stuck to us, stayed around day and night, at home and in foreign lands. He certainly came along on our first real vacation, a trip to Bangkok and Hong Kong.

To arrange our journey, we chose a well-known Swiss travel agency that specialized in transporting hordes of tourists all over the world. Air fare, hotel, and ground travel were included in the price of the package. In Zurich we boarded a plane filled to the brim with pleasure-seekers. Our first refueling stop was Teheran, where the airport was crammed with crates and boxes all marked "IBM," and these were surrounded by swarms of heavily armed, fierce-looking security guards.

In Bangkok clutching our health certificates, which solemnly attested that we were immune to cholera and smallpox, we passed customs, hopeful that our luggage would be among the mountains of bags and suitcases piled on top of each other. We boarded a large bus, happy to be in Thailand. During the lengthy ride into town our travel consultant briefed and warned us: beware of phony guides. They might lure us to places of ill-repute where we could be robbed or even killed; beware of fortunetellers and be as rude to them as possible (he never told us why) ; always take the excursion buses of *his* company, as only *they* would take us to the honest and reliable stores where Thai silk and jewelry could be bought at reasonable prices, but, he went on, it was still a good idea to bargain (he never mentioned that he or his company might get a commission on every purchase).

Then he told us, with a smirk on his face, about the great pleasures provided by the famous Bangkok massage salons:

"Gentlemen, you enter a glass enclosure where beautiful Thai girls are seated. It is a one-way glass. *They* cannot see *you*, but *you* are able to calmly pick the 'physiotherapist' "—here he laughed at his own joke—"that your body desires."

He mentioned the going rates and how much to tip the "masseuse" for services beyond the call of duty. "The hotel clerk will advise you as to which establishment to patronize," he added, leaving us gentlemen with a warm feeling of being in secure hands.

Our luggage was miraculously deposited in our rooms. A small, neat Thai servant entered, folded his hands as if in prayer, and bowed. "I am your loom boy," he announced. When he returned with the four extra pillows I had requested, he stacked them on my bed, one on top of the other, then stepped back and doubled with laughter. He was a jolly little fellow, spoke English fairly well, and urged us to use only the Shinawa excursion buses because one of his brothers was a driver and *he* would take care of us. He also recommended a restaurant that belonged to his uncle, "with velly clean ladies' looms."

We were booked to see the klongs (canals) the next morning, but we canceled out—too tired from the long flight.

Friends in Lugano, Switzerland, had written to their friends in Bangkok, and it was because of their charming hospitality that we didn't have to join the group of noisy vacationers in the "company bus" (the one that would stop at the reliable and honest stores, and would keep stopping and stopping until everyone finally had made purchases).

We saw the loveliest, most graceful Thai girls performing traditional dances in their gorgeous costumes, we saw all the wonderful temples, and we were ushered through the King's palace, where Anna and the King of Siam had educational problems with his many children. We dined at, among other places, the Thai Tong, where our choice of several fish and crustaceas was prepared in a wicker basket immersed in steam. We met many Thai people and came to admire their serene outlook on life, their wise moderation in matters sacred and secular.

We were taken to Wat Trimitr and saw the "golden Buddha." About fifteen years ago, during a real estate transaction, the owner removed from his property a heavy worthless cement figure. During the removal the figure was dropped; it broke open and revealed a solid gold Buddha. In the fifteenth century, when that peaceful little country was threatened by war, monks had covered their treasure with cement. Apparently, all who knew about that well-guarded

secret were killed, and it was not until the accident occurred that this national treasure was discovered.

In Bangkok I looked up a friend of olden times. Her hair was now white, but the eyes and spirit were young, funny, and impertinent. It was she who took us on the trip we had canceled the morning after our arrival, a beautiful boat ride through the klongs—a maze of interlocking canals where a floating market of hundreds of small craft loaded with farm produce, fruit, vegetables, meats, spices, and wondrous flowers, ply their trade to people who live along the canals in houses standing on piles and stilts. It was an unforgettable sight.

In Hong Kong, a huge metropolis with squalor and riches side by side, we ate the best, the very, very best Chinese dinner imaginable, at the Mandarin Hotel. But when I asked them for their recipes, suddenly they could no longer understand English and answered in Chinese.

From Hong Kong we returned to Thailand and there rejoined our group for the flight to Zurich. An ambulance drew up to the plane, and a lady was carried up and deposited in the seat next to us. She was heavily bandaged, with one arm in a cast, and she told us that she had been on the boat ride through the klongs (the one we missed) when their boat had been rammed by a motor launch and capsized. One elderly lady had died instantly, her head had made contact with the propeller, and everybody had been dumped into the dirty brown water. Some who couldn't swim nearly drowned, and everything they carried—wallets, binoculars, and glasses, money and traveler's checks, jewelry and cameras—was LOST. The bandaged passenger had had to spend nineteen days in the hospital until she was pronounced well enough to travel.

That day we thanked our angel from the bottom of our hearts for holding his wings over us!

Truite au Bleu

The best, the tenderest, the gentlest fish in *truite au bleu* . . . that delectable aquatic friend.

I hereby *forbid* you to use frozen trout. The trout *must* be alive. Have ready a rapidly boiling court bouillon in a large skillet or fish poacher, and kill the fish with a short, hard blow on the head. When you clean it, take care not to handle it too much, because it's the slimy surface of the fish that will later produce the lively blue color. Now gently lay the dear departed in the court bouillon, remove the skillet immediately from the fire. It should steep for seven to eight minutes, according to size. You have my permission to sing *"An einem Bächlein helle . . ."* from *"Die Forelle,"* the famous trout song of Franz Schubert, but it is not absolutely necessary.

After many years as a trout fisherman and as a trout eaterman, it behooves me, in all modesty, to claim that I have perfected the art of properly preparing trout to its highest peak. I am right-handed, so I lay the trout with its head to the left on a warm plate. I now address it with reverence, as you would a golf ball at a championship match, and gaze with pleasure at the lovely blue color and the red dots. Don't gaze too long, because the fish might get cold. I now insert a fish knife near the gills and gently lift the skin toward the tail end. Be most careful not to touch the underlying meat. After having removed the skin, I draw the fish knife tenderly along the middle of the trout and lift the meat of the upper part away from me and place it on another warm plate. I now attack the lower part of the trout, being very careful to lift the meat off the bones, so I do not wind up with a mouthful of fishbones. I then turn the fish around! (When I am in a restaurant or when my little wife is watching, I use a knife and fork, but if I am alone I grab the fish by its head and tail and just flip it on its other side.) I now repeat the performance, and—on my knees—please don't forget to take out the cheeks, for they are the choicest parts of a trout. All this should be done fast and elegantly, so the meat won't get cold. Have ready hot melted butter, boiled new potatoes, and just a spinkling of minced parsley. If you feel the natural urge to have a second or third trout, be patient, for they should be freshly steeped. Serve them with a light white wine.

When I was young, a *long long* time ago, I often camped in the Sierra Nevada next to trout streams. To crawl out of your warm sleeping bag, catch a wriggling fish, and panfry it is quite a good breakfast, but it's nowhere as delicate as *truite au bleu*. My tent and my sleeping bag are gone—today I am a spoiled old Sybarite who craves a comfortable bed, soft mattress, three pillows, and next to the bed a telephone so I can call for nourishment anytime starvation is grinning in my face. No more Wild West for me!

Switzerland—Die Schweiz,
La Suisse, La Svizzera

I had always planned to retire at the age of sixty-five. I worked toward that goal, aware that retirement should be a self-willed action. Actors in particular always have to be aware that, with advancing age and the constant demand for new faces, their chances of remaining part of the scene will slowly diminish.

For me to stop acting and to remain in the United States, a land where I had been part of all the media of entertainment since 1930, was unthinkable. I knew damn well that if I stayed on I would still buy *Variety* every Wednesday to find out what was going on, and scan all the theatrical pages and columns for new projects in my field. I knew that every time I saw a show, turned on the TV set, or went to a movie the tiny worm of the actor's vanity would gnaw on my insides: "*I* could have played that part," "*I* might have been right for that role," and the result would be pain and disappointment.

An unemployed old actor, when asked why he wasn't working, answered, "I have passed on the torch to the younger generation." And to forestall my ever making such a remark, I moved to Europe. *There* I can be retired—in *America* I might be unemployed.

Switzerland has acquired an unfortunate international image. So many stories about the gnomes of Zurich, about numbered accounts that hide supposedly ill-gotten funds, have overshadowed the virtues of that lovely land, the oldest TRUE democracy in existence since the year 1291.

We rented a modest house in a small community near Zurich,

that beautiful cosmopolitan city with its excellent theaters, good opera, and many museums, and art galleries.

We found that the locals in our small village, though very fond of tourists, were rather reserved toward us, maybe because we had trouble understanding their peculiar dialect, Schwyzerdütsch. Not that they were unable to speak proper German, mind you, but it seemed to be too much trouble. The Schwyzerdütsch are known for their deliberate, unhurried ways. I knew a man who had had a nervous breakdown in Bern. The hotel called in a renowned physician. After a lengthy examination he spoke: "Yes . . . it is serious. You'd be well advised to stay in your room, preferably darkened. Avoid the intake of food; do not smoke or consume alcoholic beverages; abstain from relations with women. And, *most important,* keep yourself entertained."

Frugality is their key word: a woman saw an old man bending down and pulling up grass from between the cobblestones: "What are you doing, my good man?" she asked. "Lady, I am taking this grass home and will make soup. You see, I have no money to buy anything else."

"Do you mean to say that you have no money *at all?*" she asked in an incredulous voice.

"No, dear lady, NO money."

"Why, that's terrible," she said with deep sympathy, "then you will have to touch the *principal!*"

A very staid Swiss banker once told me, "To live off one's interest is being a spendthrift. One should live off one's *compound* interest!"

A lady who lived in Thun told me the following story. She had gone to a dry goods store. "I would like to buy six buttons for my husband's pants," she said. The salesgirl stared at her and after a long pause said:

"That's not possible."

"Why not?" the lady asked, amused.

"Because it's not possible," was the same answer.

The girl thought awhile and then said, "I'll ask the manager."

She went to the back of the store and disappeared behind a curtain. After a while the manager peeked out from behind the curtain

and he looked strangely at the lady who wanted to buy buttons for her husband's pants. The girl returned and said with finality:

"It's not possible."

"But why not? There must be a reason." The lady was becoming impatient.

"Because," answered the girl, "we only sell buttons by the dozen."

"Then please give me a half-dozen," said the lady.

"Gladly," answered the girl, and brought the buttons.

Zurich is bursting with superb restaurants; there anyone's tastes can be satisfied. Our favorite is the old Kronenhalle, the meeting place after the opera and theatre. The owners have always been art collectors, and it is possible—and most pleasant—to sit and dine under an original Picasso, a Van Gogh, a Chagall, or a work of some other great master. The food is excellent and relatively reasonable. The same waitresses have been there for decades and know nearly all their customers by name: Lilli is in charge of actors and writers; Elsa takes care of painters. The groups are seated separately, and when celebrities like the late Carl Zuckmayer, Max Frisch, or Friedrich Dürrenmatt want to dine without being stared at, there are rooms on the second floor that offer privacy. Erich Kaestner, the famous writer, supped there before he went back to Germany at the beginning of World War II, and when he returned to the Kronenhalle in 1946, Lilli said, "Mr. Kaestner, the last time you were here you forgot this," and she handed him, properly wrapped, his hat.

Lucerne has the greatest Chinese restaurant this side of the Ming dynasty. It is called Li Tai Pe, and the owner is Mr. Chi, who was once adjutant to Chiang Kai-shek and somehow felt that he might have a more tranquil, better, and more sheltered life as a restaurateur. So he opened his temple of heavenly eating in the Altstadt— the same place the great Richard Wagner used to visit while he bemoaned his exile in Switzerland.

In Switzerland the banks help immeasurably in their client's daily problems. The Swiss Fruit Growers' Association and the Kantonalbank were generous with recipes for this book.

We own a small house above Lugano—with a breathtaking view of the Alps. The house has been expanded to fit our needs; it contains my books and memorabilia and those of my father's long and illustrious career. On the lower floor, my wife, who has become a renowned ceramist, has her studio, with her potter's wheel, kiln, spray booth, and her ceramic trophies.

We think that the Ticino is the nicest part of Switzerland—not only because WE live there, but because of its climate, the beauty of the countryside, our many friends, and the convivial southern atmosphere.

As landowners and permanent residents, we join in the shouts of joy and happiness when on Labor Day all the tourists, who have been loud and boisterous and who have occupied all the parking places, disappear like a nightmare.

DIE SCHWEIZ

Peasant Bread
(Puurebrot)

1 pound flour	1 teaspoon sugar
1 teaspoon salt	1¼ cups lukewarm water
½ cake of yeast	1 small potato

Sift the flour and salt into a mixing bowl. Dissolve the yeast and sugar in the lukewarm water, stir until completely dissolved, add to the flour. Peel and grate the potato to make ⅓ cup, add to the flour mixture. Mix well, knead the dough, cover with a moist towel, and let it rise to double its bulk. Form a round loaf, lay it on a buttered pan, cut a pattern of 1-inch squares into the top with a sharp knife. Sprinkle the loaf with a little flour and set it aside in a cool place for 1 hour. Bake in a preheated 350° oven for 50 to 55 minutes. *Makes 1 loaf.*

Kappel Milk Soup
(Kappeler Milchsuppe)

Kappel is a small village in Switzerland.

2½ cups milk	3 egg yolks
½ teaspoon salt	½ cup heavy cream
A pinch of nutmeg	Seasoning salt to taste
1 bay leaf	Freshly ground pepper to taste
1 clove	Croutons for garnish

In a saucepan heat the milk, salt, nutmeg, bay leaf, and clove for a few minutes, stirring constantly. In a bowl beat the egg yolks and cream till foamy, then stir in the milk. Return to the saucepan, bring close to the boiling point, stirring steadily. Add the seasoning salt and pepper. Remove the bay leaf and clove. Pour the soup into warmed soup bowls, sprinkle croutons on the top, and serve immediately. *Serves 4.*

Pot Roast for a Wedding Party
(Betzholzer Hoochsig Aesse)

2 tablespoons oil	½ cup bouillon
1½ pounds beef for pot roast, larded (if your butcher cannot lard the meat, use 3 strips of bacon)	Seasoning salt to taste
	2 onion halves, each stuck with a clove
	¾ pound carrots, diced
Salt and freshly ground pepper to taste	2 stalks celery, sliced
	1 leek, sliced
¼ teaspoon nutmeg	1 cup cooked peas
2 tablespoons flour	1 cup sautéed sliced mushrooms
1½ cups red wine	3–4 tablespoons heavy cream or sour cream
2 tablespoons tomato paste	

Heat the oil in a roasting pan that has a cover and brown the roast lightly on all sides. Sprinkle with salt, pepper, and nutmeg. Remove the meat from the pan and keep it warm. Brown the flour in the juices, add the wine, and cook slowly, constantly stirring, till the sauce thickens. Add the tomato paste, bouillon, and seasoning salt, let simmer for a few minutes. Return the meat to the pan (if it was not larded, cover the top with the strips of bacon). Add the onion halves, cover the pan tightly, and roast in a preheated 350° oven for 1¾ hours, basting frequently. Add the carrots, celery, and leek, roast for another 30–40 minutes or till the meat is tender. If the liquid has evaporated, add more bouillon. Heat the peas and mushrooms in their liquid and keep them warm. Remove the roast from the pan, slice it thinly, and arrange on a heated platter. Discard the onion and surround the meat with the other vegetables. Add either heavy cream or sour cream to the roasting pan, mix well, heat, and pour over the meat slices. Excellent with piping hot mashed potatoes. *Serves 4.*

Boiled Beef, Zurich Style
(Boelefleisch)

2–3 medium-sized onions, sliced
3 tablespoons butter or margarine
1–1½ pounds leftover boiled
    beef, sliced
1½ tablespoons flour
1 cup dry white wine

1–1½ cups bouillon
Salt and freshly ground pepper
    to taste
Nutmeg to taste
1–2 tablespoons heavy cream

Sauté the onions in the butter, then add the beef and simmer for a few minutes. Add the flour, wine, bouillon, salt, pepper, and nutmeg, and cook for about 20 minutes at low heat. Add the cream at the last minute, stir. Serve with piping hot mashed potatoes or boiled noodles, and with a fresh green salad. *Serves 3–4.*

Stuffed Breast of Veal
(Gefuehlte Kalbsbrust)

Stuffing:

1 roll, cut into small pieces,
    soaked in ¼ cup milk, then
    pressed dry
¼ pound ground veal
¼ pound ground pork
1 medium-sized onion, chopped
    fine
¾ cup diced cooked ham
1 tablespoon finely chopped
    parsley

2 tablespoons flour
1 egg
1 tablespoon cognac or dry white
    wine
¼ cup cooked ham cut into
    small pieces
Salt, freshly ground pepper, and
    seasoning salt to taste

Roast:

A breast of veal, 3–4 pounds
    (have your butcher cut a
    pocket in the breast)
Salt, pepper, and nutmeg
1 tablespoon oil

1 cup white wine
1 cup (approximately) chicken
    bouillon or consommé
Cornstarch or flour for thickening
    gravy

Mix all the stuffing ingredients with a fork and stuff the veal breast pocket. Sew the opening or fasten with skewers. Rub the meat with salt, pepper, and nutmeg. Heat the 1 tablespoon of oil in a roasting pan, place the veal in it—sunny side up—and roast, uncovered, in a preheated 350° oven for 40 minutes. Add ½ cup of the wine and a little bouillon, cover the pan, and roast for another 20 minutes. Then add another ½ cup of wine and the remaining bouillon, and roast for another 50–60 minutes, basting frequently. Skim the fat from the drippings, add more wine or bouillon if more liquid is needed, and thicken with cornstarch or flour. Cut the veal in long crosswise slices and serve with the hot gravy. This is delicious. *Serves 4–6.*

Veal, Zurich Style
(Zürcher Geschnetzeltes)

3 tablespoons oil
1½ pounds veal cut into strips
    ½ by 1 inch
Salt and pepper
1 scant cup sliced mushrooms
1 medium-sized onion, chopped
    fine

1 tablespoon flour mixed with a
    pinch of nutmeg
½ cup dry white wine
¼ –⅓ cup bouillon
½ –⅔ cup heavy cream
Salt, pepper, and Lawry's
    seasoning salt to taste

Heat the oil in a skillet, add the veal, and sauté quickly until light brown. Remove it from the skillet, season it lightly with salt and pepper, cover, and keep it warm in a deep plate set over hot water. Add the mushrooms and onion to the skillet and sauté for a few minutes. Sprinkle with the flour and add the white wine, stirring. Add the bouillon, let cook for a few more minutes. Add the cream, salt, pepper, and seasoning salt, stir. Return the meat to the sauce, heat, and serve immediately. This dish is delicious when served with a Potato Pancake, Swiss Style (see Index), and a crisp green salad. *Serves about 3.*

Veal Kidneys Kronenhalle
(Rognons Flambés Kronenhalle)

A well-known restaurant in Zurich, the Kronenhalle serves this excellent dish.

4 veal kidneys	2½ tablespoons cognac
Lemon juice	¼ cup heavy cream
¼ cup butter	½ teaspoon dry mustard
¼ cup chopped scallions	Salt and freshly ground pepper
A pinch of sage	to taste
A pinch of oregano	Chopped parsley for garnish

Peel off the outer fat and the thin membrane of the kidneys, cut out the fat and tubes underneath, slice them thinly, then soak them in a mixture of equal parts lemon juice and water for 1 hour. Remove them and wipe dry. Melt the butter in a skillet, add the scallions, sage, and oregano, and sauté the scallions till they are tender. Add the kidneys and cook over moderate heat till they are lightly browned, 2–3 minutes. Heat the cognac, add it to the kidneys, and ignite. When the flame has died down, add the heavy cream, which has been mixed with the mustard, and cook for 1 minute, or till the sauce thickens. Season with the salt and pepper, stir, and sprinkle with chopped parsley. This dish is superb when served with piping hot rice. *Serves 4–6.*

Pork, Rafzerfelder Style
(Schweinsteak, Rafzerfelder Art)

Marinade

1 cup dry red wine	3 peppercorns, crushed
½ cup sour cream	Lawry's seasoning salt to taste
¼ teaspoon each of rosemary,	
tarragon, and dill	

Pork chops

4 pork chops, ¾ inch thick,
  without the bone
Nutmeg
Flour
1 tablespoon oil
¼–½ cup heavy cream

Freshly ground pepper to taste
Salt to taste
2 tablespoons coarsely chopped
  almonds, browned lightly in
  butter

Garnish

2–4 apples, cored, peeled, and
  halved

Apple juice for boiling apples
Lingonberry or currant jelly

Combine the marinade ingredients. Flatten the chops a little with a mallet or other instrument, sprinkle with a little nutmeg. Cover with the marinade in a bowl, cover tightly, and let stand in the refrigerator for 4–5 days, turning the meat at least once a day. Remove the chops, dry them with paper towels, set them aside for a few minutes to prepare the apples for garnish.

Boil the halved apples in apple juice to cover for 15 minutes, till they are slightly soft but *not* mushy. Put them on a plate, cut side up, and fill with the jelly. Set aside.

Sprinkle the chops with a little flour on each side. Heat the 1 tablespoon of oil in a large skillet, and sauté the chops for 3–4 minutes on each side. Remove them from the skillet and keep them warm. Strain the marinade, add it to the skillet juices from sautéing the meat, and boil till slightly reduced. Add the heavy cream and bring to a boil. Season with salt and pepper. Pour the sauce over the chops and sprinkle the almonds over them. The apples are served as an accompaniment. This very tasty dish is often served with hot buttered noodles. *Serves 4.*

Pork Hot Pot
(Alt Zürcher Topf)

1 tablespoon oil
½ pound sliced bacon, chopped
1 pound shoulder of pork cut in
   ½-inch cubes
2–3 medium-sized onions,
   chopped
2 cloves garlic, minced
2 tablespoons flour
1 pound white cabbage, cubed
4–6 medium-sized carrots, sliced

½ teaspoon salt
½ teaspoon pepper
A pinch each of nutmeg, thyme,
   marjoram, and dill
½ cup dry white wine
⅔–1 cup chicken bouillon
4–6 medium-sized potatoes,
   cubed
Chopped parsley for garnish

Heat the oil in a large skillet, sauté the bacon and pork cubes till
golden brown. Add the onions and garlic and sauté for another few
minutes. Sprinkle the flour over the meat, mix well, then add the
cabbage and carrots. Cook over a very low flame, add the seasonings, white wine, and mix well. Then add the bouillon and let the
meat cook slowly, tightly covered, for 1 hour. Add the cubed potatoes, cook slowly for another 20 minutes (you may have to add
more bouillon). Just before serving, sprinkle with chopped parsley.
Serves 4.

Smoked Sausage with Potato Salad
(Bassersdorfer Schueblig mit Kartoffelsalat)

2 pounds potatoes
½ cup hot bouillon
6 smoked sausages
1 tablespoon dry mustard
Salt and freshly ground pepper
   to taste
2 tablespoons yogurt
2 tablespoons oil
2½ tablespoons vinegar

1 medium-sized onion, chopped
2 cloves garlic, minced
2 tablespoons chopped parsley
1 tablespoon chopped chives
1 medium-sized sweet pickle,
   chopped
1–2 tomatoes, peeled and cut into
   small pieces
1–2 tablespoons mayonnaise

Boil the potatoes in their jackets until done, about 30 minutes. Pour off the hot water, let them dry a little, then peel and slice them while they are still warm. Pour the hot bouillon over them. Put the sausages in cold water to cover, bring to a boil, turn off the heat, and let the sausages stand in the very hot water for 15 minutes. Set them aside. Make a salad dressing of the mustard, salt, pepper, yogurt, oil, and vinegar, mixing thoroughly. Add the remaining ingredients to the potatoes, pour the salad dressing over all, mix very gently with two forks, and serve with the smoked sausages. This dish is very special. *Serves 6.*

Potato Pancake, Swiss Style
(Zürich Roesti)

6–8 medium-sized potatoes, scrubbed and unpeeled	2 tablespoons oil
2 tablespoons butter	Salt and freshly ground pepper to taste

Boil the potatoes in salted water for only 15 minutes: they should be half cooked. Drain them, cool overnight, skins still on, in the refrigerator. Peel them and shred them coarsely using the shredder side of a grater. In a heavy skillet, heat the butter and oil, add the potatoes, salt and pepper, and cook the potatoes as a single large pancake, covered, over medium-low heat till the underside is brown and crusty. Put an inverted serving plate on top of the skillet, and, holding the skillet handle with one hand and the plate with the other, turn them over quickly, letting the pancake fall onto the serving plate with the browned side up. Excellent! *Serves 4.*

Potatoes with Onion and Bacon
(Kartoffeln mit Zwiebeln und Speck)

*3 slices lean bacon, cut into small
  pieces
1 large onion, chopped fine
2 tablespoons butter
1 clove garlic, crushed
6 medium-sized potatoes, peeled
  and cut into ⅛-inch slices*

*1 cup chicken bouillon
1 stalk celery, chopped
A pinch of basil
Salt and freshly ground pepper
Chopped parsley
Grated Parmesan cheese*

Fry the bacon and onion in the butter in a medium-sized skillet. When the onion turns golden, add the crushed garlic, then the potatoes and the bouillon (the potatoes should not be completely covered by the bouillon). Add the celery, basil, a pinch of salt, and then pepper to taste. Cook over medium-low heat, stirring once or twice, till the potatoes are done, about 20 minutes. Sprinkle with chopped parsley, place on a heated serving dish. The grated cheese is best served on the side. *Serves 4–6.*

Apple Fritters
(Apfel Beignets)

*¾ cup sifted flour
A pinch of salt
1–2 tablespoons sugar
1 teaspoon baking powder
1 egg, beaten
⅓ cup milk
½ tablespoon oil*

*2 medium-sized apples, peeled
  and cut in short strips
  (about 1½ cups)
2 tablespoons raisins
Oil or butter for deep frying
Confectioner's sugar*

Make a batter of the first 7 ingredients, mix till smooth. Stir in the apples and raisins. Into a large skillet drop the fritters by tablespoonfuls into very hot oil or butter, press them flat, and cook till they are golden brown, about 4 minutes. Drain them on paper towels, then sprinkle them with confectioner's sugar. Delightful! *Makes 15–18 fritters.*

Apple Pie from Affoltern
(Affolterner Opfelwaehe)

1 package of frozen puff pastry
2 pounds apples, peeled, sliced
⅓ cup sugar
5 eggs

¾ cup apple cider
¾ cup heavy cream
⅓ cup additional sugar

Place the rolled-out pastry in a 12- by 18-inch cookie pan at least 1 inch deep. Prick the pastry with a fork in several places to keep it from buckling. Cover the pastry with the apple slices, bake in a preheated 400° oven for 15 minutes. Mix well the ⅓ cup sugar, the eggs, apple cider, and heavy cream, pour carefully over the apple slices, place back in the oven and continue to bake for 20–30 minutes. During this second baking period, add a little of the ⅓ cup additional sugar every 5 minutes, sprinkling it over the top so that it will caramelize. When the pie is finished, cut in squares and serve while it is still warm. This is delectable. *Makes about 14 squares.*

Rhubarb with Cream
(Rhabarber mit Sahne)

1 pound rhubarb, peeled
2 cups water
A scant ½ cup sugar
Cornstarch

A few drops of lemon juice
Heavy cream
Sugar
Vanilla extract

Cut the rhubarb into 2-inch pieces and wash them. Cook the water and sugar down to a thin syrup, add the rhubarb, and poach it for 15 minutes. Do NOT stir it. Remove the rhubarb with a slotted spoon and place in a serving dish. Thicken the juice with a little cornstarch, cook it for a few minutes, add the lemon juice, then pour it over the rhubarb. To the heavy cream add sugar to taste, a few drops of vanilla extract, and mix well. Serve the cream on the side. This refreshing dessert goes well with ladyfingers. *Serves 4.*

LA SUISSE

Cheese Fondue

1 clove garlic, peeled
1 cup dry white wine
⅔ pound Gruyère cheese, grated
*   coarsely*
A generous ⅓ pound Swiss
*   cheese, grated coarsely*
A scant ¼ pound Appenzeller
*   cheese, grated coarsely*

2 tablespoons kirsch
4 teaspoons cornstarch
Freshly ground pepper to taste
Nutmeg, a dash
Bread cubes ¾ inch square with
*   plenty of crust*

Rub the bottom of a fondue pot with garlic. Pour in the white wine and one third of the mixed cheeses. Place the fondue pot on the stove, begin stirring in a figure-8 motion, and keep on stirring as you add the rest of the cheese mix. Cook over moderate heat, stirring all the time, till the mixture begins to boil and bubble. Add the kirsch and the cornstarch, bring to a boil again. Quickly season with pepper and nutmeg, bring the fondue pot to the table, place it on an alcohol burner, and adjust the flame so that the fondue will simmer all during the meal. Each person will spear a cube of bread and dip it into the cheese, giving it a good stir each time.

To enhance the joy you experience, you have my permission to dip each speared cube of bread into a glass of kirsch *before* you dip it into the hot cheese—it will make the meal an unforgettable moment, color your cheeks, and free you of whatever inhibitions you happen to have. Serve with a light white wine.

There are some incurable carnivores who insist on eating meat every time they sit down down to dine; they should be served thinly sliced prosciutto garnished with sour gherkins. *Serve a generous ¼ pound cheese per person.*

Kaasi Fondue

A generous ¼ pound Swiss
cheese, grated
¾ pound Gruyère cheese, grated
A scant ¼ pound Appenzeller
cheese, grated

A scant ¼ pound Walliser
cheese, grated

Proceed as with the recipe above—Cheese Fondue.

Fondue Bourguignonne

A light red wine served with this fondue is delicious.

Oil enough to half fill the fondue pot
3 pounds fillet of beef cut into very thin slices, 1 by 3 inches

Bring the oil to a boil, spear a slice of meat on the tip of your fork, twist it around the fork, dip it into the boiling oil, and leave it there as long as you want to—raw, medium, well done. Before you put the meat into your mouth, remove it from the fork and spear it with another fork; otherwise you might get a painful burn on your lips and tongue. You may use bamboo spears if you like, then you won't have to spend time changing forks. Before you eat each cube, dip it into any of the four sauces given below. All of them should be prepared well ahead of time. *Serves 5–6.*

Rémoulade Sauce

½ cup mayonnaise
½ cup sour cream
1 teaspoon chopped chives
1 teaspoon minced onion
1 teaspoon chopped capers

1 teaspoon chopped parsley
A pinch of dry mustard
A few drops of Worcestershire
sauce
¼ teaspoon tarragon

Mix all ingredients well and chill. *Makes about 1 cup.*

Dill Mayonnaise

> ½ cup mayonnaise   2 tablespoons chopped parsley
> ½ cup sour cream   1 tablespoon minced onion
> 2 tablespoons dill weed   A few drops of lemon juice

Mix the ingredients well and chill. *Makes 1½ cups.*

Curry Sauce

> 1 cup mayonnaise   ¼ teaspoon powdered ginger
> ½ cup heavy cream   Bouillon, enough to make the
> 1 tablespoon chopped chutney   desired consistency
> 1 tablespoon curry powder   Lemon juice to taste
> ½ teaspoon peanut butter

Mix the ingredients well and chill. *Makes about 2 cups.*

Sauce Piquante

> ½ cup ketchup
> ½ cup chili sauce

Mix the ingredients well and chill. *Makes 1 cup.*

The following three salads are excellent accompaniments to Fondue Bourguignonne, given above. They should all be made very fresh and well chilled. Chutney and pickles are also usual additions.

Cauliflower Salad
(Blumenkohl Salat)

Dressing

> Olive oil   Dry mustard
> Mayonnaise   1 small cauliflower
> Worcestershire sauce   Pitted black olives
> Garlic
> Salt and freshly ground pepper
>   to taste

Prepare the dressing from the first 6 ingredients in proportions of your choice. Boil the cauliflower for 10–12 minutes, break it into flowerets, and mix with the dressing. Cut the black olives into small rings and sprinkle over the salad. Serve very cold.

Celery Root Salad
(Selleriewurzel Salat)

1 small celery root	*5 walnuts, chopped*
A pinch of salt	*1 apple, peeled and grated*
1 teaspoon lemon juice	*1 tablespoon honey or sugar*
2 tablespoons seedless raisins	*1 cup sour cream*

Peel the celery root, cut it into thick slices, and boil it in water to cover to which a little salt and the lemon juice have been added, cook till the slices are *al dente,* drain well; let them cool. Mix in the remaining ingredients very carefully and serve cold. Something new and quite different—good.

Rice Salad

1 cup uncooked rice	*1 teaspoon chopped chives*
6 tablespoons olive oil	*2 tablespoons chopped cucumbers*
3 tablespoons vinegar	*1 tablespoon chopped scallions*
1 teaspoon salt	*1 large, ripe tomato, peeled and*
1 teaspoon pepper	*chopped*
¼ teaspoon dried tarragon	*4 tablespoons cooked peas*
1 tablespoon chopped bell pepper	*1 tablespoon chopped pickle,*
1 tablespoon chopped celery	*sweet or sour*
1 tablespoon chopped parsley	

Boil the rice till it is cooked *al dente,* and in a colander rinse it under *hot* water, shake out any excess water and let the rice dry for a moment. While it is still hot, thoroughly mix in the olive oil, vinegar, salt, and pepper, let cool for a while. Add the remaining ingredients, mix thoroughly, and let stand in the refrigerator till serving time. This salad is very tasty and very out of the ordinary. You'll see! *Serves 4–6.*

Polynesian Rice

This dish may be served instead of the preceding recipe—Rice Salad—as an accompaniment to *Fondue Bourguignonne*. It is just as good and just as different.

1 cup uncooked rice	*1 tablespoon lemon juice*
2 cups orange juice	*1 cup drained pineapple tidbits*
¼ teaspoon salt	*½ cup toasted slivered almonds*
1 teaspoon grated lemon rind	

Combine the rice, orange juice, and salt in a medium-sized saucepan, bring to a boil, stir lightly, reduce heat, cover, and simmer for 20 minutes or till the rice is tender. Drain and chill. Add the grated lemon rind, lemon juice, pineapple, and almonds, mix well. Serve chilled.

Café Diable

Using amounts of ingredients to suit your taste, mix some sugar with powdered cloves, pieces of orange rind, pieces of lemon rind, and a cinnamon stick in a chafing dish. Pour prepared coffee into the dish and heat it. Add 1 ounce of brandy per person and flame it, let it flicker for a moment, then enjoy this very tasty beverage.

Turkish Coffee

1½ cups water	*2 tablespoons very finely ground*
4 teaspoons sugar	*coffee*

In a small heavy saucepan, bring the water and sugar to a boil, take off the fire, add the coffee, stir well, then carefully put the saucepan back on a low flame and bring to a boil again, then allow the brew to rise 3 or 4 times more. Add a few drops of cold water to settle the grounds, pour it immediately into demitasse cups. Very Turkish. *Makes 4 demitasse cups.*

LA SVIZZERA

We live six miles away from the Italian border. Crossing over used to be a very simple thing. Through the window of our car I would show our American passports and the border guards, seeing our Swiss license plates, would wave us through. True, there were always a few customs inspectors who would put on a big show. I remember a mild one who—all smiles—inquired if we had anything to declare. When I answered, in a voice suitable for such occasions, with a firm *"Niente,"* his smile broadened. "Really, nothing?" he inquired patiently. Then, in a gentle way, he slowly shook his head, surprised that we would want to put something over on HIM—a friend—and his eyes implored us to give up the silly game and confess. *"Niente!"* I repeated, and my smile matched his. Our eyes held for a spell, then suddenly he turned away as if to say, "Oh what the hell, I'm a nice guy—I believe you," and he motioned us to drive on.

And there were the strict ones. No smiles distorted their pitiless expressions. They would take our passports, turn page after page slowly, and, with great suspicion, compare my face with the passport photo. Instinctively my face took on the same bland expression as that in my passport. They would lean into the car to make sure that the features of my wife corresponded to the image in her passport, and finally, satisfied of having done their duty well and finding no fault in us, they would say, "Okay," thus indicating that they were able to speak English.

Lately it has all changed. The economic situation in Italy is deteriorating at a galloping pace. Driven by the red scare, billions of lire are being smuggled daily over the border to be converted into the hardest currency in the world, the Swiss franc. Gold in ingots, bullion, and coins, also rare stamps, jewelry, and valuable paintings are being brought here to safety. The Italian way of levying taxes is partly responsible for the flight of so much money from the country. Italy is the *only* country I know where the tax declaration of a citizen will be ignored; where the tax inspector will come—

unannounced—and invade your premises, be they office, factory, or private home. He will look at your furniture, your paintings, count your silver, open the closets and count the ladies' furs, the gentlemen's clothes, he will note what car you drive, what year the car was made, how your garden is kept. He will then make an arbitrary judgment of your worth and put you down for the amount *he* thinks you should pay in taxes.

The burden of proof to the contrary is on *you*—the citizen. Of course you may sue the government, have a long-drawn-out trial that enriches the courts but mostly the lawyers, OR—and I hear that it is often done—you will try to make an arrangement with the tax assessor. It is whispered that in such dealings money changes hands, under the table, before a suitable settlement is arrived at.

To protect her currency, Italy has issued new directions—but has failed to publicize them properly. Today, if I want to drive into their country, I have to stop at the border, walk over to the customs office, and fill out a document stating how many lire I am carrying on me; also how much and what kind of foreign currency, including traveler's checks. I have to produce these moneys, and only then do I get that document signed and countersigned, stamped and counterstamped.

Nowhere at the border are there notices visible to drivers indicating that such a new law exists; no customs inspector who perfunctorily asks, "Any merchandise?" draws your attention to the fact that you should get out and obtain such a document. Ninety-eight per cent of the Swiss population have never heard of one, and awful things can happen and have happened:

A Swiss citizen crossed the border into Italy to attend a funeral, was stopped by a highway patrol and asked to empty his pockets. He produced the 750 Swiss francs he was carrying, was arrested, accused of smuggling, the money was confiscated as well as his car ("because it had been used for smuggling"), and after a lengthy trial in which he swore that he had never even heard of the new law (which had geen passed by the Italian Government only two days before his apprehension), he was fined the equivalent of twenty thousand Swiss francs.

A friend of ours had a similar experience. He was going on a business trip overseas and carried a large amount of money. On the way to the international airport in Milan his car was stopped, everything was "confiscated," and a huge fine imposed. These incidents and the frequent strikes (often lasting only a few hours but nonetheless irritating) are some of the unpleasant aspects of today's Italy—an otherwise wonderful country, desperately trying to get out of the economic and political mess it finds itself in.

The beauty of their country is unsurpassed, the people friendly, warm, and generous, gay and musical. Of course, those who make their money from tourists are always trying little tricks, a condition that is the same the world over, but in Italy it is done with so much charm. Many years ago my parents were dining in Naples, in a small waterfront restaurant, and the waiter added up the bill: *"Pasta, sei lire; brodo, quattro lire; vitello milanese, otto lire; dolce e vino, otto lire . . ."* and then very fast: *"Quando se va—dieci lire!"* (If I can get away with it—ten lire!) My father, who spoke excellent Italian, asked, *"Che cosa vuol dire: quando se va—dieci lire?"* The waiter smiled apologetically and said with a shrug, *"Allora, non va!"* (So it won't work!)

Once in Bologna my wife and I had a waiter who tried to add his mother's birthday, his telephone number, and the ages of his children to my bill. When I picked him up on it, he laughed, winked, and said, *"Un scherzo!"* (A joke!)

Venetian Fish Soup
(Zuppa di Pesce alla Veneziana)

3 pounds white-fleshed fish	*½ cup olive oil*
Salt and freshly ground pepper	*2 cloves garlic, chopped*
1 small onion, coarsely chopped	*½ cup dry white wine*
2 bay leaves	*1 cup chopped canned tomatoes*
2 sprigs parsley	*½ teaspoon powdered saffron*
½ teaspoon thyme	

Trim and cut the fish into slices ½ inch thick. Boil the trimmings, including the head, for 40 minutes in 3 cups of water with salt and pepper, onion, 1 bay leaf, parsley, and half the thyme. Strain this stock. In a large skillet brown the fish slices in the olive oil, garlic, and remaining bay leaf. Add the stock and the rest of the ingredients, simmer for 15 minutes. Remove the bay leaves. When serving

the soup, try to keep the slices of whitefish as intact as possible.
Serves 5–6.

Minestrone alla Milanese

2 medium-sized onions, sliced
7 tablespoons olive oil
1 pound ground beef
1 cup navy beans, soaked
    overnight
1 cup chopped carrots
½ cup chopped white turnips
½ cup chopped fresh string
    beans
¼ cup peas, fresh or frozen

2 stalks celery, chopped or diced
2 tablespoons chopped parsley
2 cups shredded white cabbage
½ cup sliced mushrooms
2 medium-sized tomatoes, very
    ripe, peeled, cut up
1 clove garlic, crushed
1 cup uncooked vermicelli
2½ quarts water
Grated Parmesan cheese

Sauté the onions in the oil for 6 minutes over a low fire, then add
the ground beef, brown for another 7 minutes. Add the beans and
vegetables, simmer for about 10 minutes, stirring occasionally. Add
the 2½ quarts of water and the vermicelli, simmer for another 20
minutes, stirring frequently. If the soup is too thick, add a little

chicken bouillon. Serve with lots of grated cheese on the side. *Serves 6–8.*

Stuffed Eggplant Nini
(Melanzane Riempite Nini)

4 medium-sized eggplants,
    unpeeled
1 pound ground beef
3 tablespoons finely chopped
    parsley
5 tablespoons bread crumbs
1 teaspoon garlic powder
2 eggs, beaten
1 cup chicken bouillon

1 tablespoon chopped onion
Freshly ground pepper to taste
¾ cup grated Parmesan cheese
Oil for frying
1 cup heavy White Sauce (see
    Index)
Additional bread crumbs
Nutmeg

Clean the eggplants, remove the stems, and slice them in half lengthwise. (They can also be cut and stuffed as for stuffed peppers.) Scoop out the insides, leaving a wall ½ to ¾ inch thick all around. Mix together the beef, parsley, bread crumbs, garlic powder, eggs, bouillon, onion, pepper, and Parmesan cheese. In a large skillet, cook the eggplant halves in the oil till they are brown inside and soft outside. Drain them, place them on a cookie sheet, and fill with the meat mixture. Make the white sauce, then cover each eggplant with some of it, sprinkle with bread crumbs, then with nutmeg. Bake in a preheated 350° oven for 40 minutes or till done. This dish can be made ahead of time and reheated before serving. *Serves 6–8.*

Angela's Cioppino
(Cioppino all'Angela)

1 cup butter
¼ cup olive oil
2 medium-sized onions, chopped fine
2 bell peppers, diced
2 cloves garlic, minced
1 20-ounce can tomatoes or 6 large, ripe tomatoes
1 6-ounce can tomato paste diluted with 1 can water
1 bay leaf
1 teaspoon paprika
Salt and freshly ground pepper to taste

6 peppercorns
1 cup dry white wine
¼ cup dry sherry
1 tablespoon grated orange rind
2 pounds striped bass cut into 2-inch pieces
1 pound raw shrimp, shelled, deveined, and boiled
1 pound cooked crab meat
1 pint shucked clams
1 pint shucked oysters
2 small lobsters, boiled and meat removed from the shells
2 tablespoons chopped parsley

Heat the butter and olive oil in a large skillet, add the onions, peppers, and garlic, sauté till brown. Add the tomatoes, tomato paste, bay leaf, paprika, salt, pepper, and peppercorns, cook for 1 hour—*very slowly*—covered, then add the wine, sherry, and orange rind. Place the fish, shrimp, and shellfish, layer by layer, in a kettle. Pour the sauce and some fish cooking liquid over the seafood and simmer, tightly covered, for 20–25 minutes. Serve in soup bowls. This is a wonderful dish. *Serves 10.*

Boiled Beef with Soy Sauce
(Manzo Lesso con Soia)

2 tablespoons vegetable oil
1 pound boneless stewing beef cut into 1-inch cubes
3 tablespoons soy sauce
3 tablespoons dry sherry

1½ teaspoons sugar
3 scallions, cut into 1-inch pieces
1 cup water
1 tablespoon Sambuca (Italian liqueur)

Heat the oil over high heat in a skillet with a cover, add the beef, and sauté, stirring, till the cubes are well browned. Add the soy sauce, sherry, and sugar, mix well. Cook for about 3 minutes, then stir in the scallions and 1 cup of water, bring to a boil. Cover the skillet and cook for 30 minutes over a medium flame. Sprinkle the Sambuca over the beef and cook for another 10 minutes. This goes very well with piping hot boiled rice. *Serves 4.*

Braised Veal Shanks
(Osso Buco)

2 veal shanks, cut into 2-inch pieces by your butcher	1 clove garlic, minced
½ cup flour mixed with ½ teaspoon pepper	2 carrots, diced
3 tablespoons butter	1 stalk celery, diced
3 tablespoons oil	1 teaspoon salt
¼ teaspoon ground sage	1½ cups dry white wine
¼ teaspoon rosemary	1½ cups chicken bouillon
1 medium-sized onion, chopped fine	2 tablespoons tomato paste
	Gremolata (given below)

Dust the veal shank pieces with the flour, heat the butter and oil in a skillet, add the shanks, and brown on all sides. Place the veal in a Dutch oven, sprinkle them with the sage and rosemary, and add the onion, garlic, carrots, celery, and salt. Cover tightly and braise for 10 minutes, either on top of the stove or in a preheated 350° oven. Then add the white wine, bouillon, and tomato paste, simmer, covered, for 2 hours. *Serves 6–8.*

Gremolata
Combine 1½ teaspoons chopped parsley, 2 cloves of garlic, chopped fine, and 1 tablespoon grated lemon rind. Sprinkle over the finished veal shanks, which are delicious served with hot buttered *fettuccine*.

Veal Cutlets Milano
(Costolette di Vitello alla Milanese)

2 large veal cutlets
¼ teaspoon salt
¼ teaspoon nutmeg
1 egg, beaten
3 tablespoons bread crumbs

3 tablespoons grated Parmesan
  cheese
3 tablespoons butter
2 cups cooked saffron rice

Season the cutlets with the salt and nutmeg, dip them into the egg.
Combine the bread crumbs and grated cheese, bread the cutlets in
this mixture. Sauté them in the butter in a skillet over medium-low
heat for 15 minutes. Serve the cutlets on top of piping hot saffron
rice. *Serves 2.*

Lamb and Eggplant Parmigiana
(Agnello e Melanzane alla Parmigiana)

2 medium-sized eggplants
1 clove garlic, minced
½ cup chopped onion
3 tablespoons cooking oil
1 tablespoon flour
1 large can tomatoes
2 teaspoons sugar
1 teaspoon salt

½ teaspoon basil
½ teaspoon oregano
1 tablespoon chopped parsley
2–3 cups cooked lamb cut into
  ½-inch cubes
½ pound mozzarella cheese,
  sliced
½ cup grated Parmesan cheese

Peel the eggplants and cut them into 2-inch cubes. Simmer them
for 10 minutes in a little salted water, drain and pat them dry.
Sauté the garlic and onion in the oil till they are tender, stir in the
flour, tomatoes, sugar, salt, and herbs, stirring well, simmer for 15
minutes. In a greased 2½-quart casserole, arrange half of the
eggplant and half of the lamb. Top with half of the sauce and half
of the cheese. Repeat these 2 steps. Then sprinkle on the grated
Parmesan cheese. Bake in a preheated 400° oven for 20–30 minutes.
This is an excellent dish. *Serves 6–8.*

Veal Steaks Campione
(Costolette di Vitello alla Campione)

4 veal steaks ¾ inch thick	*Cornstarch*
Salt	*½ cup heavy cream*
Paprika	*½ cup butter*
Seasoning salt	*Freshly grated Parmesan cheese*

Season the steaks with salt, paprika, and seasoning salt. Roll them in cornstarch, dusting off the excess. Place them next to each other in a large rectangular ovenproof dish, cover with the heavy cream and dabs of butter. Sprinkle grated cheese liberally on top and bake, covered, in a preheated 375° oven for 30 minutes. This is veal at its best. *Serves 4.*

Breast of Turkey with Truffles
(Tacchino con Tartufi)

6 uncooked slices of turkey breast	*Bread crumbs*
Flour	*Butter*
2 eggs, beaten, a few drops of	*Salt*
water added	*White truffles*

Pound and flatten the turkey half breasts, then dust them with flour, shake off the excess, then dip them in the beaten egg. Roll them carefully in bread crumbs, patting them well into the meat. Sauté the turkey cutlets in butter in a skillet over low heat, turning them once. Add salt. Just before serving, place paper-thin slices of white truffles on the cutlets. (White truffles are not to everyone's taste because of the powerful odor, so use discretion.) *Serves 6.*

Quail à la Cossi
(Quaglie alla Cossi)

The measurements depend on the number of birds you serve.

2 or 3 quail per person	Half oil and half butter
Salt and freshly ground pepper	Rosemary
Bacon, 1 slice for each bird	White wine
Sage	½ cup heavy cream

The quail, which have been plucked and cleaned, should be lightly rubbed with salt and pepper outside and salt only inside. Then wrap each quail in a slice of bacon. Join 3 birds together by running a skewer through them side by side. Sprinkle them lightly with sage. In a large skillet with a cover, heat the oil and butter, add some rosemary, then *carefully* and *slowly* brown the birds. Add some of the white wine till it comes a quarter way up the birds, and let them simmer, covered, for 40 minutes, basting frequently with some of the wine. When the birds are almost done, add the heavy cream to the pan liquid, let simmer for another 10 minutes. Strain the sauce and serve. The quail are usually served with *Polenta* (see Index).

Chicken Hunter Style
(Pollo Cacciatore)

A 4-pound broiling chicken, cut into serving pieces	2½ tablespoons tomato paste and an equal amount of water
Flour	
Olive oil	1 teaspoon marjoram
2 medium-sized onions, sliced fine	1 cup dry white wine
1 clove garlic, minced	Salt and freshly ground pepper to taste
1 bay leaf	3 large bell peppers, cut julienne
4 large ripe tomatoes, cut in small pieces	¾ pound mushrooms, sliced fine

Dredge the chicken in flour and brown in a large skillet in olive oil. Transfer to a large saucepan. In the skillet where the chicken has been browned, sauté the onions and garlic for a few minutes, then add to the saucepan along with the bay leaf, tomatoes, tomato paste, marjoram, and wine. Add salt and pepper, then simmer, covered, for ¾ hour. Separately sauté the bell peppers in olive oil, then add the mushrooms and sauté for about 6 minutes. Transfer the peppers and mushrooms to the large saucepan and simmer, covered, for about 20 minutes, till the chicken pieces are tender. *Serves 3–4.*

Risotto

¼ pound butter
1 large onion, chopped
1 pound rice
2–2½ quarts chicken bouillon

1 teaspoon salt
½ teaspoon fennel seeds
½ pound grated Parmesan
    cheese

Melt half the butter in a heavy skillet, sauté the onion till golden brown. Add the rice, stir well so that all grains will be coated with butter. Add 1 cup of the bouillon and, while stirring for 10 minutes, slowly add ⅔ of the remaining bouillon. Add the salt and fennel seeds, cook for another 10 minutes while slowly adding the rest of the bouillon. By this time the rice should have absorbed all the liquid, place it in a warm bowl, pour over it the rest of the melted butter, and sprinkle with the cheese.

Sliced chicken livers, sautéed, or mushrooms can be added to this recipe, in which case leave out the fennel. *Serves 8–10.*

Polenta—Cornmeal Mush, Italian Style

1 pound cornmeal
2½ quarts cold water, or 1½
    quarts water and 2 cups
    chicken bouillon
2 teaspoons salt
¼ teaspoon onion salt

⅛ teaspoon nutmeg
    (optional)
4 tablespoons butter
½ pound grated Parmesan
    cheese (optional)

Place a medium-sized saucepan in a larger one half filled with warm water (or use a very large double boiler). Set on a medium fire. Add the cornmeal and mix well with 2 cups of the cold water. Heat the rest of the water (or water and bouillon) and add to the cornmeal, stirring constantly. Add the salt, onion salt, and nutmeg, and, while stirring continuously with a wooden spoon, cook for an hour over a medium fire. Place the polenta on a buttered serving dish and serve hot. Just before serving, stir in the 4 tablespoons of butter and the grated cheese. This is a delicious, dependable dish. *Serves 10.*

String Beans with Ham
(Fagiolini con Prosciutto)

1 pound fresh string beans
2 tablespoons olive oil for frying
¼ pound boiled ham (or leftover cooked), sliced
1 clove garlic, minced

1 small onion, chopped fine
Salt and freshly ground pepper to taste
Chopped parsley for garnish

Cook the string beans in boiling salted water till they are almost tender (cook them with a copper penny in the water so they will preserve their color). Place the cooked beans in a colander to drain. Put a tablespoon or so of olive oil in the same saucepan, add the ham, and cook over a low flame for 1 minute. Add the beans, garlic, and onion, cook for another 3 minutes. Season with salt and pepper. Sprinkle with parsley and serve immediately. Slices of dark bread are delicious with this fine dish. *Serves 4.*

Tomatoes Taverna Flavia
(Pomodori Taverna Flavia)

These tomatoes are delicious. A half of one per person is enough as an accompanying touch; a whole one is fine as a first course. Taverna Flavia is a lovely restaurant in Rome. It is favored by locals and not many tourists.

4 medium-sized ripe tomatoes
½ bunch of scallions, chopped
   fine
1 clove garlic, chopped fine
1 cup bread crumbs

A small bunch of parsley,
   chopped fine
Salad oil
Salt and freshly ground pepper
   to taste

Trim the stem ends of the tomatoes, slice them neatly in half *horizontally.* Mix together the scallions, garlic, bread crumbs, parsley, and enough salad oil to make a thick paste. Add salt and pepper. Spread a generous 1 tablespoon of the mixture on each half, bake in a preheated 350° oven for 25 minutes. These tomatoes are delectable served either hot or cold.

Spaghetti Sauce Bolognese
(Ragù Bolognese)

4 tablespoons oil for sautéing
6 medium-sized onions, chopped
   fine
1 clove garlic, minced
1 large bell pepper, chopped fine
1½ pounds ground round steak
1 large can tomatoes
1 bay leaf

1 tablespoon Lea & Perrins
   Worcestershire sauce
4 dashes of Tabasco sauce
Salt, pepper, celery salt, and sage
   to taste
1 can button mushrooms
Tomato juice

Heat the oil in a large skillet with a cover, add the onions, garlic, and bell pepper, sauté till soft. Add the meat, brown it, stirring frequently. Add the tomatoes, bay leaf, Worcestershire sauce, Tabasco, salt, pepper, celery salt, and sage. Add the mushrooms and their liquid. Cover the skillet and simmer for at least 30 minutes, adding tomato juice bit by bit as the liquid evaporates. This sauce is wonderful served over many kinds of pasta. Try it! *Makes about 2 cups.*

Green Sauce Nini
(Salsa Verde Nini)

This is a very good sauce that goes well with almost any cold meats
—for example, cold boiled tongue—and it is excellent as an accompanying sauce for *Fondue Bourguignonne* (see Index).

2 slices white bread, soaked in water and pressed dry	¼ teaspoon salt
3 hard-cooked eggs	Freshly ground pepper to taste
1 cup olive oil	3 bunches of parsley, chopped
3 tablespoons vinegar	1 small onion, chopped
2 tablespoons prepared mustard	1 teaspoon small capers
	Sour cream for consistency

Put all the ingredients except the sour cream into a blender and
process till the sauce is very smooth. Add enough sour cream to get
a thick consistency. You can keep this sauce in the refrigerator for
quite a while. *Makes 2½–3 cups of sauce.*

Pesto—Basil Sauce

Pasta is often served topped with *pesto* and some butter. It is then
served at the table along with grated cheese. Also, a tablespoon of
this unique sauce—none other quite like it—can be added to mine-
strone just before serving.

2 cloves garlic	A handful of fresh basil leaves, chopped fine
A pinch of salt	1 teaspoon finely chopped parsley
10 pine nuts or walnuts (the latter chopped)	1 cup and 2 tablespoons olive oil
3 tablespoons and 1 teaspoon freshly grated Parmesan cheese	

In a mortar, pound together the garlic, salt, pine nuts or walnuts,
and grated cheese till they are mixed and rather fine. Add the basil
and the parsley, continually pounding and grinding, gradually add

the olive oil till the sauce is thick and smooth. *Makes about 2 cups of sauce.*

Pears Taverna Flavia
(Pere Cotte Rosse)

6 large Bosco pears, 1 per person　　*A pinch of salt*
1 cup sugar　　　　　　　　　　*1½ cups red wine*
Juice of 1 lemon

Peel the pears, leaving on the stems if possible. Place them in a Pyrex bowl that has a cover. Add the sugar, lemon juice, and salt, and cover the pears with red wine. Put the bowl in a preheated 350° oven, turning the pears once, for 1 hour.

Pears in White Wine
(Pere Cotte Bianche)

Prepare these as in Pears Taverna Flavia, the recipe preceding.

Zabaglione—A Delicious Dessert

2 cups dry Marsala, Madeira, or　　*6 tablespoons superfine*
*　　sherry*　　　　　　　　　　*　　granulated sugar*
6 egg yolks

Pour the wine in the top of a large double boiler and set it over boiling water. Add the egg yolks and the sugar. Beat these vigorously with a wire whisk, and continue to do so till the custard that is formed doubles in bulk and begins to thicken. Remove from the heat and serve it *at once,* piled high in large stemmed glasses. This dessert is delicious and it's spectacular—the higher it is piled the better. *Serves 6.*

Cheesecake St. Anthony

Crust

> *About 16 graham crackers, crushed fine, 1⅓ cups*
> *¼ cup softened butter*
> *¼ cup sugar*

Blend these ingredients well, press evenly against the bottom and sides of a 9-inch pie plate.

Filling

> *2 eggs*   *1 teaspoon vanilla extract*
> *12 ounces cream cheese*   *½ cup sugar*
> *2 tablespoons heavy cream*   *¼ teaspoon cinnamon*

Place the eggs in a blender, start it at low speed, gradually adding the cream cheese, heavy cream, vanilla, and sugar. Pour the mixture into the crumb crust, sprinkle with the cinnamon, and bake in a preheated 375° oven for 20 minutes. Let it cool.

Topping

> *1 pint sour cream*   *2 tablespoons sugar*
> *½ teaspoon vanilla extract*

Place the ingredients in the blender, mix them thoroughly at low speed. Spread the topping on the cooled cheesecake and bake in a preheated 375° oven for 5 minutes. Allow to cool, then place in the refrigerator for at least an hour before serving. This cheesecake is superb! *Serves 8–10.*

Ricotta Cake
(Torta di Ricotta)

Crust

> *1 cup flour*   *¾ stick of butter*
> *A pinch of salt*   *1 egg yolk*
> *4 tablespoons sugar*

Combine the flour, salt, and sugar in a bowl, work in the butter with your fingertips. Then mix in the egg yolk and form a dough lightly into a ball. Wrap this well in aluminum foil and chill for 1–2 hours in the refrigerator. Then roll out the dough on a floured board to about ⅛ inch in thickness (or thinner) so it will fit into a 10-inch springform cake pan—the sides and removable bottom. Flute the edge. Chill for 30 minutes. With a fork prick the bottom and sides of the shell and bake in a preheated 350° oven until lightly browned, about 15 minutes.

Filling

    2½ *tablespoons butter*
    ¼ *cup sugar*
    3 *eggs, separated*
    1 *pound ricotta*
    2 *tablespoons seedless raisins*

2 *tablespoons chopped, blanched*
  almonds
Grated rind of ½ lemon
2 *tablespoons sour cream*

Cream the butter and sugar till fluffy. Beat in the egg yolks, then add the ricotta, raisins, almonds, and lemon rind. Fold in the stiffly beaten egg whites and the sour cream. Fill the crust and bake in a preheated 350° oven for 30–45 minutes. This cake has a delicate flavor and a fine texture. *Serves 8–10.*

The Poor Stewardess

We have a friend who used to be a hostess for one of the big airlines. She told us the following stories:

⋯⋗⊶⊶⊸⋖⋯

It was in Las Palmas, in the Canary Islands, that a lady wanted her highly prized show dog, a German shepherd, flown to New York to try to win another blue ribbon for his mistress at the Westminster Show. The dog was crated, delivered to the airport, and placed in the hold of the plane. But the departure was delayed for several hours, so a member of the ground personnel, an animal lover, felt sorry for the poor beast broiling in the compartment. He wanted to take the dog for a walk, but as he reached into the crate to take hold of the leash the dog pushed his hand away and escaped. The horrified animal lover hailed one of those "follow me" cars that guide the planes to their parking places, and gave chase. The dog led him all through town, finally disappearing down a side street. However, after a few minutes the dog chaser found the animal again, quietly sitting in front of a butcher's shop. He coaxed the dog into his car, the dog was put back into his crate, and the plane took off.

Next day the owner of the dog called Las Palmas airport: "Has my German shepherd arrived safely in New York?" she wanted to know.

"Oh yes, madam, he left on schedule."

"That's strange," replied the lady, "because he is lying right here next to me!"

The wrong dog had been shipped to New York; the lady sued, the butcher sued, the butcher's dog had to be flown back, and the show dog missed the dog show.

Our friend also flew as stewardess from Rome to New York, with a stopover in Shannon, Ireland. At that time the health authorities in Shannon were especially strict; before anyone was permitted off the plane, a health inspector boarded and sprayed the ship. About one and one-half hours before landing in Shannon a stewardess rushed into the cockpit.

"Captain," she gasped, "we have a rat on board!"

"Oh, my gawd," moaned the captain, "that's all we need. They'll put us in quarantine for a month! Here," he ordered, "take that fire hatchet, kill the rat, put it in an airsick bag, and I'll throw it out of the window while we are taxiing."

The girl was lucky. She caught the rat and had just brought it, properly executed and laid to rest in an airsick bag, to the captain, when a second stewardess rushed in.

"There's another rat on board!"

The girls were lucky again, the second rat suffered the same fate as the first, and at the moment the plane wheels touched ground in Ireland out of the window flew the two airsick bags.

When the plane was nearing New York, an old lady who was sitting at the back called to the hostess:

"Dear miss," she whispered in a trembling voice, "I had right here in this bag"—and she showed an empty satchel—"two dear

little chinchillas. They are gone . . . they must have escaped . . .
Could you help me find them? They are very valuable creatures."

"Of course, we will, madam," said the stewardess with great
concern. "After the plane has landed in New York, I shall stand by
the door and make sure they don't slip out; and when all the pas-
sengers have disembarked we will look for your two little friends."

And they did—the whole crew—for nearly an hour they searched
. . . and searched . . .

Das Oktoberfest

The *Oktoberfest* is to the good people of Munich what Disneyland is to the Americans. Disneyland is a year-round spectacle, but the *Oktoberfest* is wisely restricted to the last two weeks of September and ends on the first Sunday of October. Thus the name. Attempts to change the name to *Septemberfest* have been successfully resisted.

Its origin was modest enough: On October 17 in the year 1800 a horse race was arranged in a meadow on the outskirts of Munich to celebrate the wedding of Bavaria's Crown Prince Ludwig to his designated bride, Theresa, Princess of Sachsen-Hildburghausen.

In due time he became King Ludwig I (and a well-known connoisseur and gourmandizer of beautiful women, among them the famous Lola Montez, who nearly cost him his throne), and the meadow became known as Theresien Wiese. The following year the festivities were repeated and considerably improved by the addition of a Punch-and-Judy show, a shooting gallery, a display of farm products, and the dispensing of Bavaria's greatest national product: BEER!

From then on, the populace clamored for their annual *Oktoberfest,* and the modest country fair became more and more elaborate until it grew into today's awe-inspiring event. For sheer magnitude and the consumption of edibles and liquids it is unsurpassed in the world.

Opening day the festivities begin with the formation of a parade in the center of Munich. Six thousand paraders assemble, led by the *Bürgermeister,* dressed in ancient robes, with the chain and insignia of his high office. He is surrounded by representatives of outlying communities, of other German cities, and of the old artisans' guilds

—the bakers, the butchers, the tailors—all dressed in what they claim are historic costumes.

All of Munich's many breweries show off their enormous beer wagons, piled high with barrels, each drawn by eight huge brewery horses, their manes combed and curled into ringlets, their tails braided with many-colored ribbons, their coats brushed to a shine. The wagons are followed by gaily decorated flatcars carrying the servers—the beer dispensers and cask tappers, in long leather aprons, wielding the tools of their trade, the mallet and spigot. Waitresses, disguised as maidens and wearing dirndls, prance about. Hefty females mostly, they have to be able to pick up, carry, and serve at least eight one-liter steins of beer at a time—four in each hand. They are loudly acclaimed by the male onlookers, often with bawdy pantomime, and the waitresses respond with sophisticated banter.

Behind them march the brass bands of each brewery. The big restaurants, not to be outdone and trying to cash in on the publicity, also send their delegations and *their* bands. In all, I counted thirty-one music-making groups, all blowing lustily away—fortissimo—and each one playing a different tune.

Slowly the mass of humans—including rifle and gun clubmen dressed as hunters—the beer barrels, and the festive officials roll out to the Theresien Wiese, which is already packed with expectant revelers. The six biggest breweries—Hackerbräu, Hofbräu, Paul-ander, Thomas, Pschorr, and Löwenbrau—have their own big tents. These huge shelters seat between four thousand and five thousand people, employ 250 waitresses and 150 waiters, have their own kitchens, their own chicken broilers, their own spits (one claims to have the biggest grill in the world—every day three well-fed steers slowly turn in cleverly balanced rotation over and between charcoal fires, with a seven-foot butcher carving away at the delectable animals). At the entrance to the Löwenbrau tent, a forty-foot lion opens his jaws every forty-five seconds and roars the prerecorded commercial: "LOOOOOEEEWENBRAUUUUUU!"

But all this hilarity does not begin until the procession has arrived and the *Bürgermeister*—usually very nervous because this is not one of his regular functions—taps the first cask of beer and starts it flowing. Twelve cannon shots boom out, and with much screaming and shouting, with whistling, yodeling, and overdone enthusiasm, the *Oktoberfest* is officially opened.

Recently I went to Munich to do "research" on that happening, and I learned that there are 760 licensees who offer culinary thrills and exhibit every imaginable form of roller coaster, daredevil motorcycle performances, carrousels, shooting galleries, *Geisterbahnen* (where one rides in dark caves and suddenly monsters jump up to frighten you and help you to release your inhabitions about screaming in public).

I was informed that 4,750,000 liters of beer were consumed during those weeks; 485,000 grilled chickens and 1,100,000 sausages were gobbled up, and 72,600 pork and veal shanks were eaten (they are called *Haxen* and are a great and wonderful specialty of Munich). I also learned that 4,700,000 people (children were counted as people) attended the *Wiese;* that *outside* of the beer tents sixteen chicken grillers had concessions, including the world famous Wienerwald, which was not very popular with the other chicken grillers because Wienerwald undersold them. Also, 17,5000 *Steckerlfisch* were sold (they are mackerel that are speared through the mouth by small wooden *skewers—steckerl—*and laid on a bed of charcoal; they taste quite good, but eating them at the *Oktoberfest* is a messy undertaking because they are handed to you on a piece of paper—no fish knives, no forks, no plates, no napkins, and no finger bowls).

Every sweet that was ever introduced to the eating public can be had—even Pepsi-Cola and Coca-Cola, but those are drunk mainly by children and saints. There are 175 men in the fire brigade, twelve ambulances, two emergency hospitals, and there is a group that specializes in handling drunks, because the beer in Munich is very powerful stuff. It is *süffig*—it goes down your throat well enough, and when you are thirsty the first swallow is one of the most desirable sensations that humans know—but suddenly your ears turn a light shade of blue, and if you try to get up you will find that something is holding onto your feet.

Beer is dispensed in one-liter steins only, and societies for the prevention of *"schlechtes Einschenken"* (meaning not filling the stein with the amount one has paid for) spring to life. The customers grumble—I saw one furious customer who had brought a measuring glass to prove that he was being cheated—but no waitress worth her tips would stand for such shenanigans. If one is lucky, one gets two thirds beer and one third foam.

The biggest seller—aside from the beer—is grilled chicken. It is just rubbed inside and outside with salt and pepper, a few sprigs of parsley are shoved into the cavities, and on the grill they go. I don't know why—whether it's the way they are cooked or the general mood and atmosphere—they never taste as good as they do on the *Oktober Wiese*.

Try them sometime!

Oxtail Soup
(Ochsenschleppsuppe)

1 oxtail (about 2 pounds),	*4 peppercorns*
disjointed	*½ cup diced celery*
½ cup sliced onions	*1 cup dry red wine*
4 tablespoons butter	*1 tablespoon flour*
8 cups water	*1 teaspoon sugar*
1½ teaspoons salt	*½ teaspoon vinegar*

Brown the oxtail and onions in 2 tablespoons of the butter. In a large saucepan combine the oxtail, onions, water, salt, and peppercorns, simmer, covered, for about 4 hours. Add the celery and wine, simmer for ½ hour longer, till the celery is tender. Strain the soup, chill it, degrease it, and reheat. Separate the meat from the bones, cut it in small pieces, and set it aside. In a skillet brown 1 tablespoon of the flour, add the remaining 2 tablespoons of butter, and stir till blended. Add the stock slowly. Correct the seasoning with the sugar and vinegar. Add the meat. Serve very hot. *Serves 6.*

Sauerbraten
(Marinated Pot Roast)

3½ pounds rump of beef, larded
(or floured and seared in
fresh bacon drippings till the
beef is browned)
Salt and freshly ground pepper
¾ tablespoon additional salt
¼ cup sugar
6 cloves
3 juniper berries
4 cups dry red wine

2 medium-sized onions, chopped
2 bay leaves
1 teaspoon peppercorns
1 leek, chopped
3 tablespoons oil or Crisco
1 cup cider vinegar
6 gingersnaps, crushed
1 cup sour cream
A little flour or grated raw
potato for thickening

Rub the meat with salt and pepper and place in an earthenware bowl. Combine the ¾ tablespoon of salt, sugar, cloves, juniper berries, wine, onions, bay leaves, peppercorns and leek, bring to a boil in a saucepan. Pour this marinade over the meat (it should be completely covered—add some water if necessary). Place the bowl in the refrigerator for 5 days, turning the meat at least once a day. Remove the beef from the marinade, and run the liquid through a fine sieve. Heat the shortening in a large skillet and sauté the meat slowly till it is brown on all sides. Then add the marinade, vinegar, and gingersnaps, cover tightly, and simmer for at least 3½ hours. When the meat is done, remove it to a heated platter, add the sour cream to the sauce, thicken it with a little flour or grated raw potato. Strain the sauce and serve it separately with Potato Dumplings (see the next recipe). *Serves 4–5.*

Potato Dumplings
(Kartoffel Knoedel)

1 pound potatoes
3 tablespoons flour
1 egg
½ teaspoon salt
Freshly ground pepper to taste

½ teaspoon nutmeg
2 tablespoons minced chives or
parsley
Flour for coating dumplings

Boil the potatoes in their skins the day before, do not peel. Let them stand at room temperature till you are ready to make the dumplings. Then peel and rice them. Blend in the 3 tablespoons of flour, egg, seasonings, and chives or parsley, blend till fluffy. Drop the mixture by tablespoonfuls into flour, turn them to coat completely, and shape into balls 1½ inches in diameter. Drop them into gently boiling water or meat broth, cook for about 12 minutes. Serve them immediately. *Makes 12 dumplings.*

Sour Meat Balls
(Königsberger Klopse)

2 small rolls
1 small onion, grated
1 tablespoon melted butter
1 egg yolk
½ pound finely ground beef

½ pound finely ground veal
Salt to taste
A pinch of pepper
A pinch of allspice
Bouillon for boiling meat balls

Sauce

2 tablespoons butter
3 tablespoons flour
3 cups bouillon
2 tablespoons heavy cream
2 tablespoons dry white wine

Juice of ½ lemon
1 egg yolk
2 tablespoons capers
2 tablespoons cooked pearl
    onions

Remove the crusts from the rolls, soak the rolls in water, then press out the water. Sauté the onion in the butter. Mix the rolls, onion, and the egg yolk thoroughly with the meats, add salt, pepper, and allspice. From this mixture form 12 meat balls, then drop them into boiling bouillon. Let them boil for 10 minutes, then remove with a slotted spoon.

To make the sauce: In a large skillet, blend the butter and flour over low heat to make a white sauce. Add the 3 cups of bouillon, cream, white wine and lemon juice, blend well. Then add the egg yolk, which has been beaten with a little water. Add the capers and pearl onions. Do not let the sauce boil any longer, for the egg will curdle. Place the meat balls in the sauce and keep hot.

Stuffed Veal Roast
(Kalbsbraten)

1 medium-sized onion, chopped	*½ cup dry white wine*
1 medium-sized carrot, cut	*½ cup bouillon*
julienne	*½ pound mushrooms, chopped*
1 stalk celery, cut julienne	*½ cup chopped chicken livers*
3 tablespoons oil	*2 tablespoons butter*
A 3-pound veal roast	

Sauté the onion, carrot, and celery quickly in 2 tablespoons of the oil in a skillet, then remove them to a roasting pan. Add the remaining tablespoon of oil to the skillet, brown the veal roast in it on all sides, then remove it to the roasting pan. Roast the veal, covered, for 1½ to 2 hours in a preheated 325° oven, basting with the wine and bouillon. When the roast is done, remove it and the vegetables to another container, cool, and place in the refrigerator overnight. When the meat is completely cold, slice it into ½-inch slices and set them aside. Sauté the mushrooms and livers in the butter, spread that mixture between the slices of veal, tie them in the shape of a roast. Place the veal in a baking dish, cover with a thick White Sauce (given below), place in a preheated 350° oven, and bake till the top is golden. Serve immediately. *Serves 6–8.*

White Sauce

2½ tablespoons flour	*Salt and white pepper to taste*
2½ tablespoons butter, melted	*A pinch of thyme*
1 cup scalded milk	*A pinch of nutmeg*

Mix the flour and butter in a saucepan, add the milk and seasonings, blending thoroughly, and bring to the boiling point but do not boil. Stir till thickened to the right consistency.

Veal Cutlets à la Holstein
(Holsteiner Schnitzel)

6 veal cutlets, pounded ¼ inch	*¼ cup chicken bouillon*
thick	*6 eggs, fried sunny side up*
Salt	*6 rolled anchovies for garnish*
4 tablespoons flour	*Capers for garnish*
6 tablespoons butter	

Salt each cutlet and make small incisions around the edges. Coat one side of each cutlet with flour. Sauté them in the butter in a large skillet, floured side first, till they are golden brown. Remove them, place them on paper towels for a minute, and arrange them on a heated platter, keep them warm. To the same skillet add the bouillon and mix with the pan drippings, bring to a boil, and pour over the cutlets. Place a sunny-side-up egg on top of each cutlet, place an anchovy in the center of each, and decorate the rest with a few capers. A delight to see and taste. *Serves 6.*

Bavarian Shanks of Veal
(Bayrische Kalbshaxe)

2 shanks of veal from the hind	*2 carrots, diced*
legs	*1 stalk celery, chopped*
Salt and paprika	*1 cup chicken bouillon or water*
Flour	*2 tablespoons cornstarch*
1 cup oil	*1 cup dry white wine*
1 pound crushed veal bones	*Lawry's seasoning salt to taste*
1 large onion, chopped	*Juice of 1 lemon*

Rub the shanks with salt and paprika, dredge in a little flour, and in a roasting pan that has a cover, brown on one side in the oil with the veal bones. Turn the shanks over and brown them on the other side, adding the onion, carrots, and celery. Add 1 cup of bouillon or water, cover, and roast in a preheated 350° oven for 2 hours, basting frequently. Remove the shanks to a hot platter, discard the crushed bones, and skim the fat off the pan drippings. Dissolve the cornstarch in the white wine, add to the drippings (if necessary add a little more bouillon), and boil for 2 minutes. Season with the seasoning salt and lemon juice. Serve with noodles or potatoes and a green salad. *Serves 6–8.*

Bavarian Pork Shanks
(Bayrische Schweinshaxe)

2 *shanks of pork from the hind legs*	*¼ cup Crisco*
Salt	*Caraway seeds*
Freshly ground pepper	*Chicken bouillon for gravy*
Paprika	*Flour for gravy*

Season the shanks with salt, pepper, and paprika, brown them lightly in the Crisco in a roasting pan that has a cover. Roast them, covered, in a preheated 350° oven for 2 hours. Remove the shanks from the pan and place on a heated platter. Now cut a crisscross pattern with a knife in the shanks' skin, rub in salt and caraway seeds, and roast, uncovered, for another 30 minutes till the skin is crisp. After having taken the shanks out of the roasting pan, skim off the fat, scrape the pan drippings, add enough bouillon for gravy, and thicken with a little flour mixed with water into a paste. Cook till the gravy is of the right consistency. Serve the shanks with dumplings and with sauerkraut or salad. *Serves 6–8.*

Stuffed Potatoes
(Gefuehlte Kartoffel)

8 *large potatoes, baked, or boiled in their skins*

Filling

¾ pound creamed cottage cheese	1 *teaspoon paprika*
1–2 *tablespoons milk*	1 *teaspoon dry or prepared mustard*
½ cup chopped cooked ham	*Salt and freshly ground pepper to taste*
1 *tablespoon minced onion*	
1 *tablespoon chopped parsley*	
⅛ teaspoon caraway seeds	

Mix the cottage cheese and the milk. Add the remaining ingredients and mix thoroughly. Slit the hot potatoes lengthwise, skins still on, and squeeze at both ends to open wide. Keep them warm. Place the filling in a pastry bag, fill the potatoes, and decorate the tops in a desired design. Sprinkle with additional parsley and serve immediately. This is quite special. *Serves 8.*

Schwaebische Spaetzle

1 pound flour	*2 cups cold water*
7 tablespoons farina or cream of	*¼ cup melted butter*
wheat	*¼ cup grated Swiss cheese*
4–5 eggs	*Bread crumbs*
1 teaspoon salt	

Mix the first 5 ingredients thoroughly—BY HAND—for 3–4 minutes. Grind one third of the dough through a colander into salted boiling water, cook for 5 minutes. Remove with a slotted spoon and rinse in hot water. Do this twice more with the remaining two thirds of the dough. Put some of the melted butter in a casserole, add a layer of *spaetzle,* pour some butter over it. Add a thin layer of grated cheese. Repeat with a second layer of *spaetzle* and another layer of cheese. Repeat with a third layer of *spaetzle* and one of cheese. Top with bread crumbs that have been browned in butter. Keep warm in a very slow oven, then serve. *Serves 6–8.*

Apple Salad
(Apfelsalat)

¾ cup apple juice	*2 tablespoons chopped walnuts*
Juice of ½ lemon	*1 tablespoon chopped almonds*
A little sugar, to taste	*2 tablespoons raisins*
A pinch of salt	*Whipped cream as decoration*
A few drops of vanilla extract	*(optional)*
6–7 apples, peeled or unpeeled,	
as you wish	

Mix the apple juice, lemon juice, sugar, salt, and vanilla. Grate the apples coarsely, or chop them fine, and add them to the apple juice, mix well. Add the nuts, mix well, and place portions in cupped lettuce leaves. Sprinkle with the raisins. Decorate with freshly whipped heavy cream if you wish. This is good to look at and even better to taste. *Serves 6–8.*

Sand Waffles
(Sandwaffeln)

½ pound butter
4 eggs, separated
1 cup less 1 tablespoon powdered sugar

1 cup flour
1 cup potato flour
Grated rind of ½ lemon

Cream the butter, gradually add the beaten egg yolks, the powdered sugar, flour, potato flour, and lemon rind, mix well. Add the stiffly beaten egg whites, mix lightly. Put spoonfuls of the batter into a buttered waffle iron, cook till they are golden, and dust the tops with powdered sugar when you serve them. *Makes 6–8 waffles.*

Honey Cake
(Honig-Kuchen)

2 cups unsifted flour
¾ cup brown sugar
1 tablespoon baking powder
2 teaspoons cinnamon
¼ teaspoon cloves
¼ teaspoon nutmeg

1 teaspoon baking soda
¼ teaspoon salt
1 cup buttermilk
¼ cup honey or dark corn syrup
1 egg, well beaten
Butter

Mix the dry ingredients, then add the remaining ingredients and mix well. Pour into a well-greased large loaf pan, place in a pre-heated 350° oven, and bake for 45–60 minutes. (You may also add chopped almonds if you like.) When the cake has cooled a little, turn it out on a serving plate, then right side up, and slice thickly, spread with butter. *Makes 14–16 slices.*

INDEX